NURSE MOLLY

The Journey of a Lifetime

Rosie Weston

Copyright © 2021 Rosie Weston

All rights reserved, including the right to reproduce this book, or portions thereof in any form. No part of this text may be reproduced, transmitted, downloaded, decompiled, reverse engineered, or stored, in any form or introduced into any information storage and retrieval system, in any form or by any means, whether electronic or mechanical without the express written permission of the author.

The views expressed in this work are solely those of the author and do not necessarily reflect the views of the publisher, and the publisher hereby disclaims any responsibility for them.

ISBN: 9798491692361

Significant events and people, too numerous to mention, who moved in and out of her journey are characterized with a touch of poetic license and deftly woven into this human tapestry. In addition, pseudonyms are used throughout; events and places are disguised to preserve the anonymity of those who shared Molly's journey.

PublishNation
www.publishnation.co.uk

To Hub – my zest for life and living.

CONTENTS

CHAPTER 1: BUILDING FOUNDATIONS	1
CHAPTER 2: EXPANDING HORIZONS	37
CHAPTER 3: A TASTE OF TOWN LIFE	56
CHAPTER 4: IS IT A DREAM?	71
CHAPTER 5: ON THE WARDS	110
CHAPTER 6: WHOOPS! NEW TIMES AHEAD	144
CHAPTER 7: FAMILY AND FUN	166
CHAPTER 8: NURSING BECKONS	183
CHAPTER 9: WAS IT ALL IN VAIN?	224
CHAPTER 10: LOVE: IT'S PRIZE AND PRICE	259
CHAPTER 11: RASPBERRY SPONGE PUDDING!	287
CHAPTER 12: GWEN STURDY	309

ACKNOWLEDGEMENTS

To my inspirational family for the absolute joy and enrichment of their constant presence and the anchor they provide throughout times of challenge and celebration.

To my nursing colleagues and friends including Sheilah, Dorothy, Steve, DSM - the portrayer of stories, and especially to daughter, Joy for the time and resources they have so generously made available.

To Tabbie Browne for guiding me towards the helpful and professional resources of Gwen at PublishNation.

CHAPTER 1

BUILDING FOUNDATIONS

INTRODUCING MOLLY:

Molly's story is defined by her overriding passion to be a Nurse. It is a journey which begins in a farming community before the introduction of the 'cradle to the grave' National Health Service (NHS); antibiotics and corticosteroids; and the unforeseeable advances in science and technology. It encompasses aspects of poverty in the 1930's; political incorrectness; a war to end all wars and its aftermath.

It is a lifetime, which unfolds within a strict value system and codes of practice in which respect and the upholding of one's good name and reputation was paramount. Even the shoes were cleaned to sparkling perfection before being taken to the cobblers for repair!

Molly's life is spliced with a rare sense of fun, a love of the arts and the spirit of adventure. Numerous engaging characters appear along the way; perhaps one of the most intriguing is Molly's imaginary friend, Gwen Sturdy. Molly described her childhood relationship with Gwen as "the essence of friendship and the person I aspired to be." It is a 'friendship' that lasts a lifetime but changes significantly over the years. But to know Molly, to respect her passion to be a nurse and all that inspired her passion is to have some understanding of her roots, her home life and what made Molly tick as a person.

AN INDOMITABLE DYNASTY:

Wills, Molly's father and her mother, Rose came from backgrounds rooted in the traditional beliefs and values of the times; her father from farming stock and her mother a miner's daughter who had entered the genteel and rarefied world of Gentleman's Service. Gentleman's Service related to the many employees who lived-in at the large country estates and the elegant homes of wealthy affluent members of society to provide for the needs of the family as cook, lady's maid, butler, groom etc., they lived together in a real-life 'Downton Abbey' empire. The 'servants', or 'old retainers' as they were sometimes known were expected to uphold the same standards and discipline as 'the family'. In so doing, people living in the neighbourhood respected the polish and sophistication the servants acquired from the big house – a style that was transferred unconsciously, almost by osmosis, when they married and had a family of their own. Rose preserved the traditions to perfection as she insisted on the same niceties of behaviour in her own home.

Rose was full of tales about Gentleman's Service, its traditions, discipline and fun. For example, the risky chances taken by the young kitchen maids to hasten the process of making early morning tea by using warm water from the over-night stone hot water bottles - the tea was known as 'toe-broth'! The title 'Mrs' was given to the Head Cook as a mark of respect; the eminent position of the Butler, which Rose likened to the captain of the ship; and the chauffeurs and coachmen who displayed the polish and sophistication of the cars or horse-drawn coaches they drove. Rose told how Sunday church routine was a compulsory requirement of the household. The servants, led by the Butler preceded the family to take their places at the back of the church, where they stood until the family entered and were seated in their private pew at the front of the church. Rose found great camaraderie in the Servants' Hall – a communal area assigned to the employees where friendships were formed, secrets exchanged and woes shared. On special occasions such as Christmas and other times of celebration, the Servants' Hall community would unite in rare frivolity. Rose loved dressing up, she recited poetry like a professional artiste, sang like a bird, coaxed a tune out of the piano and from thereon her 'theatrical' talents blossomed!

At one time Rose held the appointment of cook in a highly esteemed boarding school and she delighted in recalling the pranks the boys would play. For instance, they knew when it was cake-baking day in the kitchens. As Rose prepared to serve tea on these occasions, she would find her cap missing from its place only to be taunted by mischievous faces grinning round the kitchen door saying, "Your cap for some cream buns, Rose!"

However, the fortunes of the two families in the early decades of the 1900's were vastly different; Wills' father, Josiah certainly came from the most colourful background. Josiah Lange was a respected member of the local farming community and Wills followed in the same tradition. A rare tin photograph shows this relationship to perfection. Josiah, a well-built, stylishly dressed man with an imposing moustache is seated next to a neighbouring farmer, with Wills as a young child standing at his knee. Josiah, in today's terms would have been known as a person who 'thought outside the box'; he was an inventive opportunist. As his children grew older, Josiah began to explore opportunities, which lay further afield. With the agreement of his wife Lisa, Josiah left for Canada to stake a claim on land to develop as a future farming enterprise and home for his family of two sons, Jack, the elder, Wills, and his two daughters Pricilla (known as Pru) and Martha.

In the fullness of time, Josiah returned having succeeded with unimaginable stories of opportunity laced with hard work and endeavour. Meanwhile Lisa, having realized the full extent of the venture, sadly changed her mind. Josiah tried hard to settle back on his farm and to his old way of life but he became a disillusioned and sad man. Tragically, he died and the management of the farm was left in the hands of his family. The two sons lacked the ability to work together; Lisa and her two daughters became distracted and lost enthusiasm for their 'women's work' of looking after the hens, and managing the dairy – cooling the milk and preserving the cream to make butter and cheese.

Jack and Wills were totally different personalities. Jack was a quiet, reserved sort of man who did not readily take to the rigours of farming but preferred to be 'toffed-up' posturing with his silver headed cane at County Fairs and the weekly market. By contrast, Wills had farming in his blood; he was a handsome chap, a very sociable character and inevitably a hit with the girls for whose attention they vied at the local dances where he twirled them around with great abandon during the Gay Gordon's and the Lances.

Wills and Rose had an on and off courtship but during this time of family upheaval their relationship was quite strong. The partnership between the two brothers did not improve and there were many disruptive disagreements. However, in good faith that 'things would right themselves' Wills and Rose were married, they lived on the farm and Molly was born in the City's Hospital for Women in the early 1930s.

The fortunes and way of life of the Lange family were seriously disrupted by Josiah's sad and untimely death; the family eventually broke-up and the dispersal of the farm was mishandled. Rose and Wills never talked about these times, even their wedding day was shrouded in silence. But over the years relatives from both families helped Molly to put together a rather sad picture.

When Rose was discharged after the birth of her baby they returned to live on the farm whilst the family Josiah left behind tried to make a go of things but Rose found the situation unbearable. Wills and Jack could not agree; their mother, Lisa, became a sad and unhappy woman; and to make matters worse Molly was a sickly, miserable baby who could not be consoled. Rose found the farmhouse a cold and dreary place compared with the comfort of her family home and the luxury to which she had become accustomed in Gentleman's Service.

Taking a very brave step, or perhaps a desperate one, Rose left Wills and returned to her family home with Molly. In these times Rose's position brought shame to the family and she was left in no doubt that it was not the way to go on; or in the words of an old idiom ... "you've made your bed, now you must lie on it."

Meanwhile, Wills made every endeavour to make a fresh start by bidding at farm auctions but the money, including Rose's savings, was dwindling and Wills' final attempt at an auction for a farm in Kent ended in disaster. Returning home, Wills' only option to provide for his family was to gain employment either as a bailiff, or farm worker. It was a sad end but the esteem within which the local farming community held Wills stood him in good stead. He was soon offered work with a cottage adjacent to the farmhouse, home of his employer and the family were reunited. However, the whole tragic saga had a devastating effect on Rose with her genteel ways and expectations of a position in the social hierarchy of a local community. In many ways it seemed that neither Rose nor Wills, nor their marriage ever recovered.

With the demise of the farm came the dispersal of the rest of Josiah's family. Molly had little memory of Grandma Lange; perhaps her most vivid was of Granny living in a tall Edwardian Villa in a smart part of town and the vast upstairs room where she lay on what was, in effect, her deathbed. Wills' sisters, however, trailed through Molly's life in different ways.

By contrast, Rose's parentage came from a coal mining community. Rose's father, Jack Dolman, was a quiet, gentle man who was said not to have 'made old bones'; he died as a result of a pit accident. Rose's mother, Ada, was a harsh disciplinarian who ran the family home with military-like precision. Ada, usually referred to by her maiden name as Granny Bunce, the matriarch of 'the Dolman Girls', passed on to the next generations a set of values and an indomitable spirit for which they were renowned. The Dolman's had eight children; one baby boy died in infancy and the two surviving boys who worked in the local coalmine until they left home and eventually married, were only vague memories in Molly's mind, but the five girls, Molly's aunts, the second generation 'Dolman Girls', formed a closer and more meaningful bond. Molly remembered with fondness a photograph of the 'Dolman Girls' that was sadly lost when the last known custodian died. The sepia photograph showed the 'Girls' standing in profile, according to height. They were dressed in the fashion of the day with high-neck blouses, calf length tunics and high button-up boots. Their long straight shiny hair hung down to their waists with the exception of the youngest, Jane, whose curly hair is dressed in ringlets.

The 'Dolman Girls' were not only gifted with an indomitable, independent spirit, they were handsome women and quite adventuresome. Amy, the eldest, achieved distinction by attaining status as a businesswoman and the celebrity of a cathedral wedding. Faith, the second eldest married into a well-heeled local family and lived in one of the large well-to-do houses within a short distance from the family home. Rose, Molly's mother, the middle daughter who married Wills was the least robust of the five girls. Helen, the second youngest, a pretty, genteel lady and gifted needle woman became a lady's maid in Gentleman's Service until she married a wealthy Westmorland farmer, and Jane, the youngest lived with her mother in the family home where she continued to live after she married Bill, a local builder and highly esteemed bowler in the town's cricket team.

Together, the 'Dolman Girls' produced nine grandchildren for Granny Bunce. Molly, an only child until the age of three when sister Kate was born, was fascinated by the little people she sometimes met at Granny's and who she was told were her cousins. So rather typical of Molly she went home to invent a playmate, an honorary 'Dolman Girl' she named Gwen Sturdy! Others never saw Gwen, except perhaps on one occasion. A family photograph shows Molly sitting on a chair in the garden holding baby sister Kate on her knee and behind the chair is an ill-defined, cloudy, ghost-like image, which Molly claimed to be Gwen!

Molly well remembers the Dolman home as an end house in a terraced row of miner's cottages. When she closes her eyes today Molly can smell the coal fire and the steam of the copper boiling in the kitchen on washday. The living room in which Granny sat like Queen Victoria in a large fireside chair surrounded by furniture, which shone like mirrors – a testimony to the ever-prevailing smell of Mansion Polish. It was an awe-inspiring place to visit and Molly was always glad to know Gwen was there too. The parlour was out of bounds to 'little folk' – Molly hated the cool, uninviting room anyway, particularly when she began to understand the sad memories it held for her mother. Rose was always beleaguered by severe headaches following a fall from a swing-boat at the fair aged seven. She would tell of the comfort she found in the cool of the parlour and by lying with her head on the cold tiled hearth of the fireplace.

A large, ornate organ with its long red velveteen seat stood majestically in the corner. When Molly did sneak into the parlour she would climb on the seat, imagining Gwen hopping on beside her. As she pretended to play the organ Molly felt she experienced the delight her mother once described of making music on the beautiful instrument.

One of the greatest attractions of visiting Granny Bunce (Molly always silently thought of her as Granny Grumps), was the bakery that stood at the bottom of Granny's garden. The smell of fresh bread and temptation of cream horns - these flaky pastry rolls filled with jam and cream were hard to resist and only provided as a special treat for exceptionally good behaviour! By contrast, if someone was 'out of sorts' they would be told, "Never mind, cheer up we will go a walk round the cemetery in a minute."

Time passed until on one visit to Granny, Molly found her in bed – unheard of!! So, climbing the dark steep stairs Molly whispered to Gwen, "Well, I wonder what on earth we are about to find?" And when they arrived in the bedroom Granny lay in her large ornate wooden bed covered by snowy-white bed linen and bolstered upright by pillows. She wore a white mop cap with a deep lacy frill around the brim, a white nightdress with long sleeves and a high buttoned up neck. Granny seemed unnaturally mellow and smiling; Molly's aunties were visiting too. Granny began to remonstrate with her youngest daughter, Jane, "Bring me the pancheon, some flour and butter I want to make a pudding for Molly." The ingredients were supplied and Granny kneaded them together with great gusto scattering flour everywhere. A piece of dough was eventually produced, placed in the pudding basin and given to Jane to put on to boil. Sadly, Granny did not survive but this lasting memory of her feisty spirit and resolve was to remain with Molly – so did the guilt Molly experienced by calling her Granny Grumps when she was really such a lovely, smiling old lady: Gwen had never been impressed by Molly's disrespect anyway.

After the death of Granny Bunce, her five daughters became the next generation 'Dolman Girls', with her granddaughters to follow – not forgetting honorary member Gwen!

FAMILY LIFE:

Situated within this intergenerational and matriarchal dominated dynasty, was Molly's family unit. Into which Molly 'created' Gwen one warm sunny afternoon whilst playing in the paddock adjoining her back garden. She would tell how Gwen just appeared whilst she was singing and dancing in her pretend world with the fairies and the woodland creatures in her secret 'Fairy dell' - a hollow surrounded by trees. In the beginning Gwen only came to life in the 'Fairy dell' as she joined Molly to sing and dance, or pick the long-stemmed daisies peeping through the grass to make a daisy chain necklace, or a crown to sit in their hair. The imaginary friendship lasted a lifetime but of course, over the years the relationship changed from the expressive childhood delight in the human-like friendship to one of an indelible memory gradually absorbed within Molly's subconscious reservoir of life experiences. Gwen probably became a subliminal influence - Molly's alter ego, maybe? In adult life Molly would sometimes smile and wonder if a person was unintentionally recognising the influence of their alter ego when they said, "It was against my better judgement that I decided to ..."

Pretend friends are sometimes compared with fictional characters created by an author (Gleason, Tracy 2013). But to Molly, 'Gwen Sturdy' felt like a 'real-life' friend rather than a figment of her imagination. The day Molly introduced Gwen to her home they were greeted by the smell of sizzling bacon; Molly's mother, Rose kneading the dough to make tea-time bread and iced buns; and Kate, Molly's baby sister lying asleep in the corner of a large sofa. The family pets gave an aura of comfort too. A tortoiseshell-coloured cat, the matriarch of the surviving feline family, lay in front of the fire alongside her son a magnificent young black cat with ragged ears – the battle scars from his 'nights on the tiles'. The atmosphere of contentment seemed supreme but beneath this seeming tranquillity, Gwen sensed an indefinable undercurrent of sadness, of which Molly seemed unaware or maybe chose not to acknowledge.

MAN'S WORK:

Molly's father was rarely seen in the home except for mealtimes and evenings; quite usual in the 1930's where a strict division of family labour was assigned with the man's role as the provider. Wills worked on the farm busily rearing generation after generation of cattle for the market and dairy cows to produce milk and the by-products of butter and cheese. Breeding was not always a straightforward activity, sometimes a cow would not have enough milk to feed her young, or the calf couldn't suckle which left Wills having to hand rear the new-born. A trick he performed by placing his hand in a bucket of milk to encourage the calf to suckle his fingers and in so doing to take the milk so essential for life. Wills called these struggling animals 'suckie-mullies' and was delighted when he could tell a success story of the calf being weaned back to its mother, or to a foster mother.

Likewise, in the lambing season a new-born lamb suffering from failure to thrive was wrapped in a sack and taken home where Rose waited to lay the little creature in a warmly lined cardboard box next to the kitchen fire. Rose delighted in these little lambs, she cared for them day and night, fed them with a bottle and teat and the lamb, responding as if to its mother, would bleat each time Rose came near. When the time came it was notoriously difficult to part with a Cade lamb and the experience for Rose, Kate and Molly was no different. But they remained undaunted. On one occasion the family named an orphaned lamb Shirley. Shirley followed Rose around the kitchen bleating and wriggling her squiggly tail; they both revelled in the pleasure each gave the other. Time came when Shirley was allowed outside and she found the hen run. Molly giggled and she knew Gwen was just as amused to watch Shirley mimic the chickens pecking on the ground; they were convinced that was how the lamb learned to nibble the grass! But Shirley could not stay as a house pet forever and so the choice laid between the cattle market or returning to the flock – thankfully, the flock won!

On the land, Wills undoubtedly saw his role as custodian for 'Mother Nature'. The foundation of good husbandry lay in firstly, ploughing, harrowing and fertilizing the land to restore nourishment to the soil. 'Hedging and ditching' usually followed. Hedge laying was an exacting skill and one at which Wills was particularly proficient. The annual maintenance of hedges bordering the fields and roads involved pruning out the old wood, splicing and laying the new shoots. It was a crucial activity by which the ravages of winter were repaired and re-growth stimulated in the hedges to ensure protection of the land from the searing winds that blew across the open fields and to provide a home for the nesting birds in the spring. Such was the regard and value associated with the preservation of hedgerows and the craftsmanship required for their maintenance, the National Hedge Laying Society was formed in the late 1970s with the Duke of Cornwall as its esteemed Patron. Clearing the ditches was equally important to encourage free flowing drainage to prevent waterlogged soil and flooding. Little did the family know then that many years later these were to be Wills' final acts of devotion to his beloved 'Mother Nature'.

Springtime followed in seasonal succession and the seeds were sown for the next summer's harvest. During the time of growing, the seedlings were protected from predators by Wills' handmade scarecrows which stood in the fields like Lowry-figures with their posturing messages of hope and despair; hope for a flourishing season and pride in a job well done, despair in the thought that the crops might fail. To the girls' delight Wills recited his home-made ditty to them and they quickly became word perfect:

My name is Johnny Scarecrow and Tammy is my friend.
Each year we pose like mannequins as guardians of the grain.
Dressed in the latest fashions with our straw hair nicely cut, we
save the seed from thieving birds and distract greedy crows.
The crows are wily birds who see through the disguise but when
our friend the fierce North Wind blows and gives us unexpected
life, we fox these cheeky creatures and give them a surprise.
We like the friendly nimble field mice that snuggle down within
our straw; although they tickle and make us wriggle and
disturb our sleep with their snores.
When the crops grow tall and strong, we toff-up in our best bib
and tucker to celebrate a job well done at the Scarecrow
Festival Supper.

It was to be several years before mechanisation eased the manual effort of farm work. But when it did Wills' beloved Fergie Tractor was his pride and joy.

To make a living from the land and to be a worthy custodian for 'Mother Nature' not only required all Wills' knowledge and skill but a commitment by the rural community of which the church was an integral part. The first Sunday in May was dedicated as Rogation Sunday when services would be held in the fields seeking God's blessing on the fruits of the earth, the labour of all who worked the soil, and the farm animals. Molly enjoyed the church service in the field and she was sure Gwen did so too, it was always a disappointment when the weather caused the congregation to withdraw to the church.

Another tradition known as 'Beating the Bounds' was associated with Rogation. On this occasion the local people, led by the Vicar and Church Wardens, met to walk the boundaries of the Parish and say prayers for a successful harvest, the wellbeing of the Church, and the parishioners. One version of the prayers offered at Rogation time, expressed sentiments that might be seen to lie at the heart of Wills' family:

Bless this good earth and make it fruitful
Bless our labours and give us the things we need for our daily lives
Bless the homes of our Parish and those who live in them
Bless our common life and care for our neighbours.

The church was a focal point of village life. In addition to its spiritual ministrations, the church or chapel provided social activities; it also had an important welfare function for the out of work and less well-off people of the village. Many children were taught to read and write at Sunday school; they learned religious verses that were spoken and sung with the same enthusiasm as the nursery rhymes!

The village school was a Church of England establishment and with the reigning Monarch as its temporal head, the Royal Family commanded great respect. On special occasions, such as Coronations, Jubilees and Royal births the school children were presented with a commemorative china mug — Molly still prizes her collection.

During Molly's early days at school, she well remembers the day the headmistress announced that the Royal Train would be coming through at 11am. The railway track could easily be seen from the playground and the children lined up in eager anticipation. But the Royal Train just whizzed through belching black smoke like any other train, the only activity to be seen was the fireman feeding the greedy fire with shovels of coal. Molly's account to Rose was clouded with disappointment because she had not seen the Queen wearing her crown and waving through the carriage window. The village was steeped in patriotism. King George V1 ascended to the throne in 1936 following the death of his father and the subsequent abdication of his elder brother, Edward. The King's young, pretty, smiling wife, Queen Elizabeth, was adored, as were the two royal children, princesses Elizabeth and Margaret Rose. It was not unusual for parents to name their children after the princesses, adopt their style of dress, or the ways in which they dressed their hair. Rose was a keen follower of Royal fashion!

In addition to the local church, each year a visiting mission, founded in 1916 for the purpose of sharing the message of Jesus, came to stay in the village. The arrival of the Village Mission Caravan with two Deaconesses, known as 'Sisters', brought a carnival-like atmosphere. Throughout the year the whole village anticipated the occasion; it was certainly an event to which Rose, Kate and Molly looked forward; and much to Molly's delight Gwen was also swept along with the excitement.

The Sisters parked their caravan in a field near the centre of the village and with easy access to the vicarage. During the day they visited the schools and housebound people in the village and surrounding area. Most evenings religious gatherings were held in the caravan – when the numbers were too large the congregation overflowed on to the grass outside.

The caravan was equipped with a small pedal organ, which the Sisters played with great gusto to accompany the singing. One of Molly's favourite songs was written by Nellie Talbot ...

Jesus wants me for a sunbeam to shine for Him each day,
In every way try to please Him at home, at school, at play,
A sunbeam, a sunbeam, Jesus wants me for a sunbeam,
A sunbeam, a sunbeam, I'll be a sunbeam for Him.

During these gatherings they read the Bible together, the Sisters made the reading easier to understand through simple explanations and graphic illustrations. Although the messages gave moral guidance, in effect they were so familiar they might have been like stories from the comics if Molly had been allowed such luxury! So, Molly and Kate eagerly waited to hear the stories from the Sunday School Annual they found in their 'Christmas stocking' each year ... stories such as Jesus walking on the waters of Lake Galilee to calm the fears of His disciples in their little fishing boat; or of the feeding of the five-thousand crowd who had gathered to hear His teaching. Molly's love of story-time was bolstered by Rose's talent in making the stories come alive; such as the story of Samuel from the 'Old Testament' and how he woke in the night hearing a voice calling his name. Rather frightened by this he spoke with his father, Eli, who after listening carefully told Samuel to go back to bed, and if it happened again to say, "Speak, Lord, for your servant is listening." Molly would quietly say to Gwen in bed, "What if He calls me and I don't hear because I am sleeping – what would I do?" "You will know," Gwen assured Molly. Almost inevitably another of Molly's favourite songs, which the Sisters often sang to conclude their service, was:

Tell me the stories of Jesus I love to hear;
Things I would ask him to tell me if he were here;
Scenes by the wayside; tales of the sea;
Stories of Jesus, tell them to me. (William Henry Parker, 1885)

The Mission's visit was a lovely welcome to spring or autumn interlude and a memory that lasted the whole year through.

As the seasons changed Wills harvested the hay and cereals for cattle feed, bedding, or for the market; he built hayricks, turnip and potato camps as protective storage for cattle food in the winter. The potatoes were also used for home consumption and stored as 'seed potatoes' in the dark until they 'chitted' with new roots for next year's planting in Wills' kitchen garden.

Harvesting of cereals such as barley and wheat took place towards the end of the summer. It was an intensely busy time of heavy, dusty and thirsty work from dawn until dusk. Rose and the girls took Wills' teatime cake, sandwiches and 'pop bottle' of tea to the fields. They loved this novel experience, which allowed them to share time with Wills who would point out the wildlife chasing hither and thither out of the way of the harvester. As they sat in the shade, he might give Molly and Kate a crust, or a bit of his cake – he often left some tea in the pop bottle, which Molly knew Gwen agreed to be the sweetest drink ever.

When Wills came home at dusk, he would shed his shirt in the privacy of the back hall of the house and Rose would dust away the chaff and seeds, which had seeped through his clothing and stuck to his damp skin. The next stop was a warm bath. But never too tired to enjoy the beauty of nature, sometimes before taking his bath, Wills called the girls outside to witness a murmuration of starlings sweeping their way across the sky in the fading daylight making the most amazing patterns and swirls as they prepared to roost for the night.

The Harvest Festival, an ancient tradition to celebrate a safe harvest, was held near to the autumn equinox. This time of great rejoicing, which consumed the interest of the local community, was heightened by the appearance of an exceptionally bright full moon, known as the Harvest Moon. Considerable effort was taken to decorate the church and school with sheaves of wheat and corn brought in by the farmers; fruits, vegetables and flowers gifted by the villagers (in later years dry foods such as pasta, flour, rice and tin foods were included) and after the festival, the food was shared with people in need. The harvest hymns were sung with great enjoyment, such as one particular favourite

Come, ye thankful people, come, raise the song of harvest home;
All is safely gathered in, ere the winter storms begin. (H. Alford (1820 -71)

At home, Wills took great interest in his vegetable garden, fruit bushes and trees to produce food for the family. He always added a special touch of colour by planting flowers between the rows of banked-up potatoes and marigolds alongside the broad bean rows to stave off the black fly! Wills had a great fondness for the birds that inhabited his garden; he chuckled as he watched the blackbirds with their excited calls and playful skittering as they sped across the ground to take their flittering flight into the air. Sometimes, Wills would just stand and stare as he listened to the musical sound of the song thrush or engaged with the cheeky robin as it sat on the handle of his spade cocking its eye for a worm. All these delights he taught the girls to know and appreciate, quite accepting that Gwen would be listening too!

For a while, Wills kept chickens, Rhode Island Reds were his favourite breed. The 'Reds' liked to roam freely; on the whole they were friendly birds but could unexpectedly become a bit skittish and aggressive. The cockerel strutted around with an air of arrogance and his strident call to his harem, which in return attracted their low crowing responses, could be heard across the village. It was strange how analogies of bad behaviour were often drawn from the animal kingdom. For instance, one day Molly came home from the Infant school having been taught to whistle, only to be admonished by Rose saying, "A whistling woman and a crowing hen is neither good for God nor men." Gwen knew Molly quite liked the rhyme but did not really understand its meaning at the time! On another occasion, Wills and Rose were contemplating a move to a new house. Noticing the girls' excitement, Rose cautioned them not to expect too much, "there are black crows in every cupboard (meaning faults)." Preparing to leave after looking round the place and making sure Gwen had too, Molly came skipping up to her parents saying, "It's alright we've looked in all the cupboards and there are no black crows here." Rose was quite used to Gwen Sturdy being given a point of view! Nevertheless, they did not move to the house.

However, Wills' chicken flock experienced a sudden disaster when one morning Rose was delegated to collect the eggs and open the doors of the pens so that they could enjoy the freedom of the chicken run enclosed by wire netting. Rose forgot to close the outer gate behind her and off the chickens went in all directions. Molly was called to help her mother as she chased hither and thither trying to catch the hens that by now had scattered down the field and were hiding in the hedgerows. The episode caused Rose to become anxious and breathless from her efforts, plus the concern that Molly might be late for school. The situation triggered a severe anxiety asthma attack, to which Rose had been prone since her early teens. So from past experience Rose knew she must rest and relax but the incident unsettled Molly, which disturbed Gwen too. Before the family came home for lunch Rose had begun to recover and to her great relief found that the chickens had all made their way back home – largely thanks to Molly who had scattered several handfuls of corn inside the pen before she went to school! But Wills' chicken keeping days were over!

In addition to his garden and the wildlife, Wills had other interests to which the girls were NOT privy. For instance, he read the Daily Mail, listened to the news and the boxing matches on the wireless – Freddy Mills was the star of the day. They were certainly never allowed around the farm!

WOMAN'S WORK:

So much for Wills' role in the family as provider, Rose however, had different responsibilities. The 'woman' of the house was assigned the role of homemaker combined with rearing a family. Molly and Kate consciously and unconsciously absorbed such attributes and know-how from the cradle!

Monday, for instance, was always washday and criticism heaped upon those housewives who did not conform, or who had not 'pegged out' before 8am – quite an achievement considering the absence of labour-saving laundry aids at this time. When Rose was eventually persuaded to have a washing machine she tutted with disdain at the "waste of electricity" and the "sheer idleness" but she soon succumbed to temptation and never looked back! Housewives were very competitive and further criticism could be expected as neighbours compared the brightness of their 'whites' as they hung on the washing line. 'Whites' that were rather grey and did not glisten in the sunlight brought shame on the housewife. Reckitts Blue Bag was used in the final rinse as an aid to perfect whiteness. But the 'Blue Bag' had a dual function in Molly's home, Rose stored one in a jar on the kitchen windowsill to be handy as a first aid measure for insect bites and stings.

Tuesday, devoted to the ironing and airing of the family's clothes and household linen had less exposure to neighbourly critique! The ironing was undertaken by alternately using two flat irons heated on the fire, or hob. Before use, the irons were first wiped with a cloth and the temperature tested by a spray of spit, if the spit danced down the iron like a ball then the iron was too hot, if the spit just sizzled it was not hot enough, there was a well-judged in between which Rose often confirmed by holding the iron near to her cheek! The electric iron was a wonderful invention but such aids also depended upon whether the home was connected to an electricity supply.

Wednesday, and Market Day with a day's outing to town on the village bus. Thursday was set aside for cleaning the upstairs rooms – even to dusting the wire springs under the bed! But on one afternoon each month the Women's Bright Hour held at the chapel took priority as Rose set off ready to participate in various ways.

Friday, in anticipation of the weekend was a busy day. All downstairs rooms were thoroughly cleaned and time set-aside for a visit from Mr Groves, the representative from Patterson's

High-Class Grocers. Mr Groves came each week to take Rose's order for delivery the following Tuesday – the present today system of 'shopping online'!

And so for the weekend with Saturday devoted to window cleaning plus any 'extras', and preparing Sunday meals. Sunday was solely devoted to church and religious or other respectful activities such as singing, playing religious music on the piano, reading from the Sunday School Annual, drawing and colouring bible story pictures. All sewing, knitting, skipping, or playing ball was suspended - needless to say, Rose always found ways around having a bit of fun! Of course, there was no television at this time, newspapers were not taken on Sunday and the wireless, which was turned on for the news on weekdays, remained silent.

But once each year the home had a major overall known as 'The annual spring clean'. This was a frantic event, almost like a religious ritual. Every nook and cranny in the home was cleaned from top to bottom: cupboards and drawers were cleared and their lining paper renewed; home decorating was also part of this ritual and Rose's aim to "wallpaper a room in a day" was sacrosanct. Rose stripped off the old wallpaper whilst Wills attended to the early morning milking and after breakfast, they would begin the meticulous job of repapering the room. Wills always left Rose the defining touch of placing the ornate border between the top of the wall and the ceiling whilst he returned to the farm to milk the cows and bed down the animals for the night. The final adornment was to replace the heavy winter curtains with pretty, light summer curtains – all homemade by Rose. And so each room in the house took its turn in rotation each spring.

Eventually the seasons rolled around and Wills' garden produced a fine selection of fruit and vegetables ready for jam making, pickling and preserving. These home industries, in which the girls became involved, began with the ripening of the fruit and vegetables and ended in the late autumn when eggs were collected from the hens and preserved in Isinglass in anticipation of the usual decline in egg laying during the winter. Eating and cooking apples were neatly laid in a spare bedroom on a bed of straw - strictly not touching each other. And on Christmas Eve, Rose placed one of the lovely crisp eating apples, an orange, a few brazil nuts together with the Sunday School Annual and a few novelties in Molly's and Kate's Christmas Stockings to hang on the foot of the bed for Christmas morning.

Home industry in all its forms was both a hobby and a necessity! In addition to preserving fruit and other food for the winter, the home economy of 'Make do and Mend', irrespective of wartimes, was one that continued throughout the year. Garments, such as jumpers, cardigans, socks and scarves were knitted by Rose, aided by the girls, and when the garments began to show signs of wear and tear, they were repaired until the repair became too unsightly or cripplingly uncomfortable! When this happened to the socks for example, the knitting would be unpicked from toe to ankle and a new foot knitted on the sock – not necessarily in the same-coloured wool but Rose would settle for "a good match" to keep the socks going!

Thrift was a virtue and an obligation on the housewife, so when clothing was beyond all repair it still had a job to do! Garments were cut into strips, say 6"x1", then with the aid of a pegging hook the strips were woven into their final home – an empty animal feed sack provided by Wills to reappear as a colourful 'Pegged Rug'. (Some women washed the sacks and made them into aprons!) Pegging a new rug was a wintertime activity and one in which all the family participated whilst sitting around the fire on a winter evening. Molly would frequently sense Gwen's guidance when choosing a colour, from the strips of material; sometimes Rose would make the choice easier by drawing a pattern on the sack. From time-to-time Wills joined in the challenge of making a pattern, probably a farm animal, a bird, or the moon if he could find the right colours! Molly and Kate loved it when Dad joined in – he made it such fun!

Next, the bedding would be inspected for wear and tear. Sheets worn in the middle would be rejigged by 'turning sides to middle'; when the sheets had "gone too far," the good bits would be made into pillowcases, or handkerchiefs lovingly embroidered by Rose and the girls. Some families used straw filled mattresses called paillasses and at the end of harvesting fresh straw would be saved to top up the worn filling.

Again, just like the four seasons, each day was organised according to mealtimes with four meals a day. Breakfast – cereal, fried bacon or lambs' kidneys on bread dipped in the fat; dinner – a roast, or stew with vegetables and appropriate complements such as dumplings, Yorkshire pudding, stuffing, or a pastry case for meat pies. This course was followed by a fruit pie, suet pudding or jam roly-poly: teatime included fruit, sandwiches and cake; and finally, suppertime with cheese on toast, or toasted teacakes.

There were also certain traditions to be observed. Fish instead of meat was always eaten for dinner on Fridays; and all meals were prepared from seasonal produce. For example, hot cross buns and Simnel cake were only eaten at Easter; mince pies and oranges at Christmas, probably because there was not such easy access to world-wide markets but there was also a foreboding saying, "Food out of season, trouble without reason" – home preserved plums and runner beans for Christmas were an exception!

Molly, like all the children, walked home from school for her mid-day meal. The table was the place where food was eaten and nowhere else, certainly not in the street. All mealtimes were a disciplined and well-polished performance. A pristine white tablecloth with meticulous table settings adorned the table with Wills, seated at the head carving the joint with the precision of a surgeon. One's cutlery was manipulated with the delicacy of a ballerina's hand; the food politely served; and table manners observed with military-like discipline. For example, mealtimes were expected to be taken in an atmosphere of calm companionship - 'small talk' rather than raucous conversation. If Molly's voice did get rather loud and shrill, she would be likened to a Corncrake – the secretive little bird with its rasping call that Wills often pointed out in the tall grasses. No particle of food was wasted and everyone's plate was expected to be clean at the end of the meal ... not scraped clean that was considered vulgar. All leftover meat and veg was re-cycled as soup or bubble and squeak; bread was recycled as bread-and-butter pudding ... it was a mortal sin to throw away bread – the 'Staff of Life,' declared the Holy Bible. If recycling was beyond the imagination the last resort was the 'pig-swill' tub! Finally, Molly and Kate were expected to ask permission to leave the table and to thank Rose for the meal – Wills always acknowledged Rose's efforts ... with his usual form of address he said, "Thank you, Mum that was very nice," or "That was different Mum, very tasty, thank you."

Molly and Kate were not allowed to wander freely around the farm, particularly during the busy times, such as market day when the animals were being assembled in the transport, or during harvest-time when the heavy thrashing machines would pound away in the rick-yard. Wills would call to Rose, "Mum, keep the girls inside." However, on one occasion Kate slipped the net. Witnessing Wills arrive home with a blood-stained cloth around his hand saying he had taken off the end of his thumb in the thrashing machine – Kate went to investigate. She returned with the larger part of Wills' thumb dangling on a piece of skin! For all Molly's bravado and passion to be a nurse it was a sight she found extremely distressing as she inwardly looked to Gwen for consolation. Wills sought medical advice but reconstructive surgery was not as advanced in these times and his peculiarly shaped thumb-end was a permanent reminder of that fateful day.

But there were fun and family times too. In addition to harvest-time in the fields, Wills gave one other concession to his enforced boundaries - a ride through the village in the pony and trap to take the milk churns to the station in time for the evening Milk Train. The girls enjoyed this treat and Molly always made sure there was a space for Gwen to sit next to her on the side seat of the trap. To this day Molly talks about feeling the thrill of the warmth of the late afternoon sun, or the crisp cold of winter with the wind blowing through their hair. The gentle nestling together of Molly with Gwen beside her was a wonderful feeling as the trap swayed to the clip-clop rhythm of the horse's hooves cantering through the village in the heart of the English countryside.

It must have been over half a mile to the station. On the way they passed the village pub, always known by the name of the landlord as 'Bob Fairy's'. The village blacksmith's, 'Smoky Joe's', on the opposite corner would often be lit up by scarlet and white flames from the forge together with the added interest of sparks from the hammer as it shaped the metal. The smell that came from the Blacksmith's was like no other, particularly in the process of shoeing a horse when smoke and an earthy, steam-laden aroma would rise up as the hot horseshoe came into contact with the horse's hoof.

The road was lined on either side with rather nice houses – until a very high black corrugated iron fence appeared heralding the entrance to Miss Goodwin's Sweet Shop, where every Friday teatime Wills took Kate and Molly to spend their weekly penny on Palm Toffee. The girls would stand on their tiptoes peering over the counter as Miss Goodwin took out her shiny little hammer to break the slab of toffee into pieces, and weigh out 'one penny-worth' each. Sometimes Molly would whisper, "Do you think we should have something different for a change, Gwen?" but Gwen always said, "No thank you," knowing that the choice of sweets approved by Rose was very limited: no sherbet or pear drops – they gave one acid-indigestion; no dolly mixtures - they were just sugar and water and rotted one's teeth; and definitely no liquorice that was made from 'Blackman's blood'!

What lay behind Miss Goodwin's corrugated iron fence was always a mystery to Molly. That is until later in life when she retraced her steps down memory lane to find the fence, which was barely shoulder high, hid Miss Goodwin's flower garden, a little shaded arbour surrounded by trees and a vegetable plot.

Riding on, an entrance to a farm appeared on the left side of the road and on the opposite side, a gate to the fields where manure from the farm was piled ready to scatter on the land. This particular spot on the journey to and from school always raised a smile as they remembered the day Molly gave chase to one of her classmates, Bobby, a red head they called 'Copper knob'. On taking fright at Molly's approaching threats, Bobby ran straight up the heap of manure – sadly as he came down the other side, he found he had lost his shoes! Molly received the sharp end of his mother's tongue and avoided further contact with her until Molly felt it had all 'blown over'. But Gwen noticed that the lad's mother, a wily old bird, would never miss a chance to intimidate Molly!

Continuing on the ride in the pony and trap through the village, they came to the 'Co-op shop'. Rose didn't shop at the Co-op she thought it was 'common', although she was a member and had a 'divi number', but in Rose's eyes, Patterson's was the place to be seen to shop … and that is what she did! Opposite to the Co-op stood the Methodist Chapel attended by Molly and her family; next door stood the large impressive house where the Superintendent lived – an awesome figure in the chapel, and one who was treated warily.

On the 'milk run' Wills would normally turn left into the station at this point but if he were to have continued up the road a short distance beyond the Chapel he would have passed by a row of picturesque thatched cottages, homes to some of the poorest families who frequently benefited from Wills' benevolence. The plight of the children haunted Wills. A short way beyond the cottages and immediately before a railway bridge, Wills would have passed the village school before crossing over the railway bridge and round a sharp corner where the large imposing spire of the Anglican Church (the Church of England) appeared like a sentinel keeping watch over the village. The landed gentry and the upper classes patronized the church, whilst the non-conformist establishments – the Methodist and the Baptist chapels attracted the 'self-made man' and the working classes. At a very early age it seemed that one's social class determined one's religious affiliation!

However, to retrace their steps to the chapel and the 'Co-op shop' the pony turned into the station yard. On one side of the yard a row of railway cottages had been built for the railway employees. Rose's chapel friend, Mrs Dillum, lived with her husband in the end cottage. Rose, accompanied by Molly and Kate, periodically visited Mrs Dillum to take tea on her lovely lawn; or sometimes they would sit in the parlour, an atmosphere in which Gwen sensed Molly's discomfort with its resemblance to that awful room at Granny Grumps! Well-drilled by Rose before the visit the girls knew exactly what was expected of them. Such formality even extended between the two friends who never addressed each other by their first names but always as "would you like a piece of cake Mrs Lange?" "No thank you Mrs Dillum, that was just nice." Although invited, to have taken a second helping would be considered lacking in social etiquette!

The milk churns were unloaded from the cart onto the 'milk table', a large wooden bench-like structure raised way off the ground by several sturdy legs. The girls were not allowed out of the trap. Holly, the horse impatiently stamped her feet and, in the summer, shook off the flies from her ears and eyes, her coat glistened and her clean warm smell was all part of the lovely evening air and the simple adventures of childhood. Suddenly, they were off again and without the heavy churns in the trap, Holly seemed to just fly, like Pegasus, through the village and back home for tea.

Wills was not the only one to provide such treats, Rose also had one or two up her sleeve. For instance, in the summer holidays, or after school, Rose would take Kate and Molly on a picnic with sandwiches, cake and tea in a 'pop-bottle'. Their walk varied, sometimes taking a route through the fields to the canal, or maybe to cross over the canal locks and on towards the banks of the river. At this particular 'beauty-spot' on the river, the water had worn away the bank to leave what they thought of as a 'sandy beach'. And it was here that the little party sat to enjoy their picnic. Sometimes a school friend would come along with Molly and on one such occasion her friend threw a banana skin into the river. Molly ran in the water to retrieve it but was soon out of her depth in a river notorious for its whirlpools. Rose stood on the bank frantically calling Molly to turn back. But Gwen's instinct warned that Molly was on a mission and Gwen only hoped that she would be conscious of her foreboding and have the good sense to listen to her mother! But Molly didn't and it was then that her school friend, who was an older girl and could swim, cautiously ventured out into the water and managed to grab the bottom edge of Molly's dress and drag her back to the bank. It was a very scary moment and one never to be forgotten.

However, there were also family outings that Molly will always remember such as the walks along the canal banks with Wills and Rose on a Sunday sunny summer's evening – a rare occasion when the family missed the church service! The girls always waited with eager anticipation to arrive at the lock keeper's cottage where he sold pop and crisps – a very rare treat indeed! Wills, always on 'nature watch', would point out the little creatures inhabiting the canal banks and name the variety of fish swimming just beneath the surface of the water as if to tease the fishermen sitting patiently on the canal banks waiting for a catch!

Molly often showed by her chatter and singing how much she enjoyed these family outings, although the relationship between Rose and Wills seemed rather cool and devoid of fun. Perhaps, the relationship could be attributed to the conventions of this time where the impropriety of public demonstrations of affection was closely observed. Although Molly, to some extent, seemed to accept the formal ways of her parent's relationship as normal, Gwen always wondered whether propriety lay at the heart of their seemingly distant relationship, or was it a wide chasm where love was floundering and trying to regain its place? Molly was a happy child but for some unexplainable reason she constantly seemed to need permission to spontaneously show her love to the father she adored; feelings that were transferred to Gwen and caused her much sadness. Cuddly Kate was very different. She was a plump little girl with rosy cheeks, dancing blue eyes and curly blond hair. Kate would quite naturally hold her father's hand as she skipped along and at home cuddle up on his knee, sucking her thumb and playing with a length of soft cloth she called her 'nummy-num'. Wills affectionately nicknamed her 'Wumpty'.

Gregarious, fun-loving Wills could seem constrained in the home, although from time-to-time sparks of his vivacious nature burst forth to the delight of his daughters. At heart Wills was a strict disciplinarian; a man of high moral standards but undeclared faith – that is until he experienced a religious conversion in his late forties. Wills would recall this dramatic encounter as one of being hit by a bright light and flying from his bicycle into the hedgerow near the local railway level crossing. The signalman on duty seeing Wills fall ran down to help and comfort him as he listened to Wills confused but animated account of what had happened. The signalman was a member of the local Pentecostal Church who understood and guided him into his church. Wills was a witnessing Christian until his life's end. Following Wills' religious conversion, the Pentecostal Church filled much of his life – he read the Holy Bible avidly, highlighting passages with special meaning and making notes in the margins on his understanding and insights.

Wills was a caring and compassionate person, always conscious of the needs of others in the village – the sick, the poor and lonely. He came into the kitchen on many occasions to ask Rose to "put up a plate for old Mrs Tams, her arthritis is bad again and she will not feel like cooking;" or "a box of your newly baked buns for the Smith family" … father was out of work again; or, "a thick jumper and a bowl of soup for old Joe, in yon cottage it will be a bit bleak in this snow." Wills became affectionately known as 'the village help', long before the role of Home Help was defined by the 'Welfare State' in the late

1940s! It was from her father that Molly learnt the true meaning of compassion that undoubtedly equipped her for the challenges she had set herself to become a nurse.

There was only one time, as far as it is known, that Wills' generosity was his downfall. On one rare occasion Wills joined Rose and the Vicar taking tea together. Wills, seeing how much the Vicar was enjoying Rose's homemade scones and the plate was empty, asked, "Another scone, Vicar?" The Vicar, disregarding social etiquette and much to Rose's discomfort replied, "Well, Mr Lange that would be rather nice," - there were none left! Not to be daunted, Rose took the empty plate found some rather dated raspberry buns in the pantry, cut them in half, placed them over the fire on the griddle, laced them with raspberry jam and cream and hey presto Vicar!

TALENTS AND MAKE BELIEVE:

Rose was a talented lady; a 'scholarship' girl whose home circumstances in a mining community prevented the fulfilment of a great potential. Rose left school aged 12 to work as a live-in maid for an elderly brother and sister, and was able to contribute to the family's income back at home.

However, life was kind to Rose; her eventual journey through Gentleman's Service produced a very polished and accomplished lady. Rose taught her girls to read, write, deal with simple numbers and to remember and appreciate verse long before they attended school. Roses investment was soon rewarded when Molly started school and she won the 'Ovaltine Essay' prize. Molly always attributes her love of the power of the pen to her mother; and to her father the wisdom to respect it.

Rose was a also creative needlewoman whose delicate crochet work adorns the tablecloth she prepared for her 'bottom drawer'; now a heirloom for future generations! The girls' interest was soon captured by Rose's ability to knit, sew, and embroider plus the more practical skills of mending and darning! The art of making peg-dolls was pure recreation; a novel experience involving the creations of intricate small items of clothing to fit a clothes peg, a happy face to be painted on the knob of the peg and 'the head' topped with duck, or chicken down for hair - the shoes were added by dipping the tips of the peg into a bottle of black ink!

Etiquette, however, was supreme in the household "you will get nowhere without gentility" (*knowing how to conduct yourself*). Rose was a prim upright figure with white hair surrounding her youthful face with the softest pink skin; a neighbour's child once said to Rose, "Your face looks just like sunshine Mrs Lange," and so it did when life was going well for Rose. Each morning found Rose well-groomed and dressed in accordance with the requirements of the day – "you never know ..." she would warn! As the girls grew older, they became familiar with Rose's behaviour in response to the doorbell. Before answering, she would titivate her hair and rehearse her greeting in front of the hall mirror, "Oh! Good afternoon, Vicar," she would mouth – a typical present day Mrs Bouquet!

Although, Rose perhaps felt that her marriage had denied her the social position to which she aspired, Rose numbered amongst the 'elite' of the village ladies who organized garden parties and summer fetes where the food was sumptuous. Molly, although a small child at the time, well remembers the mischievous atmosphere at one garden party, and Gwen's distain, when, in the face of food (and clothes) rationing during the war, the hostess recklessly remarked, "I wonder what Lord Woolton, our Food Minister, would say if he could see us now?" And, almost in defiance she served generous portions of homemade trifles and strawberries adorned with lashings of cream; ham on the bone with a variety of salads and mayonnaise, rich fruit cake and pastries!

Rose was also renowned for her more sophisticated accomplishments such her poetry recitations, recitals of classical readings and songs at various festivals and church events, notably the monthly meetings of 'The Women's Bright

Hour'. 'If' by Rudyard Kipling and 'The Wreck of the Hesperus' by Henry Wadsworth Longfellow, were the most vividly remembered by the girls; not only the story the poems told but primarily, for the dramatic way in which Rose told them! Molly knew the poems by heart, including all the expressions that went with them! The reciting of Kipling's 'If' felt like a philosophy lesson, which laid down a set of life-rules (albeit perceived as rather sexist today). Rose's undeniable thespian talents came to the fore in her rendition of 'The Wreck of the Hesperus'. The girls with their dolls and cuddly toys, and the cats included, would wait with anticipation for the part where Rose tossed back her head with a rakish laugh, and holding a clay pipe aloft saying ...

"The skipper, he blew a whiff from his pipe and a haughty laugh laughed he."

As the poem progressed through the throes of a shipwreck, tears began to flow from her audience as Rose proceeded ...

"Father answered never a word, a frozen corpse was he'...
The form of a maiden fair ... salt sea was frozen on her breast ...
Salt tears in her eyes ... her hair like the brown seaweed on the billows fall and rise ...
Christ save us all from a death like this."

The girls loved it, although they would be inconsolable with sadness, which Gwen too absorbed!

Sometimes impromptu play-acting would be organised. The fairy tale 'Red Riding Hood' was a popular choice. The play was unscripted - they knew the story in every detail. Kate might act the part of Red Riding Hood, Molly the parts of Red Riding Hood's mother and granny; whilst Rose would take the parts of the woodcutter and the wolf – her glorious fox fur with its piecing amber eyes realistically springing to life as the wicked wolf as if by magic. They all knew the moment was coming but it always made them jump out of their skin when the wolf pounced on granny and Gwen wasn't exempt from such surprises!

Rose so easily created a world of make-believe and her delight in 'dressing up' brought fun and entertainment to the girls, For instance, pretend 'concerts' or 'tea parties' with Rose dressed up in exaggerated fashions of the day; Molly and Kate would also be toffed-up for the occasion in large brimmed hats together with other items of over-sized and over-stated finery from the family trunk. These pretend events invariably included serving finely cut egg and cucumber sandwiches and Angel cake to her 'visitors'; mimicry like 'taking off' the Vicar's wife, or amusing 'small-talk', and items of entertainment – perhaps a recitation, or singing accompanied by Rose on the piano. Rose's piano playing was a classic turn in itself because she had developed the habit of playing one handed – the left hand playing the right-hand notes! Rose always told how she was naturally left-handed but the school teachers made her use her right hand and rapped her knuckles with a cane if they caught her doing otherwise. Molly and Kate who were taking piano lessons made their contribution to the entertainment too.

By contrast, another regular pass-time was to 'play church', probably to ease the solemnity of the real experience and to make the message easier for children to digest, or maybe Rose just liked taking a 'rise' out of the Vicar! Playing 'Church', usually took place in the warmth of the family kitchen in the winter when the weather was too bad to venture out to attend the evening service. Rose, standing on the large deal kitchen table behind one of the girls' desks as the pulpit, would play the role of the Minister to give an hilarious take of an over-zealous, 'tub-thumping' preacher; she would sing the hymns with great gusto, Molly played the piano imagining Gwen by her side – sometimes they feared Rose might fall off the table. Kate might stand at the door to 'meet and greet' the 'congregation', to be seated on various chairs and the large sofa. The 'congregation' comprised Gillian, Kate's favourite rag doll who had the most imposing presence with her saucer-like face surrounded by golden locks of plaited wool and painted with startling blue eyes framed by long eye lashes, a rose bud mouth and round rosy cheeks. Sitting next to Gillian, Molly's beloved large china black doll named 'Sambo' would be surrounded by numerous cuddly toys and pet cats. Kate took the collection; chocolate drops were placed on the collection plate and then eaten at the end of the service. The whole event had to be seen to believe!

But nothing seemed to compare with the bedtime routines! Until electricity arrived in the village paraffin lamps lit the home; a paraffin heater, which cast diamond shaped patterns on the ceiling supplemented the heating, and a candle lit the way to bed. In the winter the cold was extreme as the wind blew across the wide-open space of the surrounding fields. Rose wrapped two shelves from the fireside ovens in towels and placed them in the bed before bedtime to make it nice and warm. Finally, Rose crept in between Molly and Kate to tell her stories under the bedclothes.

At times the stories would feel rather spooky with every situation vividly described and accompanied by Rose's unique sound effects! For instance, it was particularly eerie when Rose took them into 'Benjamin Bunny's' dark burrow, or the holes in the river banks where 'Bertie Beaver' and his family lived, and at Christmas time to fly amongst the tree-tops with the mischievous cackling witches on their broom-sticks who, Rose warned, took accounts of any unseemly behaviour to Santa!

Rose always put the evening to bed by saying prayers – with Molly making sure that Gwen was included! Rose's usual prayer was an extract from the 18th century Charles Wesley hymn and one the girls knew by heart as if reciting a poem –

Gentle Jesus meek and mild, look upon a little child,
Pity my simplicity, suffer me to come to thee.
Loving Jesus, gentle lamb, in thy gracious hands I am,
Make me Saviour what thou art, live thyself within my heart.
Amen

In the morning, when Rose had departed and it was time to get up, reality struck! The girls' breath was 'smoky' in the cold air of the bedroom as the frost glistened on the inside of the windowpane. A quick dash was made downstairs to find their clothes warming on the large guard in front of the fire and they enjoyed the comfort of dressing in its warmth.

But Rose's constructive play carried expectations too! From a very early age, Molly and Kate were expected to contribute to church and village events, particularly the Sunday School Anniversary, a summer event with the children sitting on a tiered platform at the front of the church. Molly had no problem when her name was announced, she would always stand up and perform with aplomb; a sensation of exhilaration would swell within Gwen too. Kate, however, was shy and although she would stand when her name was announced she would then burst into tears – up came big sister, Molly, who took over word perfect. Rose could never understand how Molly was able to achieve this performance with such perfection because she was never observed to consciously learn, or practise Kate's pieces! But Molly was a budding image of her mother's talents and theatrical nature!

The Sunday School Anniversary event was the showcase of the year. Clothes were not bought willy-nilly in these days but the Anniversary was the second of three occasions during the year when new outfits were expected. The first was Easter, complete with a boater – a straw one decorated with buttercups and daisies if Easter was late and the weather fine. The third, an autumn outfit for Harvest Festival. One autumn outfit of a navy-blue velour coat, black lace-up shoes, knee high blue socks and a red poke bonnet was particularly striking. Both girls were always dressed the same for formal events. they looked like the two royal princesses!

The poorest families tried hard to observe the tradition of new outfits. Some paid a weekly amount on a local outfitter's 'club-card'. Other mothers with creative minds and skilful fingers, like Rose, were able to convert hand-me-downs from the older to the younger children, or clothes passed on from other families, the final garment being unrecognizable thanks to a clever twist in the fabric, a bow, or a mix-and-match from several garments! Once again, 'make do and mend' pre-dated the wartime slogan of the 1940s. Whilst not meaning to be unkind, Rose was always adamant that her girls' outgrown cloths would not be seen on other children – no matter how deserving.

But one-year disaster struck the Lange family. Wills loved to shop in the market on Saturday evening after milking and as a treat Molly or Kate took it in turns to accompany him. Molly thought it was such fun to sit on the top deck of the red bus in the dusk of evening, squeezing Gwen next to her father. As Molly approached the Market in excited 'chatter' with her father, its twinkling lights welcomed them and during the winter the smell of roast chestnuts would fill the late afternoon air. Wills spotting a child begging would stop with a kindly word and drop a jingle in the purse – no child was ever ignored.

Wills then continued to walk round the busy, noisy market where he would pick up a treat or two – first the fruit and veg; then the 'pies and cheeses'; sometimes the 'hardware' for a new mop-head and finally the clothes stalls. One-year Wills was commissioned to buy Molly and Kate new dresses, shoes and socks for the Sunday School Anniversary. The dresses he chose, both Molly and Gwen agreed, were a joy to behold. They were made from a salmon-coloured silky fabric with a frill at the hem and a little mock-bolero jacket attached to the shoulder seam with its scalloped edges embroidered with blue forget-me-nots. Then Wills found the perfect little black patent shoes and white socks with lacy turnover tops to complete the ensemble – Molly squeaked with delight in Gwen's ear. The day of the Anniversary arrived and humiliation struck - another girl arrived wearing the same dress! Molly and Kate's dresses were never seen again.

In spite of Molly's spirited and rather mischievous nature, she was a 'sickly girl', whose childhood was peppered with admissions to the local Children's Hospital and it was during these times when she was frightened and lonely that she felt closer to Gwen than at any other. Before the introduction of the NHS in 1948 a 'Recommendation' from a patron of a voluntary hospital was required to qualify admission for treatment. Otherwise, young and old alike, who fell on hard times such as poverty, ill health or destitution, were at the mercy of the harsh Victorian Poor Law hospitals and workhouses until the dawn of the 1930's when Local Government assumed responsibility ... but the Poor Law cast long shadows. Such was the dread that a story with a foreboding message was often told of an elderly frail mother being taken in a wheelchair and wrapped in a blanket to a Poor Law Institution by her daughter, accompanied by her small granddaughter. The elderly mother was wheeled through the door and as her daughter turned to leave her there, the little granddaughter said, "Don't forget the blanket, Mam I shall need it when I take you."

Although only young at the time, and probably reinforced by affectionate family teasing and Gwen's reminiscences, Molly remembered the family doctor, Dr Bell, visiting her. Dr Bell always wore a beautiful sweet smelling red rose in his lapel and whilst soothing Molly's forehead he would say, "Smell my rose Molly." The rose, however, was not pure ornamentation; in other circumstances the 'sweet smelling rose' would serve the same purpose as the surgeon's cane with its vented knob filled with highly perfumed potpourri to disguise the often-unpleasant smells on the wards.

Towards the end of his visit as Dr Bell prepared to leave, he sometimes shook his head saying to Wills, "I'm afraid it's the Children's Hospital and another 'Recommendation', Mr Lange." Wills would set off on his bicycle to seek endorsement of his family's worthiness (sober, God-fearing, and in work) from a member of the wealthy village hierarchy. In 1911 an Act of Parliament introduced a Worker's Contributory Scheme which entitled the workman to a retirement pension, sick pay, and admission to the List of a Panel Doctor (present day General Practitioner) for medical care but not necessarily any medicines. The Scheme did not include a workman's family. Hence the fee for Dr Bell's consultation, together with any medicines he might prescribe, were paid for through membership of one of the Friendly Societies to which most far-sighted families belonged.

Needless to say, before calling Dr Bell numerous home-made remedies were tried such as goose-grease saved from the Christmas roast to rub on the chest for a painful wheeze; a warm mixture of vinegar, butter and brown sugar to 'cut the phlegm'; a drop of Friars Balsam on a sugar lump to soothe a sore throat; or one of Rose's home-made salt bags warmed in the oven to relieve ear ache. Rose's pharmacopeia was endless – she could even put together a steam tent to ease laboured, or painful breathing!! However, the most drastic home remedy was the application of a starch poultice to treat impetigo; impetigo, scabies and ringworm were the scourge of the poor and the embarrassment of the higher orders of society. When Molly developed impetigo, Rose was quick to prepare a starch poultice. A clean cloth soaked in wet starch was applied over the scabs and allowed to dry. Once dried and stiff the 'poultice' was removed bringing debris of scabs with it and leaving raw flesh behind. The wound was then dressed with Vaseline. But before the end of the week, Molly was covered in a rash that began to blister; Dr Bell diagnosed Pemphigus so off to hospital again. The pungent smell of the medicated bandages that encased Molly's limbs and trunk was not easily forgotten. But it was forgotten and Molly, restored to health, felt even better equipped to 'play nurses' in her hospital in the garden shed with the soft toys and dolls, sometimes the family's pet cat, as her patients. In these formative years, could it have been that such experiences fostered Molly's love of nursing and her desire to help others as they had helped her?

Surmounting all these difficulties and encouraged by her mother's teaching, Molly was an eager and competent little scholar who longed to go to school. The day came when her name was entered on the School Register and Molly boldly stepped out to greet a new phase in her journey.

CHAPTER 2

EXPANDING HORIZONS

THE WAR YEARS (1939-45):

The declaration of war in the autumn of 1939 set the whole nation back in its tracks. Children did not know what to expect whilst their parents and grandparents who had experienced the First World War from 1914 to 1918 feared what might be in store. Both at home and abroad the many faces of war cast impressionable shadows on Molly's life and as her early childhood was left behind a different awareness of the adult world began to take shape. On home ground new routines and priorities were introduced as protection against the destructive air raids and enemy invasion on home soil, the trauma experienced by families torn apart by separations and loss, and against the miss-use of essential materials and limited resources. Abroad, the armed forces fought to defend the Country with heavy loss of life and limb; terrible atrocities were reported from Prisoner of War and Concentration Camps and the ultimate sadism of the Atomic Bomb.

The fear of invasion and destruction of life, family homes, and essential services by air raids was very real. To thwart the enemy's intension all types of illumination were virtually distinguished. The villages and towns across the Country were plunged into darkness as streetlights were switched off and heavy blackout curtains, or similar devises blanked out lighting from homes, factories and other buildings. Failure to comply was admonished by the Air Raid Protection (ARP) Warden, with the familiar call, "Put that Light out!" In addition, all windowpanes, particularly in public places like schools, were covered with a network of adhesive tape to prevent injury from shards of glass during an air raid. All road and railway signage were removed from public display, and the familiar warnings 'Careless Talk Costs Lives' and 'Walls have Ears', were posted to safeguard information getting into the wrong hands; in some place's curfews were put in place.

It was a frightening time in which to live: a strange silence, even at home, seemed to descend like the hush preceding something about to happen. And yet, almost as if in defiance of the War, a heightened sense of community and camaraderie was experienced in everyday life.

1939, Molly was aged 7, and war was declared. The village, situated on the River Trent, guided enemy bombers to strategic destinations, such as Rolls Royce and the construction of aeroplane engines; the home of British Celanese and parachute making; and the London, Midland and Scottish (LMS) depot central to the rail network. So, from almost day one of the war the villagers were alerted to the sound of the sirens, a howling noise giving an air raid warning. The villagers would look up to the sky to observe the German planes following the river to their destination. Air raid shelters were built in the school grounds but until the shelters were completed, the children practised the drill of piling the desks on top of each other and crawling beneath them for safety and donning their gas masks. The gas mask, a device issued by the Government, comprised a sealed headgear with a window and filtered breathing system in protection against a poisonous gas-attack by the Germans. It was a requirement for the mask, in its cardboard box to be always carried on one's person, together with the Government issued Identity Card – Molly's allocated number was RCWL 64/3; Wills' number ended /1; Rose's /2; and Kate's /4). It sometimes concerned Molly that Gwen was unprotected but Gwen gave assurance that she was included on Molly's documents and when necessary, they would share the gasmask.

Wills thought the desk protection arrangement at school was "sheer lunacy" so at the first sound of the sirens he fetched the girls home. They would walk through the village, hushed and deserted like a ghost town, to the safety of home and the air raid shelter if the raid came too close for comfort.

Wills soon organized an air-raid shelter to be sunk into the ground off the rick-yard. The shelter had a tin roof camouflaged with sods of field grass and at the first sound of the sirens, particularly at night; the family would run across to the shelter. More often than not, the planes already droned overhead making the familiar and frightening 'chug-chug' sound of the German bomber. Shells from the 'ack-ack' guns might burst overhead and the shrapnel from the casings rained down on the corrugated roof of the barns. Gwen was caught up in Molly's terror and when they plunged down into the shelter with haste, the soil steps led into a damp, cold, cave-like space dimly lit by spluttering night-lights; it was horrid. Rose was usually the last to arrive having collected the pre-prepared refreshments and locked the house door against any German invaders!

In the fullness of time Wills' inventive mind began to work on another idea; he dug a huge crater at the bottom of the garden and in it he sank the garden shed! The large wooden structure had stood on the back lawn within sight of the kitchen door where it was used by the girls as their 'play-house' – in one corner Molly organized her 'hospital' and in the other Kate's table was filled with bits and bobs. The shed made a fine shelter – homemade pegged rugs on the floor, 'black-out' curtains draped the windows (now below ground) and oil lamps gave almost enough light by which to read, a real luxury … Until!

One fateful night, resembling the 'family Von-Trapp', they were making their way down to the bottom of the garden with the sound of the sirens howling in their ears when Kate started to scream and splutter with grief - she had left her rag doll, Gillian, in bed at the house. They arrived in the shelter but Kate could not be pacified. Rose went back to the house … found the doll but in the pitch-blackness of the night became lost in the bean sticks on Wills' vegetable plot! Rose, being what might be called somewhat 'highly strung' or 'rather theatrical' went berserk in such frightening circumstances!

The shelter was never used again; instead, they took their chances in the large cubbyhole under the stairs. But even that was not without its drama. Wills had given up on such midnight excursions saying, "If I am to die, it will be in my bed," leaving Rose and the girls to make the pilgrimage without him. On one such occasion the 'All Clear' sirens were heard and the little group prepared to leave their sanctuary but the door was fixed closed – the swivel latch had swivelled into the wrong position! Banging on the door and stairs eventually roused Wills who appeared in his nightshirt to rescue them. Wills looked very solemn and displeased; they all crept back to bed without a word. However, as the years went by and they reminisced about 'tales from the air-raid shelter', this was always one of their favourites and they would laugh until they cried by its telling – even Wills. Well, they had never seen Dad in his 'nightie' before and the pink colouring on the back hem of the gown made them giggle and generate the nickname of 'Pop the pink shirt'. Rose admitted to some lack of concentration when loading the dolly tub and a bright pink blouse had been included by mistake!

During this unsettled time Molly attempted to interest Kate in cultivating an imaginary friend, suggesting, "You could name her Eileen Street. Eileen would always be with you and Gillian would have a new friend too," consoled Molly. "You will never be in any danger of leaving her behind and when you are sad or frightened, she will always be there." But pragmatic Kate was having none of it.

Undoubtedly, one of the saddest and yet a most necessary activity during the war was the evacuation of small children from the large worn-torn cities to the countryside. Two little girls, Julia and Teresa, from Liverpool were billeted with Wills' youngest sister, Martha and her husband who had no children of their own. The evacuees, aged 5 and 7, looked totally lost, frightened and bewildered. The sad appearance of these little ones would be indelibly marked on Molly's memory, as she looked the woe of poverty full in the face once again. Julia and Teresa arrived infested with head and body lice but thankfully Rose came to the rescue. Rose and Wills were deeply affected about the plight of the girls with which Martha was totally inexperienced to deal, so they were invited to stay with Molly's family most weekends. It seemed a good idea but fear gripped the girls as they entered the wide-open spaces of the village, saw the animals roaming freely about the fields and heard the bird sounds at nightfall. Molly would share her concerns with Gwen, "it must be terrifying for them and without their parents too!" Rose persevered by showering the little girls with love and comfort, she engaged them in playtimes and read stories to them; they sat at the table and ate tasty food – although this was a routine they found strange at first.

Gradually, Julia and Teresa seemed to come alive; they joined in the fun and even led the games from time to time. Molly was often inspired by Gwen's good ideas, as she whispered mischievously, "I know what it is like not to have a voice that is heard!" But that was not strictly true because Molly was acutely sensitive to Gwen's approval when things were going well, she was equally aware of Gwen's concerns when things were not!

When the war was eventually over, Julia and Teresa had grown up and wonderful friendships had developed. Molly talked to them about Gwen and her unseen presence as an imaginary friend. "Oh, do you think you can find us one?" implored the girls, "It would be lovely to know we were never alone." Molly tried to explain that she could not find them their imaginary friend because, "she, he, or it, lives within you – you just need to know how to recognise each other." "How did you find yours?" they asked. Molly told them about the day in the fairy dell when she and Gwen just found each other in the sunshine, "and once we were friends, we have always been aware of each other."

Under Rose's tutelage the girls had grown up: they had extended their horizons by being able to read, write and manipulate simple numbers quite fluently. An air of pride and confidence had replaced the poverty expressed in their downtrodden self-image and they were prepared to live life to the full. So, Julia and Teresa returned to their home in Liverpool.

The arrival of the 'Women's Land Army' was a new experience to hit the local farming community during wartime! Two Land Girls lived with Molly's family. Dorothy, a tall elegant, well-spoken young woman, previously a bank clerk and Elsie, a bonny, vivacious bright-eyed, blonde-haired girl who worked in a dress shop. The 'Girls' were a blow of fresh air in many ways. For instance, it was a novelty for them, and the farmers, to be working on the land and tending the animals. Teaching the Land Girls to milk a cow, or to supervise birthing ewes was said to be a skilled and tactful process – but 'the Girls' made it and gained respect. The Land Girls also introduced a sense of fun into the village dances and they regularly met up with Wills and two local farmers to cycle to the town cinema on Saturday nights. One of the best treats for Molly was to accompany Dorothy to her home in Sussex for the occasional weekend.

The village seemed to escape the intensity of the air raids as the war progressed but the impact of its destruction continued to over-shadow the family. Rose's youngest sister, Helen, with her husband and two children farmed in Westmorland. Also living with the family in the farmhouse were Helen's parents-in-law, farm servants and evacuees from London - thirteen in total. One fateful night everyone in the house was killed by a direct hit from a German bomber shedding a landmine on its way back to base! The photographs in the local press told the heart-rending story of the loss of life, a flattened home and business enterprise. Clothing and bedding were draped over the surrounding trees and fences like terrified ghosts fleeing the tragic scene. Faith, Rose's second eldest sister, lost her son, a young RAF pilot - a university graduate with a promising academic career. Rose's brothers were all affected by the war in different ways. Wills' family were somewhat more fortunate.

Painful memories of the war were emblazoned upon the Dolman family members and the climb back to some sort of normality was hard. Rose was deeply affected by the loss of her sister Helen, with whom she shared engagements in Gentleman's Service at prestigious households - Rose as Head Cook and Helen as Lady's Maid.

With the passage of time the ground around Wills' improvised air raid shelter shrank, leaving the shed standing on a mound of remaining ground, a situation which always amused Gwen when Molly likened it to the Biblical story of Noah's Ark stranded on Mount Arratt after the great flood.

But it took many years for Molly's world to return back to normal after the war: identity cards and clothes coupons restricted the new clothes one could buy, and food rationing continued during the early days of the NHS.

GROWING UP:

And so, the seeds of Molly's love affair with nursing, sown as a small child, took hold and germinated throughout her life. As Molly left her early childhood behind, she became increasingly involved in the sanctuary her mother frequently provided for sick relatives. A black iron bedstead brought out of store from the back bedroom to take pride of place in an alcove by the fire in the living room inevitably signalled a new arrival. Wills played his part by providing beestings, the first milk from newly calved cows, for Rose to make into delicious nutritious custard – something like junket. Wills also made available the ingredients for the saucepan of stock that simmered constantly to produce calf's foot jelly or beef tea for its restorative properties; and wood for the fire that burned day and night. Rose was always in attendance to sooth the invalids' fears and to relieve their pain. In addition, she had her own special pharmacopeia of medicines, perhaps the most notable was

'Cinder tea' for indigestion and stomach upsets. A red-hot coal would be taken from the fire and dropped into a cup of cold water to steep, the cinder would be removed and the 'Cinder Tea' sipped when suitably cooled – to the unwary, the grit at the bottom of the cup came as a nasty surprise!

As Rose's patients began to feel better, they sat in the garden whilst she read to them – John Bunyan's, 'Pilgrim's Progress' was one of her favourite tales. Together they composed jigsaws. helped with embroidery and in the making of peg-dolls, which was always an amusing exercise. Knitting seemed to be something everyone liked to do but 'French Knitting' was rather a novelty. It required an empty cotton bobbin with four tintacks set on a flat end of the bobbin, wool and a small knitting needle. The wool was threaded up through the centre of the bobbin and wound round the tacks to make stitches for a knitting process performed with the aid of the short knitting needle. As the knitting grew and poked out of the end of the bobbin it looked like a cord, which could be as long and as colourful as the extent of one's imagination. For instance, some people wound a very long cord round and round and secured it in a circle to make a cushion cover!

Wills did not encourage board games because of their association to gambling, however, Snakes and Ladders and Tiddlywinks were cautiously permitted. However, Rose, unbeknown to Wills, engaged in the rather questionable rehabilitative activity of Tasseography, 'reading teacups' from which it was purported to tell a person's fortune. It was a game they regularly played in the Servants' Hall and one with which Rose was particularly adept! Younger patients like Pru's stepdaughter, Maisey and cousin Joan, Rose's eldest sister's daughter both having come to stay with Rose to recuperate following debilitating conditions were avid participants! Even the older patients liked to indulge with mild curiosity, or amusement and the whole experience gave Molly and Gwen a particular kind of 'zing'.

'Reading the teacups' was quite a ritual and one that Rose carried out with all her imaginative flare and sense of the theatrical. The 'reading' took place following a cup of tea when any drops of tea and the tealeaves had settled at the bottom of the cup (no tea bags in these days). The cup was ceremoniously swished round in a circular movement and quickly turned upside down on the saucer. Whilst they waited with bated breath, Rose would quietly reflect on what the tealeaves might tell – usually romance, return to health, or achievement. Time to tell all and the cup was turned over to reveal the pattern left by the tealeaves. Sometimes the tealeaves would leave a trail from the bottom to near the top of the cup to foretell the arrival of news, or the promise of an exciting journey; a ring of tealeaves would cause Rose to smile conspiratorially saying, "Someone is waiting to give you a diamond ring!" A cluster of tealeaves could foretell an invitation to a party, or if the formation resembled a bunch of flowers, then ... "Expect to hear from an unsuspected admirer;" but any drops of tea left at the bottom of the cup would foretell tears and disappointment. After the 'Reading' came the inquest and "Who could it be?" became open to some rather surprising revelations and speculations!

But one day Rose was to be hoisted by her own petard, as it were! Interpreting a formation of tealeaves as a man running up the inside of Maisey's cup, Rose foretold of the arrival of hasty news. The next day a telegram arrived saying Maisey's father, Barry, had been taken seriously ill and admitted to hospital – an illness from which he was not to recover. Thereafter Rose was always more circumspect.

In addition to providing for the needs of sick relatives, any sick or frail animals received preferential care in times of need. One beautiful horse named, Diana, suffered from septicaemia following a foot injury. Diana was 'nursed' in the corner of the home paddock on a soft bed of straw surrounded by bales of hay – sadly Diana died. Wills was deeply affected by Diana's suffering and eventual death, which added to the sadness Molly was experiencing – Gwen seemed to know just how she felt.

Other animals were housed in a variety of pens at the bottom of the kitchen garden to be cared for by Rose and 'fattened up' for the table. Needless to say, Rose's love of the theatrical meant that each animal was given a personalised name and talked to, which was lovely at the time but when they appeared on the dinner table it was a different matter.

One such casualty was a very large black pig named Juggins. Juggins was a great delight. He enjoyed the freedom to roam around the garden and the luxury of special titbits when he rattled the doorknocker with his snout. On Juggins command Rose would appear saying, "Hello, Juggins," with a few grunts of her own in reply to the pig's salutation. It was a sad day when Juggins disappeared to reappear as sides of bacon hanging from ceiling hooks in the larder. Kate, knowing Molly's tender heart, would wait by the larder door and as Molly passed by she would snort loudly and say, "Hello Juggins." Gwen found Kate's sense of 'fun' most unpleasant but she was unable to influence her behaviour. Gwen realised Kate did not have the ear to hear and tried to help Molly to understand.

Hopping Hannah, a pet duck was another casualty. Hopping Hannah had a deformed leg, she hopped around the garden quacking, wagging her tail, and flittering her wings when Rose appeared. Sadly, the day came when 'Hopping Hannah' also disappeared to reappear on the dinner table – and almost life like too. To Rose, with her long career in high-class cooking, presentation was everything, like the boar's head with an orange in its mouth at a medieval banquet. And so the roast duck appeared trussed up with its head held high and placed on a bed of finely chopped cabbage as if sitting on the grass; a rabbit would be presented likewise but with mashed potato representing two white front feet and a white fluffy pompom-like tail. On one such occasion Molly and Kate started to cry and refused to partake in the meal. Wills was furious and blamed Rose for encouraging this nonsense in the first place by naming the animals and by treating them as one of the family.

"There are to be no more waifs and strays!" he said … "And no more cats either," he pronounced as a parting shot. Molly searched for Gwen's reaction; she just couldn't believe that her kindly father would really have the heart to carry out his orders when pet animals had been a part of the family since she could remember!

But Rose had a cunning trick up her sleeve. Knowing the family's tortoiseshell coloured matriarch was in kitten again she waited until the kittens were born and before they were taken away she retrieved a lovely big black ball of fur and carried it around in her apron pocket. Mother cat and kitten were re-united for feeding in Wills' absence and when the kitten became too big for the apron pocket, Rose made him a bed in the sideboard. Everyone in the know looked on cautiously when Wills was around but amazingly, the kitten never made a sound at that time! This game of hide and seek inevitably resulted in the cat being named Moses after his name-sake who, as the Holy Bible tells, was hidden in the bulrushes away from the murderous eyes of King Herod. Moses grew into the most beautiful cat and lived to a good old age - Wills never asked any questions about Moses and he gradually became absorbed into the household.

One day a new member of the household appeared named Charlie, a large black and white rabbit who came on a temporary vacation during his owner's absence. Charlie thought he was coming as the boss and behaved as if he ruled the roost. However, under Rose's charms he soon learned the house rules! Charlie hopped around after the cats (he always knew his place), lay on the mat with them in front of the kitchen fire and, just like the cats, he responded to Rose's sharpening of the carving knife on the steel at the kitchen door as a call for food – a cheeky robin was not to be left out as he joined in at the end of the parade and waited on the windowsill for his treat of fat juicy bacon rind!

It was the most amazing menagerie but the day came for Charlie to go home, they were all in tears but at least he had escaped the dining table! Charlie went home to live in his cage under the kitchen window but sadly he came to an end far worse than the dining table when the neighbour's large Airedale dog jumped on Charlie's cage and the door flew open. The Lange household regretted the day Charlie returned home.

Molly and sister Kate realised as they grew older that living in the country carried responsibilities other than to enjoy animals as pets. For instance, when a pig was slaughtered Wills would bring home the intestines and head in buckets of saltwater. Rose, with help from Molly and Kate washed out the debris from the intestines under the outdoor pump – one would pump the water and the others would open the intestine tubes to wash out the gunge; change over came when the hands under the running water were numb with cold!

When the head and intestines were cleaned, Rose boiled the head to make brawn - the cheek meat was saved to eat cold as 'chawl'. Likewise, the intestines were curled round in a basin to simmer in a saucepan until tender, left to go cold and turned out in a jellied pudding, now known as 'Chitterlings'. It was a feast the family enjoyed with bread and butter at tea, or supper times. The delicacy was accompanied by Wills' special 'sauce' based on a mixture of mustard, sugar and vinegar.

But the special prize was the brain. Rose would poach the sheep or pig brain in milk and cream to be served on toast like scrambled eggs. However, when roast rabbit was served at the table Molly and Kate would argue over whose turn it was to pick the brain out of the rabbit's skull.

However, life was not all work and no play. A day out was a great treat and the weekly market was one such occasion. Village people, mainly ladies, travelled to town on the market day bus; the atmosphere was abuzz with chatty gossip and laughter. The farmers went to the cattle market and for a bevvy, or two with lunch before returning home –usually by pony and trap when it was said that if the farmer was too inebriated the pony would find its own way home and deliver the slumbering farmer to his doorstep. The ladies would complete their shopping which might include a little luxury such as a blouse, or length of material for a new dress or apron; some ladies had taken their produce such as fruit, vegetables and homemade preserves to sell in the market. They all returned to the village by teatime on the market day bus.

But there were special days out such as a trip to the big city to shop, have tea, and meet friends or relatives. This was an occasion that Molly waited for with bated breath and one in which she always involved Gwen, especially as the bus approached the outskirts of the City. Here Molly would be transfixed waiting for the hospital to come into sight and eventually, she would be rewarded by a glimpse of the nurses in their flowing white caps attending to the patients in their beds on the hospital balconies, all the time whispering to Gwen, "one day that will be me in uniform!

It is sometimes suggested that children who have had imaginary friends are likely to become adults who are more tuned in to the needs of others. So, just as Molly seemed to absorb the prevailing atmosphere of nurturing and caring in her own home quite naturally, she always knew that one day she would be a nurse in this magical world – but it was a hard-fought battle. Molly's father said she wasn't strong enough; her mother supported her ambition but said it was too far from home; her younger sister Kate thought Molly was mad to want to spend her life in a disease ridden, smelly place – Kate had more refined ambitions as a tailoress.

SCHOOL AND SCHOLARSHIP:

Just as Kate seemed to have been born with needle and thread in her hand, so Molly with pen and paper! Molly sat for hours at her desk with the lift up lid where her pens and writing paper were stored. Both before and after winning the Ovaltine Essay Competition, Molly was rewarded by similar achievements at school. Such as her command of English in the Infants' class when in one spelling session the teacher said she was going to try some interesting new words. She wrote the word 'Coffee' on the swivel-type blackboard and turned to the class, saying "Now?" Molly put up her hand and said, "Coffee, Miss Bowen." "Well done. How did you know that word?" "Because it looks like 'toffee' with a curly 'c'. Dad takes us to Miss Goodwin's every Friday to buy toffee – Palm Toffee." As the teacher turned to the board with a twitch of a smile on her lips, Molly quickly sensing the atmosphere looked to Gwen for reassurance, "I was right, wasn't I Gwen?"

On another occasion during her time at the school Molly played a lead part as the wicked witch in the school pantomime. Gwen's encouragement helped her to rehearse her part, whilst Rose's nibble fingers and vivid imagination created a flamboyant costume, including a huge black shiny pointed hat! Molly, also learning to play the piano, occasionally played a little tune at school. So the head teacher forewarned Rose that Molly seemed destined for Grammar School. However, life took an unexpected turn and Molly's family left the village.

The new school, although much larger, seemed very little different. Molly could do the work and she had a lovely teacher, a Mrs Basset the local Vicar's wife. Everything was going well: they lived in a nice house surrounded by a large garden; the school was a short walk from home and the Methodist church quite nearby. "No crows in these cupboards!" Molly giggled with Gwen. Life couldn't be better, except in one sense. Molly was sorely missing her piano teacher, Mrs Pilliat, a musician in her husband's dance band. Mrs Pilliat sometimes played a piece of dance music and taught Molly a few of the intriguing bars. On rare occasions Mr Pilliat joined them with his saxophone … it was so much more than a piano lesson! Then Rose became seriously ill with asthma, pneumonia and pleurisy in quick succession. A fire burned in her bedroom day and night. Molly, now 'mother' looked after Kate and sat with Rose at lunchtime and after school. The doctor called regularly to give Rose treatment and help Molly to apply Kaolin poultice to her mother's chest. One afternoon, the doctor called to find this sad little family sitting on Rose's bed in the firelight. After he had examined and attended to Rose, the doctor made them all a cup of tea, he stoked up the fire and re-filled the coal scuttle, and when he found the shepherd's pie for tea on the kitchen table, he put it in the oven ready for when Wills came home.

During Rose's illness, Christmas was approaching and time for the school party. Wills pressed the girls' best dresses but could not find a clean handkerchief for them – and one never went out without a handkerchief! "Let's get you to the party, or you will miss the beginning. I will bring your hankies later," reassured Wills as he jollied his daughters along. Wills took the girls to the party and returned home to retrieve two hankies from the laundry basket; he ironed them and took them to school. Molly will always remember her dad sneaking into the school hall with the hankies to find his girls and make sure they were settled; and his glowing smile as he mouthed, "Have a good time." With no disrespect to Rose, Gwen silently reflected on how different Rose's parting words would have been – "Mind what you are doing, behave yourselves and don't let me down!"

As Rose recovered from this dreadful spell of ill health Molly was moved into the top class to prepare for the 11+ examinations to determine her next stage of education, which Miss Bowen predicted would be the Grammar School! But the move to the next class was a culture shock that left Molly bewildered. The classroom was large, the ceiling was high as were the lattice taped windows which meant that the only outside view was the sky and some rooftops. The strange two-seater desks were made of laths of wood fastened to a metal frame – not at all like the individual desks and chairs she was used to. Mr Branch, the headmaster who to Molly, appeared an elderly gentleman, oversaw the class. He was strange and somewhat frightening; he had no teeth and puffy, floppy lips that squeaked and sprayed saliva when he spoke; a huge swelling disfigured the front of his neck and he spoke with a rasping booming voice. Mr Branch dressed in a red Harris Tweed suit with plus fours, knee high socks with a bright diamond pattern and large brogue shoes. He strutted up and down between the desks with a cane, which he would bring crashing down on the desk of any pupil who displeased him. SHOCK was the only way to describe Molly's reaction in her new situation and Gwen too was deeply affected. Rose seemed unhappy. Molly often found her mother silently crying as she sat by the fireside with little awareness of her daughter's distress.

Time passed by but with Molly's growing sense of low self-esteem that Gwen could not to resolve. The day of the 11+ examinations came and went - none of the children from Molly's school were successful. Rose was aghast and summoned up the energy to investigate. Mr Branch told Rose that Molly had absolutely no chance of passing the 11+, she was too dim and poorly educated. Molly wept broken heartedly saying to Gwen, "why am I suddenly so dim-witted, Gwen? It didn't used to be like this." Gwen could only console Molly; she really did not have an answer. But Gwen's big concern was that the growing bête noire of self-doubt might blight Molly's life as her idyllic childhood days were left behind and Rose seemed too distracted to notice.

Mrs Basset, Molly's former teacher tried to save the day. The teacher called at the home to talk to Rose about Molly attending the Grammar School as a fee-paying pupil. But even with charitable assistance, Rose was adamant that what she did for one of her girls she would do for the other and no way could they afford to send them both as fee-paying students if needed.

Molly seemed to have all the spirit knocked out of her, like someone winded in a fight but she just bided her time until she moved to the senior school in town. The day dawned and Molly sensed Gwen desperately trying to infuse some optimism. It was a new world: a modern school with large glass windows, airy classrooms and teachers who seemed human. Molly responded to the wide-ranging number of subjects to which she was now introduced but hated the obligatory shower after games, or sessions in the 'gym'. Molly had never seen a shower before and was quite unsure what to do but the games mistress soon had everyone stripped off and standing naked under the tepid stream of water! Routines that even Gwen could not justify - it was all so embarrassing and too brazen for Molly.

By contrast, the pretty, quietly spoken English teacher, Miss Smith, fascinated Molly and the English classes became a life-enhancing experience. Molly was reintroduced to Charles Dickens' fictional story, 'Oliver Twist' and she couldn't wait to get home and tell Rose. When she did, the old sparkle rekindled in her mother's eyes as she recalled the story and fictitious characters such as Fagin, the pickpocket and his ill-gotten gains. Molly felt well prepared when the class discussed the novel and acted out some of the symbolic scenes with Miss Smith.

But it was her father with whom she could explore the deeper meanings as she linked the literature to the poor families in the village and the street urchins in the market. Together they spoke about the heavy responsibility often placed on the young shoulders of the older girls *and boys* in large families to become 'little mothers', sometimes to the detriment of their own schooling but which rarely dampened a sharp wit! Gradually pity and patronage turned to the respect and responsibility embedded in her father. For the first and only time in her life, Molly wondered if nursing was the best choice of career; she wanted to be part of a process that unlocked the abilities of impoverished children and improved their life chances. Little did Molly realise at the time that she would find that opportunity as a nurse.

The History teacher intrigued Molly with her flamboyant walk, her desire to be addressed as 'Madame', and her tendency to playfully 'mock' some historical indiscretions. When Molly told Madame that Miss Smith was about to introduce Charles Dickens' novel, 'A Tale of Two Cities', patting her chignon she said, "Oooh la, la! Well, we shall have to give Mr Dickens a history lesson then will we not, Cherie?" Molly wondered if Madame had French connections to give her such flare! But it was her mother's interest that surprised her as Rose spoke about the French Revolution and its association with Dickens fictional novel – she even picked out some of the characters, including Madame Defarge and her knitting with its encoded messages. Molly didn't realise her mother was such a history buff!

Miss Barnes, the Geography teacher stretched Molly's appreciation of Europe's vast landmass beyond the immediate contours of the English Chanel as it lapped on the shores of England and the coast of France. Germany with it vast resources and Black Forest landscape was put into a new perspective to the war-machine that terrorised her childhood. Likewise, she brought to life the facilities of Switzerland beyond the Ski-slopes and the function of Holland's giant windmills and complex system of waterways. 'Mother Nature', seen in this wider setting provided interests for Molly to share with her father as they poured over her schoolbooks. One day Miss Barnes gave each pupil a slice of Black Forest Gateaux, which Molly took home for Rose to sample – "not bad, nice and light," she pronounced with the old roguish smile. To Molly's delight, Rose seemed to be coming to life again as she continued to be intrigued and involved in her daughter's education.

So, life at the new school was also fun; and Drama on a real stage with rich red velvet curtains was the icing on the cake! Molly made rather different kinds of friends. Some seemed very 'grown up' and 'street wise'; they used makeup out of school, freely associated with boys and patronized the town's newly opened Milk Bar – it was the latest craze, the place 'to be seen' as if it were 'Stringfellow's Night Club'. The girls were fun to be with, light-hearted and free-spirited but Molly was never allowed to over-step the boundary of school. 'Townies' Rose called them in a disparaging tone of voice and advanced a tentative opinion that they sounded rather common. Molly sensed that Gwen was trying to convince her that Rose might have a point and on this very rare occasions Molly shut Gwen out ... Molly was growing up, she was making self-informed choices in all kinds of ways and certainly did not want to discriminate and chose her friends on such snobby values.

At this stage in her life as she moved into the adult world, Molly seemed to find herself at crossroads and it was possible that she was not finding it easy to make sense of her refocusing. This is where the wise headmistress, Miss Stone, stepped in. Towards the end of Molly's first year at senior school, having been made aware of Molly's emerging abilities, Miss Stone suggested she might like to think about transferring to the 'Junior Oxford - School Certificate Stream'. Molly was not impressed: she was vaguely familiar with these girls and found them rather aloof and snooty; they were rarely seen at break times because they had their own common room; and after Molly's experience with the 11+ she certainly did not want to expose herself to another situation in which she was going to fail.

Rose was invited to the school to talk with Miss Stone who explained that the special stream followed a different course of studies, one laid down by an external Board of Examiners leading to the award of 'School Certificate' in line with the local Grammar School. Miss Stone reassured Rose that the scheme had been introduced by the School Governors and Education Authority who held the view that opportunity at school should exist beyond the age of 11. Rose was once again 'on form'; she was greatly encouraged and confident that Molly could do well. Molly was less inclined to grasp the opportunity, a reaction that disappointed both Rose and Miss Stone. Molly was offered an incentive by suggesting she first tried the Junior Oxford Stream's 'Penfriend Group'. Attracted to the idea Molly joined the Group and enjoyed hearing about the interest she would find in knowing more about how lives were lived in other parts of the world. Molly was allocated a schoolboy living in Hungary named Dominik. However, at this moment in time Molly's mind was resolute against further concessions and no 'Pen-Friend' would change it.

But the ultimate decision came from the most unexpected direction.

CHAPTER 3

A TASTE OF TOWN LIFE

A NEW FAMILY:

Now in a state of indecision because she appreciated Rose's disappointment, Molly began to feel that perhaps she ought to give the 'Junior Oxford' class a try when the most unexpected, albeit regrettable, opportunity came her way. Uncle Barry, Pru's husband from the corner shop died.

Barry, when first diagnosed as suffering with stomach cancer, came to stay at Molly's home to be cared for by Rose in the 'sick bay' of her living room. Gradually Barry became strong enough to return home but did not sustain his recovery. When Barry died Pru, was left to manage the business with her two stepchildren, Maisey, now approaching 20 years of age and a commercial secretary, and her younger brother Paul, a pupil at boarding school with aspirations of Ordination.

It was quite beyond Pru's capabilities to manage the business single-handed. Maisey reduced her hours at work and Paul cut short his education to return home and take a clerical position in the local railway offices. Pru was inconsolable; frequently going away to stay with friends only to return home to take to her bed and receive treatment for depression. For a short period Pru tried a position on the shop floor of a stylish fashion house where she proved to be very successful but her enthusiasm was short-lived.

Pru spoke to Wills and Rose, saying she was lonely for her own 'flesh and blood' and Molly could be such support and comfort. Would they allow her to come and live with Pru to finish her last year of schooling? The decision was a hard one for Molly's parents to make – torn between concern for Pru, Molly's state of impasse at school, and the anticipated distancing of their eldest daughter. Pru won.

REFLECTIONS:

Looking back, Aunt Pru had been a familiar figure weaving in and out of Molly's early life. Molly was fond of her; she was fun, a stylish dresser, and had a swanking way of speaking from living in the South. In her mid-thirties, Pru married Barry, a widower with two children, Maisey and Paul. They continued to live in the family home in Shropshire with Barry still managing the family grocery shop nearby. Molly recalled the time she first got to know Pru's new family. It was an occasion when Rose, recovering from a debilitating time, took Molly and Kate to stay with Pru and Barry at their home in Shropshire, "for a period of recuperation," she said. But was it? Did Molly, like Gwen see the tears roll down Wills' cheek as he stood at the kitchen sink the morning his beloved family left? Without a car or telephone, the effect of the geographical distance between them alone would be considerable and the effect of the separation on the family might not be restorative but irreparable. Gwen looked on through Molly's mind's eye to wonder if Wills' and Rose's marriage had finally cracked and this was where they went their separate ways?

Depression was a rather vague concept to Molly but sometimes Gwen felt that Rose's sadness was palpable. The periodic headaches that continued after her swing-boat accident were unbearable at times; and gradually the asthma attacks became quite debilitating. After an exhausting night trying to cope with an asthma attack Rose would sometimes say to Molly as she left for school the next morning, "I may not be here when you come home; look after Kate." From the premonitions Molly had shared, Gwen knew the prospect of her mother dying filled

Molly with dread throughout her childhood. Sadly, Molly was not to know that her mother would live into her 90's and die peacefully in her bed with Molly by her side.

During their time in Shropshire, Kate, who was very young, stayed at home with Rose and Aunt Pru whilst Molly went to school with Maisey and Paul and although she was in the first class with the 'little people', they always walked home together. It seemed a very large and intimidating classroom – possibly divided into infants at one end and juniors at the other. Molly sought Gwen's advice about where she should sit. "I don't know anyone." Molly sensed that Gwen was just about to prompt her towards the first empty seat when one of the teachers came to say, "Hello." The teachers were kind and friendly and seemed to know Molly felt lonely and timid in this strange environment. But what impressed Molly most of all was the mid-morning break, which included a drink of milk from a small bottle with a cardboard cap into which a hole could be pierced to insert a straw to drink through. Never had Molly seen milk served in such a container, in fact she whispered to Gwen, "I can't believe this is cow's milk, it tastes so different!" Gwen gave gentle assurance that the milk was OK, it was just easier to serve in that way.

On the way home from school the children would often call into the family shop to buy sweets. The shop was an imposing building in the centre of the small town, where the assistants wore a traditional long black tunic-like garment under a large white apron. It was like an 'Aladdin's cave' with the smell of fresh warm bread, coffee beans being ground and served in blue paper packets; the twang of the spices and dried fruit was mouth-watering. Molly was intrigued by some of the activities of the shop assistants, for instance the delicacy with which they cut butter from a large slab and moulded it into interesting shapes with a butter-pat in each hand, followed by the art of wrapping up the butter in greaseproof paper. But most fascinating of all was the overhead tramline that connected the shop tills to a box where the cashier sat looking down over her pince-nez on all she surveyed. The cashier took the money from a rocket shaped box, docketed the amount and returned the 'rocket' containing the receipt and any change that may be due along the tramlines to the tills. Molly whispered to Gwen that she would love to go up into the cashier's box but this was never allowed.

Although her mother was sick and sad, and Molly wondered who was looking after her father, she enjoyed her time with her Uncle and Aunt. They created fun-filled outings to the surrounding hilly countryside where they would climb to a hilltop and look down on the small town – the best part was coming down the hills – sometimes Molly would roll and other times she seemed to fly like Mercury on wings of fire. One late afternoon, Molly spotted a murmuration of starlings, "Oh, just look Gwen, I do wish Dad was here to see this – he would love it. Do you think he is alright?" Gwen agreed Wills would love to have seen the birds and tried to comfort Molly by assuring her that he was likely to be doing just fine; and it might not be too long before they went home. Occupying such an intuitive part of Molly's life, Gwen began to sense she was becoming rather fretful and prompted her to talk to Rose about when they might be going home. Gwen couldn't help but share Molly's tears in conversation with her mother whilst she was having her bedtime wash that evening. Rose promised to write to Wills.

The next day whilst Molly was quietly drinking her milk in the classroom and thinking about home, she asked Gwen if she thought her father would reply, "What shall we do if Dad doesn't want us to go back home?" With Molly on the brink of tears Gwen pretended to be shocked saying, "Doesn't want you home! I bet he will be there with open arms." Each afternoon after school Molly would burst into the house asking if there was a letter from her father. But day after day she was disappointed and almost beside herself Molly would say to Gwen, "Dad doesn't want us to go back home! I just know it!" One afternoon Molly was rewarded; there was a letter from Wills arranging for his family's return. This time Molly cried tears of joy and Gwen whispered to her, "What did I tell you?"

The day eventually came when they packed their suitcases and caught the train to return home to Wills.

It had been a long journey but Molly's tiredness just disappeared when she saw her father standing on the platform with a taxi waiting outside the station. Home smelt good. Wills had a nice fire burning and a tantalizing smell of food filled the air. By bedtime everything seemed back to normal; Rose was rather quiet but Kate trailed after Wills with her nummy-num and Molly made a fuss of the cats. A lot of water had passed under the bridge, as one might say and the family now had to piece life back together again.

So Molly had fond memories of Pru and her family and the care they provided for them during such a difficult time. In due course, Molly never really knew why, Barry sold the family business in Shropshire and moved with the family to a town some twenty miles from Molly's home where he invested in another grocery shop.

The new shop stood in a central location at the junction of one steep street and another - the typical crisscross street network of a town environment. Molly and her family visited her aunt and uncle fairly frequently to bask in the warmth of their companionship and the same old magic of the grocer's shop. After their arrival, it wasn't too long before Molly crept into the shop to be with her Uncle of whom she was very fond.

Uncle Barry had a military-like figure. He was tall, well-groomed, gentle in demeanour and nicely spoken. Barry did not seem to have changed in appearance from a photograph taken during his time in the Army in which he wore the smooth quality uniform of an Officer, adorned with its military insignia and the distinctive Sam Browne belt across his chest. When Barry died, Molly was so proud to be gifted the signet ring he had worn throughout his Military Service.

The customers clearly warmed to Barry and Molly enjoyed being with him. She would watch him lift one of the brightly coloured bottles down from a top shelf to serve Mrs Danes with "a portion of Indian Brandy for me 'digestives', please Barry." Molly watched with fascination as Barry deftly used the hand operated bacon-slicing machine in response to a customer's instruction, – "Number 8 please Barry, not too thin." Molly helped Barry to make the ice cream in a wooden churn in a well-lit protected corner of the dark cellar. The cellar, which doubled-up as an air raid shelter, was a spooky place, ventilated only by the open fretwork grid at pavement level through which coal was delivered in winter for the family fire. Tuesday and Saturday were earmarked as special days when Molly eagerly awaited the delivery of cream buns and the privilege of being given the first choice of a cake to save for tea. Geoff, the errand boy had also made his mark on Molly by giving her a ride at full speed down the steep street in the front basket of the shop-bike ... later Molly always likened the scene to the 'Hovis' advert she would see on TV!

So, to be given this chance of living with them at the shop, although for the sad reason that Barry had died and her aunt was lonely, was unbelievable. Not only did it provide Molly with an escape from the 'Junior Oxford' class and the threat of more horrid examinations but also the anticipation of actually living at the shop with Paul and Maisey was beyond her wildest dreams. They had always been friendly and enjoyed each other's company. Paul seemed to have a 'soft spot' for Molly and of course Molly being the youngest of the three, was often the butt of much teasing – sometimes quite cruel, Gwen thought.

TOWN LIFE:

The prospect of living in a town was equally exciting with access to hitherto forbidden treats and the freedom of peacetime. For instance, an early evening walk through the town browsing in the colourful shop windows was magical, or calling at the fish and chip shop with Maisey. Eating the fish and chips from a newspaper cone oozing salt and vinegar whilst walking home in the dusk of the evening seemed like enjoying 'forbidden fruits!' The opportunity to work in the shop after school and the anticipation of a visit to the cinema at the weekend brought joys untold. Rose and Wills came to visit Molly from time to time and of course Molly went home for the occasional weekend – always brimming over with news of her new way of life.

The large Methodist Mission, which Molly attended with the family proved to be another novel experience. The congregation comprised many young people, and an enthusiastic choir. The atmosphere was informal and jolly and at the end of the service a supper club was held for the young people. The supper club extended its hospitality to the local Salvation Army Hostel for the homeless where the young people shared their supper, sang well-known hymns and exchanged stories with the residents. Rose was far from happy about Molly becoming involved in such a despairing environment but Wills tried to re-assure her that the homeless were human beings who had fallen on hard times – Rose was less sure. Reverend Clay, the minister, was an exuberant chap, slightly built with sharp features and a shock of black hair that resembled a chimney sweep brush. The Reverend's performance in the pulpit nearly out-matched Rose's rendition on the kitchen table as he sprinted around with arms flailing and his mop-like hair bouncing up and down – she could not understand why he didn't use Brylcreem to dress his hair like her father!

It was at the Mission that Molly met and developed a liking for Paul's friend Joe, a tall, dark-haired, handsome youth who attended the Grammar school and had his sights set on an ambitious career. Paul was not impressed, he argued that Joe was his friend and told Molly she was getting in the way. Well, Gwen speculated, probably Paul's feelings were confused even to himself. Certainly, when they arrived home after the Mission Paul would often join Molly sitting on the sofa. Gwen, sensing him becoming rather over friendly and touchy knew Molly would not be comfortable with such contact. Molly usually moved to another seat which upset Paul and his spiteful behaviour could last for days, which again Gwen thought was quite out of order.

However, Molly had the more serious business of starting a new school on her mind. Pru accompanied Molly to an interview with the headmistress who was welcoming, encouraging and genuinely seemed to think Molly had something to offer. Gwen was aware how much Molly needed to enjoy the school and tried hard to defuse any self-doubt.

The school was an impressive ornate Victorian building with very high ceilings, a large central hall from which entrance to the classrooms and cloakrooms led. Molly played netball for the school team and Gwen was equally as thankful as Molly when there were no horrid showers at the end of a sports session! Friendships began to evolve. One friend, named Marion was bubbly and full of fun, she lived nearby and attended the Mission – just the boost Molly needed mused Gwen. Another friend, Cynthia, a tall elegant girl whose parents ran a large and imposing guesthouse on the main road adjacent to the school provided a family setting which again Gwen felt would have much to offer Molly. David, a tall slim dark-haired lad of studious demeanour appeared on the scene and often walked Molly home after school - much to Pru's disapproval. But Gwen had a particular affinity to David; he seemed to be the kind of 'schoolboy friendship' that Molly was beginning to seek. Molly did indeed make her mark at the school and by the end of the second term she was nominated to stand for Head Girl but was pipped to the post by Marion.

Sadly, ill health continued to beset Molly. Having celebrated her thirteenth birthday, she was admitted to the local isolation hospital suffering from diphtheria. The ward was stark and desolate with no flowers or trimmings, few books or toys (fomites) were allowed because these were also considered to be a source of cross-infection. It was an isolating experience; the nurses wore masks and gowns and social contact was discouraged. Gwen was so pleased to be there for Molly. It was a worrying time for Rose and Wills who visited the hospital regularly but could only stand on the veranda outside the ward and talk to Molly through a closed window.

As St Valentine's Day approach, Gwen noticed Molly's mischievous spirit returning when she decided to send Joe a 'Valentine Card'! For whatever reason, the patients' post was left open to be sealed later. The next morning Sister appeared at the ward door her face purple with rage and her well-proportioned chest heaving up and down saying, "Who has sent out this letter ... secret and unsigned as well?" She then read,

'My heart is like a cabbage when it is cut in two; the leaves I give to others but the heart I give to you. X."

"I did, Sister. It is Valentine's Day," said Molly. "Not on my ward it isn't," Sister replied whilst ripping up the card. Sitting wide-eyed on her bed, Molly vowed to Gwen, that she would never behave like that when she was a nurse! Recovery from the onslaught of Diphtheria was promising and Molly eventually went home to her parents for a period of convalescence before returning to Aunt Pru and finishing her time at school.

After school or during the weekend, Paul who disliked the messy jobs in the shop such as cleaning the bacon machine, tidying the store-room, or sick visiting a family supported by his parents, bribed Molly with favours such as a visit to the cinema if she would do one of the jobs for him.

Molly rarely undertook the messy jobs but she willingly volunteered to visit Tommy, a young lad in his early teens, who suffered from a debilitating form of childhood rheumatoid arthritis; he was pale, thin and from the contours of the bedclothes, he seemed a tall lad. Tommy was mainly bedridden and had spent most of his life in the front room of the small terraced family home. Tommy was a shy and solitary young man, the eldest of a family of 4 children. It was a poor home and Tommy's room lacked the sweetness of a regular airing and changes of linen. A brief interlude at one of the new Open-Air

Schools had seemed to offer the kind of nurturing education with which Tommy should have been able to cope, was concluded due to his lack of stamina.

Much to Paul's chagrin, Molly and Tommy became good friends and she would frequently stay with Tommy rather than collect her favours! Tommy began to take a vague interest in Molly's schoolwork, particularly 'Art and Design' from which he gradually developed a liking for charcoal sketching using the back surface of old rolls of wallpaper. Tommy was an avid reader of comics and the characters soon became ideal subjects for his sketches. After leaving school aged 14, Molly studied bookkeeping, shorthand and typewriting at evening classes and again, Tommy was intrigued by the crazy symbols which he thought were quite fun. He helped Molly to practise her shorthand and eventually took more than a passing interest in it himself; they even had competitions for the fastest and most accurate dictation and transcription!

Molly's first 'paid employment' was a junior clerk position with a large stationer where she discovered the intricacies of managing the 'Stamp Book', operating the small telephone switchboard, and discreetly mixing with the 'shop-floor' whilst distributing the cash floats for the tills. An assistant in the Art Department named Lizzy, who played the cornet in a Salvation Army Band, occasionally invited Molly home for tea prior to attending a band concert on the local park, or a practise session at the Citadel. One night, Molly asked Lizzy to come and play for Tommy – it was a surprise and Tommy didn't really like surprises but this time it was different. The sound of the cornet delighted him, although his mother was clucking around and worrying that the noise would disturb the neighbours! Tommy responded to Lizzy's musical talent and toe tapping rhythm with a smile, which devoured his whole face. As the girls were preparing to leave, Lizzy told Tommy about a recording the Band had recently produced and offered to bring it for him to listen to if he was interested – "Any time" responded Tommy. Lizzy nodded and for the second time during the visit Molly noticed Tommy's smile and this time a responding blush from

Lizzy. Could it be that Tommy had found a new friend – Molly did hope so.

SETTING BACK THE CLOCK:

It was all great fun but Molly experienced no thrill like the 'Ping-Ping' of the corner shop doorbell and always hoped she was in time to help before closing time. Gwen was beginning to experience a strange sense of foreboding, the reason for which all too soon became apparent. Wills discovered that Pru was dating the undertaker who had buried Barry. Wills, whose strong moral code was now reinforced as an active member of the local Pentecostal Church, had never heard of anything so "profane and immoral" So Molly, now aged about 15 years and having spent an enjoyable and successful year in her clerical position, was summoned home. Alas, it had all seemed too wonderful to last and so indeed it all ended in tears. Molly, who was not only very upset, could not understand the logic behind the decision. Gwen tried to give Molly some insight to the possible indelicacy of her aunt's relationship in Wills' eyes, whilst alerting Molly to the possibility that her father might be missing his daughter and wanted her back home. Molly remonstrated but Gwen quietly warned Molly that she had little choice in the matter and better to concede gracefully than leave under a cloud. Molly said 'farewell' to Tommy with the promise that if she ever achieved a place at the local hospital's nurse training school, she would continue to visit him. It was a sad farewell – Tommy had changed so much and seemed to be acquiring a new zest for life and for living.

Wills bought Molly a Hercules bicycle to travel the four-mile journey from the village to work in town where Rose had secured Molly a position as junior clerk in the offices of a reputable firm of solicitors. The post was a disaster and did not last long. Molly likened the experience to the dismal office and atmosphere of 'Scrooge's' workplace. The small dark room assigned as the juniors' office had bare floorboards; a shelf stretching along two sides of the room, the side which served as a desk was provided with two high stools and the other as storage for a mountain of ledgers. Each morning when Molly entered the office, she expected to see another of Dickens' fictional characters, poor downtrodden Bob Cratchit sitting in the gloom poring over his ledgers. Even the rooms at the back of the house, which provided a living space for the caretaker's family, reinforced the image of Bob Cratchit's family. But the final straw for Molly was to be greeted by her opposite number in this dreary establishment. Ernest, a pleasant tall gangling school-leaver; a country lad who wore a thick, rough tweed suit and boots! In sheer desperation Molly exploded, "Did you ever meet anyone like him, Gwen? He is more suited to a job at the cattle market." Gwen felt for Molly and the contrast she was experiencing between her former employment. However, Molly gave it a try and was even tempted to stay after the senior partner took her under his wing by asking her to take his dictated letters and reports in shorthand and transcribe them for his approval.

To make matters worse, the winter of 1947 descended with heavy snowfalls and the village road surfaces resembled skating rinks! The snow had blown across the open fields leaving a frozen snowdrift of gigantic proportions in front of Molly's home that was too large to clear so Wills made an exit by tunnelling through the dense mound of snow!

Meanwhile, Rose stepped in to resolve the situation by explaining to the Solicitor the delicacy of Molly's health and her need for a less restricted environment! Molly's resignation was submitted and thanks to Rose's networking abilities Molly was soon established in new employment with a more suitable firm of Solicitors; and indeed, it was far more successful. Molly made two friends, the senior clerk Eileen, to whom she would eventually be bridesmaid, and Beryl, private secretary to one of the Solicitors. Beryl was a rather sophisticated, street-wise young woman who welcomed Molly into her circle of friends. Both Eileen and Beryl eased Molly into the new routines and encouraged her in the use of her night school acquired office skills. Molly's motivation for office work grew but never outweighed her ultimate goal.

Molly chanced to hear about the Church Youth Club in town. It was a lively encounter with other young people and the facility to play table tennis, or join the swimming group for lessons at the local Baths. The Youth Club fostered friendships, inevitably romances blossomed and it was here that Molly met gorgeous Vincent, or Vin as he was known. Vin, a pupil at the local Grammar School, with his blonde hair, blue eyes and "a smile to die for," was an attentive boyfriend - life was almost perfect. Whilst Molly vaguely sensed Gwen's approval of Vin she also felt her disapproval of getting too involved knowing her heart was set on nurse training. Molly could hear Gwen's warning voice saying, "Do be careful Molly, don't break his heart." Well, thought Molly, Vin has ambitions too because although still at Grammar school he had his sight set on University and could be in the same position.

Molly and Vin were inseparable. He escorted Molly on the four miles bicycle journey back to her home after the youth club and sometimes they even went to the 'Milk Bar'! They met at the weekends to explore the local countryside and picnic under the shade of the trees. One night Vin was brave enough to kiss Molly goodnight outside her home – before they could say 'smoke' the bedroom window shot open and Wills' head appeared saying, "Isn't it about time you came in, Molly?" Poor Vin, he felt so embarrassed – in future they always stopped for a kiss and a cuddle before they rounded the corner into the village!

When Vin was free from looming examinations, he accompanied Molly on a visit to Aunt Pru. Molly was thrilled that he wanted to share her joys of the corner shop and her friendship with Maisey and Paul. The visits were happy and welcoming occasions – with lovely tea and cakes but the most rewarding of all was to take Vin to visit Tommy. Although Lizzy popped in occasionally, Tommy's spirit seemed to have faded somewhat and his artwork had fallen into abeyance. But Vin's arrival lightened Tommy's mood and by the time they were ready to leave Tommy had a smile on his face. After meeting Tommy, Vin sometimes wrote to him about his schoolwork, the highs and lows of the 'Ambassador Football Team' of which Vin was a member, and the town's famous figure, 'Dr Johnson'. Following one visit to Tommy, Vin found some unusual charcoal sketches and a newspaper article on L. S. Lowry's thought-provoking paintings to send to him. Tommy's replies were either non-existent or rather infrequent but this time Vin received a reply within the week. The prompt reply was inspired by Tommy's fascination by the familiar industrial settings and activities Lowry captured in his impressionist-style art - maybe he saw something of himself in the seemingly humourless bent figures? Whatever the reason, it was heartening to know that Tommy had found another interest and contact with the world outside his forlorn little room – how wonderful it would have been to have had access to the internet and iPhones at this time!

Knowing of Molly's ambition to be a nurse, one of the Youth Club leaders introduced her to the local branch of the St John Ambulance Brigade, Home Nursing Section; this was really a step in the right direction! The class met once each week in town and worked through the St John Manual of First Aid and Home Nursing. Sometimes a doctor, nurse, or ambulance person came to talk to the candidates and much time was spent on practical exercises. In the examinations Molly came top of the class and awarded a St John Manual of her own. Vin joined her at the Prize Giving event and gave loud applause when her name was announced as the winner of the first prize. Hoping that this would go some way towards quelling Molly's self-doubt after failing the 11+ examinations, Gwen put her increasingly limited efforts into encouraging Molly and boosting her confidence for what might lay ahead.

THE GOAL IN SIGHT:

The day eventually arrived when Molly celebrated her 16th birthday, part of which she spent with Vin. Molly talked to Vin about her plans for the future, which if successful would mean a move from the town for her. They were both upset but could find no immediate solution to the distance that would be between them and the unknown challenges Molly would be facing. Sadly, and rather prematurely as Molly was to discover with hindsight, they said 'Goodbye'. I do hope I have done the right thing, reflected Molly as she left Vin - 'so do I,' thought Gwen.

Meanwhile at home, "I am eligible to go nursing," she said to her parents, whilst laughing and crying at the same time! Rose brought out her well-worn writing case and from it took a 'Basildon Bond' writing pad, bottle of 'Stephenson's Ink' and long-stemmed pen with a 'Relief nib'. Seated with pen poised Rose penned a letter in her impressive manuscript writing-style to Matron Tranwick at the hospital with the beds on the balconies and the nurses in white flowing caps; ending with the traditional 'Yours respectfully' followed by the flourish of her copper-plate signature 'R Lange'.

The days seemed endless waiting for the postman but in the fullness of time the longed-for reply arrived inviting Molly and her mother to attend an interview – MOLLY WAS OFF!!!

Matron Tranwick was a small, bird-like lady with the face of an angel and the most beguiling smile – she alone turned the tide that day. Mother was bewitched, Molly was over the moon as Matron Tranwick continued in her dignified style to "make the arrangements" for Molly to enter as a 'Sub-Probationer' (sub-pro), explaining that the Regulations did not allow her to commence General Nurse Training until she was 18 years old.

They left the interview with Rose wagging her finger and entreating Molly to take note of Matron Tranwick and that is what she had to aspire to become!

CHAPTER 4

IS IT A DREAM?

INTRODUCTIONS AND ROUTINES:

One bright Sunday in April, Molly said her farewells and left home for the hospital with Gwen in her shadow and her parent's gift of bespoke leather holdall and a matching shoulder bag made by the local saddler.

On arrival at the hospital Molly reported to Matron's office. It all feels unreal, Molly thought and indeed, Gwen too thought Molly was due for a wake-up call! Matron's reception was welcoming but brief. She introduced Home Sister, a stern looking older lady wearing a grey dress with a lace collar, long sleeves edged with deep stiff white cuffs and a red petersham belt clasped together at her waist with an impressive silver buckle; a large frilled cap completed the uniform. Matron explained that Sister would show Molly around and set out the routines to be followed. With a warm smile and her good wishes, Matron bade Molly farewell. So, Molly stepped forth into the brave, compassionate world of the National Health Service where all health care was free at the point of need from the 'cradle to the grave' – no more discrimination and 'Recommendations' for sickly children like Molly!

Home Sister began her tour of the hospital. On the way down the main corridor, she pointed out the dining room, post-racks, notice boards and cloakroom facilities. Making their way towards the Nurses' Home, Sister explained that this is where Molly would live along with other sub-pros, probationer nurses and qualified staff under the chaperonage of a Home Sister and a resident Warden. They eventually arrived and entered the first room on the middle corridor, this was to be Molly's room and she noticed her uniform lay on the bed. Sister discussed the different garments beginning with the calf-length white coat, which was not to be shortened, a stiff white belt worn loosely and not waspish, and a white butterfly cap. Following Home Sister's brief demonstration on how to make-up the butterfly cap, she presented Molly with the key to her room and continued on a tour of the main facilities in the Home. Arriving in the sitting room they found four nurses giggling in front of the fire who immediately shot to attention saying, "Good morning, Sister." In the corner sat two girls in mufti (everyday dress). Sister called them over and introduced them as new sub-pros, Molly smiled and breathed a sigh of relief as she met with her future colleagues. Sister then suggested they joined the rest of the group for lunch in the dining room at Table 9.

The three new recruits chatted together with excitement and apprehension – one girl, Hetty, was older than the others and seemed to know all the ropes. Having found the rest of the group in the dining room they introduced themselves whilst enjoying a snack lunch. Home Sister joined them to give a brief introduction to 'Who's Who' in the hospital hierarchy, followed by guidance on the immediate protocols of behaviour, hospital routines, and dress code. Finally, a tour of the main areas of the hospital during which Molly was given a further experience of hospital protocol when Home Sister was acknowledged formally and with due respect by the nurses they encountered. Gwen sensed Molly was beginning to think, "I shall never remember all this"... and felt for her!

Eventually, they all went their separate ways and when Molly turned the key and entered her room, she had never felt so homesick and lonely in her life; feelings that even Gwen's ethereal-like presence could not assuage.

LIFE AS A SUB-PROBATIONER (sub-pro):

Molly was awakened by a knock on the bedroom door by Home Sister saying, "Good morning nurse – 6 o'clock." Breakfast was served at 7am and duty commenced at 8am until 5pm on Monday to Friday with Saturday and Sunday off. Molly prepared for her first duty. She was transfixed when she looked in the long mirror on the wall of her room – such joy overcame all the agony of trying to convert a length of starched white muslin into a butterfly cap! And so to breakfast. As she left the Nurses' Home Molly caught up with Hetty, whose cap bore no resemblance to the one modelled by Home Sister!

At breakfast, Molly learned more about the sub-pros work in various hospital departments from her seasoned colleagues. The favourite departments were the Diet Kitchen with tasty morsels available and the Dispensary where Mr Holt, the chemist, a kindly father figure brought joy and interest to the seemingly mundane tasks of bottle washing and labelling. Physiotherapy Department had the reputation of being a special treat. The physiotherapists were genteel and welcoming in demeanour; the atmosphere in the department was calm and well organized even though numerous different activities were taking place.

The Department most dreaded by all the sub-pros seemed to be the Sewing Room where they worked with the seamstresses tying off, or sewing in the ends of the cotton. The noise was deafening with the sound of the whirring sewing machines as they travelled their repeated journeys up and down the hospital linen, or wove the hospital logo in red cotton on every item.

The sub-pros, by now numbering six girls aged between 16 and 18, had been told to meet in the ante-room of the library at 8.30am. Home Sister, greeted them and first inspected their appearance and corrected, or approved as appropriate – Hetty was taken to one side for a few minutes! Next, Sister allocated their departments; Molly was assigned to 'Physiotherapy'.

On arrival in the Physiotherapy Department, the senior therapist waited to welcome Molly and to give her a brief tour of the department, during which she was introduced to the patient's receiving treatment and given a brief insight of her duties. For instance, she would transport sick children from the wards to the department for sunlight treatment. These were frightened sickly children, she was told, who were suffering from conditions such as the failure to thrive, rickets and malnourishment and who needed comforting and love – it was just like hearing her father speak! Molly took patients by wheelchair from the wards to the department for treatments to repair the ravages of 'Stroke' or to ease debilitating conditions such as rheumatism and arthritis. Gwen gloried in Molly's sense of achievement when she described how she peeled off the wax from gnarled arthritic hands after they had been soaking in the wax-baths, saying, "it was gentle caring work – just what I felt I was there to do."

The end of the day exhaustion was soon forgotten as the sub-pros gathered with the 'cocoa gang' in each other's bedrooms until lights out at 10pm. Some of the junior probationers (student nurses) joined in these 'fun-times' and the sub-pros would sit agog listening to the ups and downs of training. So new friendships were made and it was during these times that Molly and Petal, an end of first year student, began a friendship that would last a lifetime.

The sub-pros attended the local Technical College one day each week to study chemistry, biology, and mathematics. Not having encountered any serious study of the hard sciences at school, Molly was intrigued by the mysteries of chemistry and biology, later she would reminisce, "I was enthralled to discover how things fitted together and worked; what could go wrong and how the wrongs might be righted." Molly would tell of her experiences in the laboratory. For instance, the intriguing soap making exercise and her dread of biology practical sessions where in the laboratory she would be expected to dissect frogs and worms – the latter had been an object of irrational fear throughout Molly's life! Gwen quietly absorbed some of

Molly's shock when presented with a lifeless worm on the table, which as she turned it over the momentum caused the worm to continue to roll as if alive. Gwen just knew that Molly would be immediately transported back to the day when sitting on the sofa with her father, she was sent into hysterics by sister Kate, who came running into the kitchen, her little fat legs springing up and down like 'Zebedee' as she spun through the door grinning from ear to ear with a big fat worm dangling over the end of her little spade. The lecturer recognized Molly's state of shock and in future the specimen was always pinned out and prepared for her in advance!

Molly was actually very successful and came top of the class in both 'lab tests' and written examinations. Knowing of the exalted education from which many of the other sub-pros had benefitted, this achievement truly amazed Molly and earned her the nickname of 'Swot', which stuck throughout her training. But Gwen knew that Molly would only work harder as she tried to bury the nightmare of the 11+ failure – she only ever seemed to compete against herself and never intentionally against anyone else! Molly's success was acknowledged in the classroom with the lecturer saying, "If you know your sciences you have a problem-solving tool." The truth and value of his pronouncement was to stay with Molly throughout her career, particularly with regard to physiology and later the behavioural and social sciences were to make their impression.

Going home each weekend, Molly was welcomed like the 'prodigal son' with a supper tray of scrambled eggs and a pot of tea. The respite gave Molly the chance to relive the adventures of the past week – mother listened agog; sister Kate thought it all so "disgusting" that her welcome was usually brief. Dad came in from the farm and like the wise old owl would listen from the comfort of his armchair and give mixed messages – his beautiful face shone with pride; his eyes twinkled with fun but occasionally he would emit a growl-like cough and gently clear his throat – when that happened Molly and her mother knew they were in danger of getting out of order. Once back in the Nurses' Home and comparing time off, the sub-pros seemed to share very similar experiences.

However, not all weekends spent in the bosom of the family were pleasant. One weekend, Molly arrived home after feeling unwell during the week; her skin seemed sore and tingling; her head itched and she was exhausted. Sitting on the sofa scratching her head, Molly's mother said, "move over whilst I have a look." A large newspaper was duly placed on the floor in front of her and Rose arrived with a brush and toothcomb ready for battle. As she combed through Molly's hair, faint tapping noises could be heard on the newspaper and after a while they surveyed the scene to find the paper littered with lice running hither and thither. Molly and her mother were shocked; sister Kate's revulsion was palpable; and father sat in his chair saying, "I told you no good would come of this and you would have it your way."

Mother hastily hauled Molly towards the kitchen sink for a 'good lathering' with green fairy soap, followed by a soaking in vinegar, after which her hair was wrapped up in brown paper and secured in position by a towel. The procedure was repeated before bedtime but sleep did not come easily. The following morning and more of the same followed by a vigorous combing with the toothcomb to remove any dead lice and unglued nits off the hair. One more session before Sunday lunch – which, by the way, was a quiet affair. Molly returned to hospital armed with the toothcomb and strict instructions to continue the process night and morning; with her father still tutting and sister Kate nowhere in sight. Thereafter, Molly was attributed with the affectionate nickname of 'Nitto'!

Following Molly's departure, out came the writing material ...

Matron Tranwick.
Dear Madam,
...
Yours Respectfully.
R Lange.

Arriving back in the nurses' home, the 'cocoa gang' was in full swing – but not for long as Molly began to share her experience. Joan, a fellow sub-pro said, "Here give me that tooth comb," and proceeded to attack her blonde curly hair. On inspection she found livestock squirming in the comb. Joan exploded with a string of expletives rarely heard in such rarefied atmospheres and disappeared to her room to attack the problem. Joan's outburst stunned them all ... such language in the Nurses' Home and from the daughter of an esteemed Derbyshire farming family, educated at a prestigious local Grammar School too!

The problem, of course arose from Molly carrying the sick children to Physiotherapy for their Sunlight treatment. The children were usually very neglected and admitted with head and/or body lice and it was part of the admission procedure to check for and treat infestation - one, which on this occasion seemed to have been missed ... but one, which Matron Tranwick assured Rose ... would be "rectified as a matter of urgency." It was expected of Molly to write home during the week and Rose reciprocated - on this occasion an up-to-date report on Molly's hair situation was required which prompted further advice from Rose!

OPERATING THEATRES AND SAM:

As the end of Molly's placement in the Physiotherapy Department approached it was accompanied by mixed feelings. Whilst eager to move on to the next step Molly knew she would miss the quiet professionalism of the therapists and the bond that had developed between her and the children in particular. However, the day came when the 'Change List' announced her next placement would be Theatres – a complex of three operating theatres and various servicing units. So, equipped with an encouraging review from the Senior Physiotherapist, she stepped forward into her new assignment with confidence, In her weekly letter home, Molly wrote ... "I shall feel really special in the 'holy of holies' of theatres, even though we are not allowed into the inner sanctum of theatre itself during operating times."

Molly spent her theatre duties in a variety of interesting ways. Sometimes packing drums with different types of dressings, theatre gowns, towels and masks ready to be sterilized in the hospital autoclave system; at other times she scrubbed the surfaces and cleaned the wheels of various trolleys and the operating table; and all the while she was absorbing medical terms and the language of nursing. One day, whilst she was replacing the 'soils' with clean surgical dress in the doctor's changing room, a young houseman stopped by to ask how she was doing and introduced himself as Sam. Sam spoke about 'the boss' and his expectations and within a short space of time they were giggling about his boss, the Senior Orthopaedic Consultant and his well-known routine of collecting food waste from the hospital kitchens to feed to his pigs. Gwen smiled because she knew that Molly was longing to tell Sam about 'Juggins', her family's pet pig but felt it was not appropriate. Sam frequently stopped by and with his ready smile he made Molly think of the lovely Vin she had left behind. Gwen was only too conscious of the association that Molly was making but secretly wondered if, in the long term, this was Molly's route to healing an old wound.

Quite unexpectedly, Molly encountered the wrath of one of the theatre Sisters. Always referred to by their surnames, Sister shouted, "Lange, pick up that empty drum off the floor immediately and never, ever let me see you do that again." A lengthy explanation of why this was unacceptable practice was followed by demonstrations of the right way to handle a drum – both empty, or full of sterilized materials. Poor Molly, on this occasion she had learned the hard way but she soon discovered her learning experiences were to be peppered with praise and encouragement as well as admonishment. The following week, the anaesthetist gave praise to the person who had cleaned and replenished his trolley just to his liking; Molly was summoned to receive due recognition!

The camaraderie within the sub-pro group was amazing; it was here that each found solace in times of despondency and celebration in times of achievement. They were teasingly classified by their origins – *townies* or *country-bumpkins* and close friendships developed. In addition to the watchful eye of Home Sister and the Warden, a senior male nurse, Mr Shepherd, seemed to have been designated as their mentor. Mr Shepherd often appeared on the scene, especially when things were not going well; he was respected as a useful source of information, advice and affectionate gossip.

The next development was a 'bombshell' for Molly and one that took all the shine out of celebrating her forthcoming birthday. At lunchtime the 'Change List' appeared on the nurses' notice board announcing Molly's forthcoming placement in the Sewing Room. That day lunch was not the most appetizing experience for Molly, even with her colleagues trying to lift her spirits. Returning to theatres the familiar atmosphere boosted Molly's morale somewhat and she commenced her task of cleaning the surgical instruments. Sam popped his auburn head round the open door as he left following the morning list to find a rather disconsolate Molly. "Hey, what's wrong?" he asked. At first Molly smiled and said, "Nothing, why?" "Because you are not you," replied Sam. Molly went on to reveal the truth of the situation and the dreaded bogey of the Sewing Room sentence. They chatted for a while and Molly explained more about the anticipated ordeal. Eventually Sam said, "I will tell you a secret … I am not altogether taken with Orthopaedics but I have to do it if I am to qualify as a doctor which has always been my life's dream … and it will be the same for you." Molly smiled. "I wish I could take you for a cup of tea but the hospital does not provide for such socialising!" Sam gestured rather ruefully. Instead, they laughed and made a quick 'cuppa' in the theatre staff room, promising to meet in town one night after duty next week.

The sub-pros only on rare occasions worked with the patients – physiotherapy was an exception. So it was a great surprise when Theatre Sister asked Molly to sit with an elderly lady in the anteroom prior to her operation. Sister explained that Mrs Jones seemed rather nervous and disturbed "Poor dear, it is all so strange to them and such a big ordeal to face ... Just talk to her gently Lange; as you might do if it were your grandma – *BUT DON'T GIVE HER ANYTHING TO EAT OR DRINK!*" Mrs Jones was indeed upset. It seemed she had lived with her problem for a long while without seeking attention because her husband was poorly and needed her to look after him. She explained that they had taken a double room in a nursing home one mile from where her daughter and grandchildren lived. "When I have had my operation, I shall share the room with my husband and we shall both be together again." Mrs Jones smiled tearfully, and hoped Mr Jones – "Bert," she added, would settle in without her. Mrs Jones talked about her wonderful family, confident that her grandchildren would make a fuss of Grandpa in his new room. Mrs Jones spoke about her ambitions for her youngest son who was applying for a senior position in a Research Institute of repute. Dolly, her youngest daughter, had recently changed careers to qualify as a schoolteacher. With a twinkle in her eye Mrs Jones explained, "Bert and I had Dolly late in life, ... 'Miss Mystery' we call her!" Time passed very quickly and when the anaesthetist came into the room Mrs Jones said, "Oh! Is it that time already?" Then turning to Molly, she said, "Thank you nurse, I do hope I haven't kept you," and off she went.

Molly continued with her routines, making a silent prayer for Mrs Jones and the success of her operation. In a reflective mood Molly closed her locker to feel a tap on her shoulder – it was Sam ... "Mrs Jones is on her way back to the ward – everything went well. Are you ready for that cup of tea in town tonight? I guess we both need one!"

Instead of going to town Molly took Sam to the corner shop! It was a lovely surprise for everyone. Sam was introduced and made very welcome; he even helped with packing away the vegetables from the shelf outside the shop window. Molly left Sam to socialize whilst she nipped across the street to see Tommy.

Tommy was pleased to see Molly but she sensed he was rather forlorn. He cheered up somewhat as he talked about Vin's recent letter and its information about Lowry, but something was troubling him. Tommy was clearly fascinated by Lowry's life; surprised by the artist's choice of a way to earn a living as a rent collector; and intrigued by the beauty of his studio and the consolation he must have found there given the drabness of his surroundings. Tommy seemed quite disturbed by what he perceived as the sadness of the artist's soulless relationship with his invalid mother who, Lowry felt was disappointed in her son.

Molly was quite taken aback by the depth of Tommy's feelings and his insight. "I must get you a book about Lowry from the library," said Molly. "I am sure there is so much more to his story than the newspaper article was able to tell." Tommy did not respond and in the silence that followed Molly could feel that was not the answer he was seeking. Tommy eventually looked at Molly and held her gaze with haunted eyes, "Do you think I am like Lowry, Molly?" Thinking Tommy was referring to Lowry's artwork, Molly said, "Well, who knows you certainly have a gift in that direction." "No Molly, I mean am I a clumsy and an unrewarding son?" Molly asked, "Why, is that how you feel Tommy?" A long and searching conversation followed in the wake of Molly's question. There seemed to be no quick or immediate answer, these were feelings Tommy needed to be helped to work through in his own way – but how? Gwen too was feeling the heavy atmosphere of despondency through which Molly was wisely guiding Tommy when his Mum came in with tea and biscuits. Her cheery face must surely help to dispel some of her son's fears; but there was a long way to go and Gwen sensed that Molly and Lizzy would have a big part to play. After teatime their chat drew to a close and Molly prepared to leave, she and Tommy clung together in quiet desolation under the weight of the burden they had shared. Eventually they slackened their embrace and with a mock push away Tommy said, "that's enough of that ... but come again soon!" His Mum joined in to lighten the atmosphere by saying,

"Yes, I wouldn't give much for your chances if Sam saw you, our Tommy!"

Molly walked up the street and away from the shop for a while whilst she controlled her tears. 'Wow!' thought Gwen. 'That touched a raw spot for Molly.' The shop door had been left open for her and she entered the room to the buzz of conversation and laughter. Sam turned to Molly, "Thank goodness you have returned, we were just going to send out the search party!" They all settled down for more tea and biscuits whilst they caught up with the ups and downs of Molly's hospital experiences.

Taking their leave, Sam and Molly decided to walk the three miles back to the hospital. It was a lovely evening and Sam, looking forward to when his Orthopaedics was over, began to talk about his plans for his next 'house job' – probably Paediatrics, or may be Gynaecology he pondered, "I would eventually like to specialize in Public Health - I think?" "In the short-term," confided Molly, "I want to be a theatre sister and in the longer term, perhaps a midwife. But a long way to go yet and 'a lot of water can pass under the bridge', as the saying goes!" In the meantime, the dreaded portals of the sewing room were quickly approaching but suddenly such things didn't seem so bad here with Sam. But the sadness of Tommy's outburst lingered with Molly.

The weekend came around once again and on her way home Molly thought about all the news she had to tell Rose, we will never get to bed; and she wasn't far wrong! But Rose also had news to share. Kate, now aged 14, had been appointed relief organist at the village church and Rose was over the moon. Kate would play for the services this Sunday – such an elevation in village society! Wills sat in his usual corner armchair looking on, Molly knew he was so proud of his daughters but he said little – if Wills had said anything at all it would have been to give his version of the Holy Bible's warning, 'knowledge puffeth up' - or, 'pride comes before a fall!'

Sunday morning arrived. The church was full; the choirboys' surplices looked sparkling white; and the organist was note perfect. Sunday lunch was a rather chattier affair than usual. Kate was hoping to get an apprenticeship with a local tailor. Rose and Wills were planning a few days away in Morecambe with Rose's eldest sister Amy. And Molly? Well, she would be enjoying her remaining days in Theatres.

Rose was desperate to know more about Sam but Molly said, "There is nothing to tell." Nevertheless, Molly was commissioned to extend an invitation to Sam to visit and she suspected that there would be a reminder in next week's letter! Teatime quickly came and time for Molly to catch the bus back to the hospital. As Molly left home, Rose came rushing after her waving a letter. "I forgot to give you this," said Rose "It's one from that foreigner." Molly recognized it as a letter from her Hungarian pen friend, Dominik – she would read it on the bus.

Whilst waiting for the bus in town Molly's heart leapt when she saw Vin approaching … but it turned into a lurch when she noticed he held the hand of a pretty girl. Gwen's all-seeing eye just looked on and waited realising that one day this was inevitable. Molly put on a brave face and remembered the joys of the old days. Vin was obviously delighted to see Molly and proudly introduced April. He wanted to know all about Molly's experience in nurse training and hospital life in general. "Has it all lived up to expectation?" Vin asked with the old familiar look of concern. Briefly relating some of the ups and down's, Molly asked how life was for him. With a sense of enthusiasm mixed with caution, Vin told of the University places they had both been awarded – Vin planned to read Mathematics and Physics, and April, English and the History of Art. April and Vin looked at each other with a smile and a squeeze of their hands. Meanwhile, April explained that she was working in Hope's, the town's prodigious ladies and gentleman's outfitters and Vin, in Patterson's, "High Class Grocer and Purveyor of Fine Foods," he said giving the establishment its full title with his cheeky smile. Vin asked about Tommy, "is he still discovering Lowry? I have written to tell him about going to University but I haven't received a reply." Molly gave Vin news of Tommy and his friend, Lizzy, she also told of the startling reaction Lowry had evoked in Tommy. Vin looked at Molly thoughtfully and assured her that he would keep in touch with the lad. Just as Molly was longing to know more, her bus arrived and with a quick and fond 'Goodbye,' Molly was waved off into the gloom of the night.

During the journey Molly's thoughts wandered hither and thither – knowing her mother would be interested to learn of Vin's association with Patterson's whose traveller, Mr Groves, called on Rose to take her grocery order. Thankfully, the turmoil in Molly's mind was soon crowded out by amusing memories of Mr Groves, a dapper man with a thin black moustache and wearing a trilby, which he waved with a flourish as he greeted Rose. Molly could visualize him sitting at the kitchen table, opening his brief case and extracting his duplicate note pad, a pencil as sharp as a fine needle and a rubber. "Now Mrs Lange," Molly could hear him say, "Are we to start with the usual?" Prompting, "sugar, butter and tea?" Mr Groves would then progress to the occasional. "Now Mrs Lange, you haven't ordered any bars of Fairy soap, washing soda, or brick salt for a while?" … "Quite right Mr Groves, add them to the order please." The conversation was so predictable; it was like the well-orchestrated dialogue of a West End play!

Molly's mind began to ponder on 'the history of art'. Last Christmas, Paul had given Tommy an art pad and drawing equipment. Tommy's 'good days' seemed to become more frequent at that time and his imagination began to take flight. It occurred to Molly that Tommy might find an added dimension of enjoyment to his talent through an understanding of the history of his art; it may also put the life of Lowry into perspective. Tommy's pending birthday, or Christmas present was solved!

Suddenly, Molly remembered she had not read Dominik's letter – he didn't write very often but when he did it was always so interesting and this time she was not disappointed, Dominik was in the process of applying for a University place to read Politics ... "Well done," Molly murmured.

It was a cool night when Molly arrived back at the hospital. Stan, the head porter at the Gate House called, "Goodnight, Nurse." The hospital did not have a clocking in and out system for professional staff and their visitors but Stan always knew who had gone out; with whom; at what time they returned; and with whom. Stan was always most circumspect about any indiscretions!

Eventually, Monday morning dawned and Molly was facing her last week in theatres. Sister warned of a busy week – "we are 'on take' all week because the Infirmary is short of beds." Sure enough, there was not a moment to breathe and Molly even got drawn in to help clean theatres between cases – she dreaded breaking anything, or not returning equipment to its right place! The sterilizing room was working to capacity, the 'scrub room' a challenge to keep tidy and re-stocked, porters were deftly replacing the anaesthetic cylinders, and the sub-pros were repacking the drums for sterilisation as though their life depended on it. Lunchtime came as a welcome break and Molly could sense the spin-off across the hospital. By Wednesday lunchtime the bed situation at the Infirmary had eased, Thursday morning the usual 'On Take Rota' was resumed and work proceeded at a more normal pace. Sr Teasle, senior theatre sister asked Molly to report to her office at 12 noon on Friday for an end of placement interview

Molly's weekly letter home was brimming over with theatre's emergency workload and news of her meeting with Vin and his girlfriend, April. Rose's reply, although primarily telling of Kate's success on Sunday and wanting news of Sam and his intended visit, contained a note of admonishment when she broached the subject of Vin ... "Such a respected family and his mother, now Head Librarian and Chairman of the Town's

Women's Guild, was held in high esteem." Slapped wrist thought Molly!!

Sister Teasle was known as a 'hard task-master' so it was with some trepidation that Molly presented on Friday midday. With brief reference to Molly's indiscretions, such as mishandling the drums, Sister gave an encouraging account of her diligence and good behaviour; noting in particular, the respect she had earned from all members of theatre staff. Sister then invited Molly to comment on how she had found the experience. In response Molly highlighted the interesting and stimulating learning experiences to which she had been exposed, concluding with anticipation to the day she would return as a probationer. The interview ended with a request to attend Matron's office at 5pm that evening. Molly left theatres with mixed feelings – the joy of having a good report was rather over-shadowed by the unexpected summons to Matron's office.

Five o'clock arrived and Molly entered the room last seen when she became a sub-pro. "Good evening, Lange," said Matron. The interview opened with informal enquiries about Molly's welfare, leading to rather more focused questions about Molly's work and studies. Matron concluded by congratulating Molly on having made such a splendid start to her nursing career. "Your college results are commendable and the reports on your conduct and diligence from both the Physiotherapy Department and Theatres show that you have achieved a very high standard." Matron went on to explain she was considering offering Molly a place on one of the next intakes to the Preliminary Training School (PTS). "I believe you will cope extremely well with the challenge." Meanwhile, I note you will be commencing your next placement in the Sewing Room on Monday … I wish you well. Thank you, Lange."

The interview was over and Molly was stunned – have I been dreaming, she wondered but of course Molly knew this was for real! Gwen, who recognized that Molly's bête noire of self-doubt was beginning to raise its ugly head hoped she would be strong enough to break the barrier.

As Molly walked down the main corridor, she met Hetty and telling her about the interview with Matron, Hetty said, "Good news kiddo – you're smart, you'll be OK." In the distance Molly saw Sam about to turn into the doctors' quarters – he waved and came towards her. "Hi Molly, I don't know whether you look better, or worse – what's been happening?" "I've been summoned to Matron's office," said Molly "Good news, or bad?" asked Sam. "Good and bad, I suppose," said Molly looking at the clock and realising time was short and fearing she would miss her bus home said, "Tell you all about it next week – Wednesday, OK?" "Fine." Sam replied with a wide grin, "Can't wait!" and off they went on their separate ways.

Molly arrived home on Friday night rather later than usual to be greeted with "Is everything OK?" And so settling down to a light supper the story unfolded. Both Rose and Wills were pleased to hear of the commendable reports and the unexpected earlier date of Molly's admission to the nurse training school. After ruminating on the news Wills said with great emphasis, "Well done Nitto but remember that is for what you have achieved – the future has yet to be earned."

Rose was still a bit sore about Vin but making polite tentative enquiries about Sam she said, "I hope you are not getting too involved – I trust you; you know. I have always taught you right from wrong." ... 'Wow,' thought Molly, 'where did that come from?'

It was mid-September, the weekend of the Village Fete and Summer Dance in the village hall. Wills was busy helping to erect the marquees and trestle tables, Rose organizing the cake stalls and Kate in charge of the Aunt Sally competition. Molly espied Ted, a lad from early school days, setting up the skittles. The years had slipped by almost unnoticed and Ted had lost the tousled look of a schoolboy to become a presentable young man. Ted and Molly chatted together and looked forward to meeting up at the village dance that evening. The Bishop accompanied by the Vicar opened the Fete, with 'Mrs Vicar' dressed up in her finery, determined to do the village proud! As Molly wandered around the various sideshows she took part in the competitions, renewed acquaintances and exchanged news with old school friends.

The village dance was a happy affair. The band was in tune and the singer crooned away to fill the air with romance. Molly was never short of a partner including Ted who was a nice lad and easy to dance with. Ted and Molly walked home together and as usual everyone would be at church in the morning.

Over breakfast, Rose wanted to know all about the evening and smiled with contentment when she heard about Ted. "Such a nice family, you know," purred Rose "his mother is so well thought of in the village and his father is a highly respected businessman." Sunday morning came and much to Molly's embarrassment Ted came and sat with Molly and her mother in 'their' pew – most intrusive because everyone always sat in their designated pew – 'a place for everyone and everyone in their place' was the village motto! However, Rose smiled and made room for Ted. 'Oh no!' Molly thought. 'Please don't play cupid again!"

Having arrived home from church Rose made a pot of tea and Molly sat chatting with her parents whilst waiting for Kate to arrive. Molly began to reminisce about various village people and the children with whom she had once been a close friend. Rose said with some amusement "Do you remember your imaginary friend Gwen Sturdy?" Both Rose and Wills chuckled as they thought of the bizarre and inseparable friendship. Molly smiled as she recalled how close Gwen had been to her, "it was like having my own Fairy Tale!" "And my goodness you needed one with all the ups and downs you faced," interrupted Rose. After a thoughtful silence whilst their cups were refilled, Molly explained that she still remembered Gwen very clearly, not as a person now because I know she doesn't exist except in my imagination but more the sensation her friendship generated. Rose and Wills raised their eyebrows with an expression of curiosity so Molly continued to explain the sensations of encouragement or caution when she seemed to be at a crossroads in life, or feel out of place in a situation. "It's probably my over-active conscience," laughed Molly ... "Or vivid imagination," quipped Wills.

Wills gave his usual cough-like 'hum-hum', followed by the view that "the mind was a funny thing and should not be tampered with." Rose was more ponderous and understanding as she reminded Molly of her own gift of 'in-sight', or 'presentment' Rose mused, "I'm not afraid of it, in fact sometimes it is very helpful – a safety net almost." Rose enjoyed reminding Molly that she too was always a very perceptive and creative child who could produce a story from nowhere to spring the most unexpected surprises, - like taking over from Kate when she fluffed her lines at Sunday School Anniversary! "And don't forget my Aunt Rose, your Great Aunt, was a clairvoyant!" Rose prompted mischievously. "That's enough of that, Mum; we don't want to go into the wickedness of Black Magic on the good Sabbath!" Wills rebuked.

They then talked about 'the mind' and its wonderful store of memories and gifts not just from this lifetime but also from across the generations. "They do not sit there idle," enlightened Rose, "they are there to be used and learned from, they help to make us what we are, like a reservoir of intellect across time – I often think you are so much like your Aunt Amy and probably a steak of Granny Bunce! Wills, who had sat silently listening, gave his cough-like 'Hum Hum' saying "Of course we are not stone, our mind is like blotting paper, the wise person recognises which impressions to ignore but learns from them; and which to value and nurture. So, use your insight wisely Nitto, do not be afraid of it, your sensitivity will make you a good nurse." Father and daughter smiled at each other with great affection. Good old Dad, thought Molly, always there when it matters! Suddenly, and quite unprovoked, the image of 'Pop the pink shirt' of the air raid times flashed before Molly's eyes: Yes, Dad was always there.

Just as all three of them were feeling they had reached the extent of their understanding and acknowledged each other's misgivings on the matter, Kate burst in as if on cue! The teapot was cleared away and lunch was served. The philosophical discussion disappeared in the presence of pragmatic Kate and the conversation turned to holidays. Molly talked about her forthcoming break, speculating that perhaps Beryl, her friend the solicitor's secretary, would be free to visit her Aunt in Brighton. Rose was assured that Molly would spend some time at home and also visit her aunts. Goodbyes were said and Molly set off to catch the bus back to the hospital.

THE SEWING ROOM:

When Molly arrived in the Sewing Room the head seamstress, Mrs Fritton, a tall slim youthful looking middle-aged lady with curly hair, was waiting to greet her with a warm smile. Molly was introduced to the other sub-pros who were at different stages of their placement. They seemed a jolly bunch and chatted together for a while before they explained the routines of checking the articles for damage on their arrival and segregating them for the seamstresses to work on. Finally, Molly was demonstrated the knack of sewing in the tails of cotton at the end of a seam, a repaired area, and at the end of the hospital logo.

Mrs Fritton, Mrs F as she became known, made the sub-pros feel they were doing an important job and proved to be every bit as lovely as her appearance foretold. Mrs F enjoyed poetry and belonged to a church choir – so for Molly it felt like being at home. Rose was always interested to hear about Mrs F and often said how much she would like to meet her. As Molly settled into the Sewing Room, she discovered that Mrs F was a widow whose young husband had died on active service during the war, they didn't have any children and sometimes Molly saw the same raw grief on her face as that of her mother and aunts when they reminisced about their lost family members.

It was so easy to share with Mrs F; she didn't pry but was interested in the sub-pros' lives – even the seemingly trivial aspects. For instance, she was particularly attentive the day Molly received a letter from her Hungarian pen friend Dominik, which as usual, was full of interest about his life and country. That day Molly stayed behind to talk to Mrs F during the coffee break and learnt that her late husband had family connections with Eastern Europe. Molly now felt she was able to explore some of the issues Dominik raised, which she had found interesting but difficult to fully understand. Mrs F recalled the long and sad history of Eastern Europe she had so poignantly learned from her husband's family. She reminisced about the effects of Communism and Fascism; the invasion of the Germans during the war and the atrocities committed to the Jews. It was a history lesson Molly would never forget, like the experience of studying English Literature through the eyes of Charles Dickens with the lovely Miss Smith. Molly was inspired by the thought that Tommy would enjoy Dominik's letters and the background Mrs F had provided.

Mrs F did not seem to have forgotten what it was like to be young; she was kind and considerate. When Molly's finger became sore from pushing the sewing needle through the hard fabric, Mrs F provided her with a thimble. Four sub-pros were assigned to the sewing Room, Hetty, Pat and Joan (who found the 'livestock' in her hair) were Molly's companions. They could get rather 'out of hand' at times with their idle chatter and their often-monotonous work was in danger of becoming slip-shod - but Mrs F had the most subtle ways of steering them back on course again!

At lunchtime, Sam caught up with Molly in the drive as he returned from the post box. They arranged to meet at the Gate House at 6pm. Molly had already given some thought about their evening out and asked Sam if he would like to call in the shop again and perhaps visit Tommy. Sam thought it was a great idea. They hopped on the tram and during their ride into town Molly talked about Tommy, the disability under which he laboured and the disturbing effect his acquaintance with Lowry had provoked.

Ping-ping went the shop bell. Paul greeted them from behind the counter and ushered them through to the house where his new girlfriend, Conny, was sharing a pot of tea with Maisey. On Molly and Sam's arrival the pot was 'topped up' and two more cups were produced. Paul introduced Conny as a friend from the Mission who was training to be a teacher – she seemed a bright intelligent girl who obviously adored Paul by the way she responded when he came through from the shop. Then it was Maisey's turn to tell about her new boyfriend, a trainee executive with Tate and Lyle Sugar Company currently completing a part-time degree before returning to his home in Canada. Pru was away on holiday with friends. So sated with the latest news and having finished tea Molly and Sam left to call on Tommy.

Tommy was delighted to see them but he was tired and looked pale – it had not been a good day. Eventually Sam coaxed him into conversation and whilst the lads were chatting away Molly went through to the kitchen to have a few words with Tommy's mother. Tommy's mother always had a smile and a cheery word but tonight Molly could feel her strain. She was worried about Tommy and what the future would hold. Lizzy was a regular visitor and she longed to take Tommy to the Citadel to hear the band but Tommy's resources were so limited that even with the help of a wheelchair and the offer of a lift in a member's car, it was still too much for him.

Molly was surprised to see how quickly the other children were growing up – two sat reading and another carving an ornament out of a piece of elm wood. They all said how much they loved Tommy and wished he could be made better. Before it was time for them to leave, they all crowded into Tommy's room to enjoy a cup of tea served with fruitcake. Tommy was so pleased to see Molly and Sam – "don't leave it so long next time," he pleaded as they left. Tonight, was not the time to share Dominik's letter – perhaps next time.

Molly and Sam set forth to walk back to the hospital – at first it was a quiet journey both knowing the other's thoughts dwelt on Tommy. Eventually Sam said, "I couldn't really understand what treatment Tommy was having, particularly his medication." Molly said she thought it was mainly Aspirin, green oils lubrication and 'tender loving care' (TLC) … the NHS was in its infancy. Sam remarked that he had read a paper in a recent edition of his medical journal describing the use of steroids in the treatment of rheumatoid arthritis and their promising effect. Molly reminded Sam about Tommy's reaction to the Lowry information and the more he and Molly talked, the more convinced Sam became that he would seek the advice of 'the boss.' Back at the hospital they arranged to keep in touch and if anything useful came out of his discussion with 'the boss' he would let Molly know pronto. As Sam left he said, "I just hope I am still here to support Tommy when his care moves forward." Molly was taken aback – but of course Sam would not be here forever, his houseman's contract would come to an end and he would be applying for his next clinical placement, which she knew was likely to be Paediatrics, or Gynaecology.

The next day when Molly returned to the Sewing Room, Mrs F sensed that something was troubling her. In the early days, Mrs F had a slight frown when Molly spoke of her friendship with houseman Sam; they were both so young and each had a long journey to qualify and succeed in their respective professions. However, one day Mrs F was somewhat comforted to hear Molly say that Sam would never be another Vin and how much she was beginning to regret not carrying on with their special friendship. But today, Mrs F felt that her fears could be realized when Sam moved on to progress his career and leave another big gap in Molly's life.

Molly shared Tommy's predicament with Mrs F who told her about the brother she had lost with a debilitating condition when he was aged 17. Mrs F never forgot Tommy and always made enquiries when she knew Molly was going visit. Just a chink of hope glowed in Molly's heart that maybe, one day she might have the opportunity to introduce Mrs F to Tommy – she would be a wonderful person to befriend him ... and the family.

After what seemed to be a very short time into Molly's placement Mrs F announced her pending retirement – "we are all devastated," Molly wrote in her weekly letter home. But with hindsight they recollected one or two ladies visiting the sewing room recently. The week before her retirement Mrs F announced that another seamstress had been appointed to replace her. "She is a homely woman, obviously younger than I and very experienced at her work, I am sure you will all get on well together." The day Mrs F retired the four sub-pros brought in a celebration cake with a homemade card and a box of chocolates. Molly implored Mrs F to keep in touch with the sewing room ... "how could I not, my dear?" she asked.

However, a rather large, sour-faced person replaced Mrs F, an ogre of a woman named Miss Goad who told them off if they stopped working to whisper and giggle and she thought Molly's thimble was pretentious. Miss Goad quickly earned the nickname of 'the toad' and life in the Sewing Room changed almost overnight.

Now the only bright spot seemed to be Bubbles, the cleaning lady-cum-general factotum, a tall woman of indefinable age, who always dressed in a wrap-a-round pinafore. Bubbles had the most distinctive walk with her rhythmically nodding head thrust forward and her body sloping towards her rear, she continually chattered in a low murmuring voice. Bubble's little face, framed by a short dark bouncy hairstyle, had a bronzed, almost weather-beaten look and was always bathed in a smile. She always seemed to be happy, often teasing the sub-pros about their boyfriends, and mimicking Miss Goad with a rather naughty, but realistic toad-like 'croak-croak'. Bubbles cleaned the non-patient areas of the hospital, like the Sewing Room but everyone in the hospital knew Bubbles, and she knew everyone else! When she met a member of the hospital hierarchy in the corridors, they too received a shot of her wit! The story is often told how on one occasion she met the Hospital Superintendent, Mr Drew, the top man, affectionately known as 'Papa' in the corridor with his retinue of medics in tow. Smiling as she approached, Bubbles nodded saying, "Good morning, Sir." Then walked on still smiling and singing, "Oh my, doesn't his mother keep him nicely, look at his lovely white coaty." Most people in the hospital were wary of Bubbles, who like some kind of apparition would appear in the most unexpected places.

Within a fortnight of Molly and Sam's visit to Tommy, Molly found a note from Sam in her post box saying he had some encouraging news and suggesting they met before sharing the possibilities with Tommy and his parents – "perhaps tomorrow about 6pm in the small anteroom of the library?" Sam had written a 'P.S.' in bold style, "Guess, what? I performed the surgery today and the Consultant assisted ME!!" Molly sent proud congratulations and confirmed their arrangement.

Sam was pleased about his achievement, which the Consultant had found most praiseworthy … "and so he should, I have recently completed my surgical house job, for heaven's sake!" Sam exclaimed. However, perhaps the most encouraging news related to Tommy's situation. First and foremost, the rather delicate issue of professional etiquette had been circumvented because Tommy's doctor was an old medical school chum of the Rheumatologist and an esteemed colleague who he met at the Local Medical Society. Second, the Rheumatologist was prepared to talk with the GP about advances in his specialty and open the door for possible collaborative initiatives. The rheumatologist realized that everything depended on gaining the agreement of Tommy's doctor, "but I can be rather persuasive," he said, "and have a couple of incentives up my sleeve!" It was very promising but they decided to remain silent until discussions were more advanced. Sam and Molly had by now both missed supper, so they took the tram into town and ate at their favourite 'Chippy'.

Molly returned to the Sewing Room the next day wishing that Mrs F had been there for her wise counsel; most of the original sub-pro group had also dwindled away to other assignments. "I feel left behind," Molly told her mother.

THE HOSPITAL CONCERT PARTY:

Christmas was looming and the hospital concert party was getting ready to produce an event for the patients who remained in hospital over the Christmas period. In due course the notice appeared calling a meeting to 'share interesting ideas and willingness to participate.' Molly and several other sub-pros arrived for the meeting. The Chairman asked each person what ideas they had and what they could offer? When Molly's turn came she said she could recite Kipling's poem, 'If', or Longfellow's 'The Wreck of the Hesperus' … "Oh! I could also do a take of Fagin from Oliver Twist!" The Chairman frowned and asked whether or not Molly knew anything more cheerful. "Not immediately," Molly replied and he moved on.

The sub-pros sat chattering together when suddenly Hetty popped up with an idea. "I know, what about 'Tales from the Sewing Room', that would be perfect?" Pondering on Hetty's suggestion they drummed up a few ideas and when the Chairman had finished going round the gathering, Hetty stood up and put the proposition … "Well done, sounds fine" said the Chairman, "but be careful how far you go!" Needless to say they had difficulty in controlling themselves as one after the other the ideas exploded. When told of the idea, Miss Goad was non-committal. Eventually, the group got down to the serious business of writing a script and casting each other into the various roles, such as 'the toad', Mrs F definitely not to be forgotten and Home Sister - really, dare they?

Actually, Miss Goad became quite interested and supportive either by consciously, or unconsciously adding to the script and offering ideas for props and costumes. Such as the day she asked if her Sandy could be represented in the sketch. No one in the sewing room had ever heard of Sandy so ears alert someone asked, "Who is Sandy!" … My pussy," said Miss Goad with a rarely seen display of emotion. The atmosphere was electric with a deadly silence; everyone with the same thought they dare not share! "Would Sandy really appear in the show?" asked Molly. "Oh no, she is far too timid." So, Miss Goad's Sandy just had to be accommodated somehow. A visit to the Children's ward did not produce a cat but a small dog on wheels that could possibly suffice with a stretch of the imagination. As they were leaving the Children's Ward Molly met Sam coming through the swing doors from the opposite direction. "Well! Hello and hello again," said Sam. "I thought they had stitched you into a pillowcase! – OK for tonight? 5 o'clock at the Gates?" Trying to clear her mind Molly hesitatingly replied, "Well, yes I think so." "Fine," he grinned.

On the dot they met at the Gates. Both of them were brimming over with enthusiasm, each trying to get a word in as they ran across the road to catch the tram. Molly insisted on having the first round to talk about the Christmas Show. Sam was intrigued with the idea of a 'Sewing Room Sketch' and, as anticipated, was quite surprised and interested in the warmth of Miss Goad's regard for her cat, Sandy. "Perhaps you have misjudged her all this time? It's amazing what you find when you scratch the surface." Molly would remember Sam's comment for the rest of her life.

"Now I have one or two surprises for you!" Firstly, Sam went on to tell her about the planned outpatient's appointment for Tommy. Secondly, he announced the forthcoming informal appointment at a London hospital renowned for clinical excellence. "The experience could give me a wonderful insight into Paediatrics but first I will look at Gynae in Manchester," he explained. "Why Manchester?" asked Molly. But she well knew the Royal Infirmary to be a highly esteemed establishment, and as Sam cheekily reminded her, "With a specialist cancer treatment centre nearby, I may get two experiences for the price of one!"

However, first things first as they agreed they would be open with Tommy tonight and try to assure him, and his family about any issues of concern. Then, as the Paediatric interview was imminent, they embarked on a brainstorming session of the points Sam needed to make and explore. They had quite a fun time bouncing ideas around, such as the quality of training and professional development; the practicalities of living accommodation, working hours, rotas and so on. As thy paused for thought, Sam snuggled up with a glint in his eye, "and where you sleep when you come to stay!" Molly rolled her eyes adding, "That's a thought, Sam, we don't want any hanky-panky!" ... "I wish," Sam countered as he squeezed her close.

Finally, they talked about the Christmas Show. Much to Molly's surprise she learned that Sam and other housemen were preparing to 'do a slot' as Morris Dancers! They had great ideas about audience participation; initially they had thought about providing sticks for them to beat time! "I know," said Sam with sudden inspiration, "We'll talk it over with Tommy tonight."

Needless to say, the corner shop was their first stop. It was closing time so Sam completed his usual routine of clearing the fruit and veg boxes from the shelves outside the shop windows. Molly went inside to make a cup of tea and there she found Pru in a contented frame of mind and eager to talk about Reg, who she had met at the dancing classes. Maisey and Paul who were just about to leave seemed to be OK with life, whilst Molly and Sam briefly described the forthcoming Christmas Show. Pru, clearly always pleased to see them, offered to entertain them for supper - "Say, after Christmas?" Molly and Sam agreed to fit in.

Tommy perked up when they arrived and eager to know all about the new treatment due to start next week. Sam reassured Tommy and his mother, as she came into the room, that it was a wonderful opportunity for Tommy, adding, "the doctors involved are the best and so keen to help you." Tommy, looked at Sam with hope written all over his face as he said, "I am so looking forward to going to the Citadel for the Christmas services with Lizzy. Do you think I shall make it?" Sam cautioned Tommy that it might be a bit early, then adding, "But see what they say, you are in the hands of experts now!" Molly and Sam began to talk about the hospital Christmas Show and the parts they were planning to play. "Who knows," Sam enthused, "we might even get you up there to see it!" The evening went so very quickly and soon Sam and Molly were heading back to the hospital.

On the way Sam said, "Now, what about this Christmas Show, we need some Morris Dancing gear. Any ideas? Straw hats seem to be a bit in short supply!" Apparently, the 'Gynae' houseman who formed part of the troupe came from Somerset, so Sam was confident he would have some 'know-how'. "Don't forget it's a pagan ritual," laughed Molly and as she thought of her mother's delight in exercising her ingenuity, she promised to see what could be produced.

The next weekend Molly and Hetty went home seeking inspiration for their sewing room sketch. Molly however, warned Hetty there was to be no lewd or suggestive remarks because her father was resolute against any 'smutty talk'. Rose was delighted to help; she hunted through the trunk and found some possible costumes and props. She gave serious thought to the cat and asked, "Could you do anything with my old fox fur?" Once again 'foxy' sprang out of the trunk as if alive! "Marvellous," said Hetty, "we can tie it round the dog and from the stage it will easily look like a randy 'Ginger Tom'! Wills sat in his chair listening but not commenting. Kate thought she made a helpful contribution by suggesting that the introductory music could be 'The Stripper' – a take on the Sewing Room stitchers!

Molly said as an afterthought, "By the way I shall need a summer frock with sewing materials such as cotton bobbins, a tape measure and scissors attached. Can you think of something either of you, please?" Kate seemed well pleased that her talents had been recognized! "Well ... Yes," said Rose "I suppose we could make a 'sewing room gown' from the bridesmaid dress you wore at Eileen's wedding – what do you think?" Molly smiled and agreed that might be a possibility. "Leave it with us," said Kate, "Mum and I will put our heads together and have some ideas ready when you come next weekend." Hetty naughtily suggested, "You could dress up as Molly Malone but you haven't really got her buxom sauciness." Wills cleared his throat - that did not go down very well, thought Gwen!

Thinking about the Morris dancers, Molly saw her father's straw hat in the cupboard – "can we borrow your hat for the Morris men, Dad? You haven't got any more, have you?" Surprisingly four straw hats were found, together with some colourful ribbon for decoration. Wills offered to search out some ears of wheat, or corn with long stems for adornment. With a flash of inspiration Molly asked, "Can I bring Sam next weekend to sort out their costumes?" Rose positively purred, "What a good idea," she said, coquettishly tidying her hair! Needless to say, when Sam heard about the straw hats and the invitation to sort out the remainder of the costumes next weekend he was well pleased.

It was not altogether surprising that Rose's weekly letter to Molly revealed an air of caution insofar as "father thought Hetty was rather worldly." Rose expressed the hope that the friendship was not too close! Sometimes Rose softened her message with a poem she remembered, or a snippet from the Sunday Companion her church newspaper! Molly treasured this fond and inspiring memorabilia all her life.

As a courtesy, Bubbles was asked about the idea of the sewing room sketch and she was delighted to think she would feature in the Christmas show – "who will be playing my part?" she asked. A rather stunned silence followed – no one had thought about that! However, Molly seemed to retrieve the day when she said, "Oh! Someone tall, dark and handsome, Bubbles." But who, they thought as Bubbles went off smiling, nodding and humming away to herself? "What about Mr Shepherd, our beloved mentor?" suggested Hetty. "Why not?" they said in unison. So, Molly was delegated to seek out Mr Shepherd who was cautiously delighted and gave an impromptu audition in which he performed to perfection! The rest of the casting followed without a hitch – Hetty being the natural to impersonate Miss Goad! The sub-pros confidently consulted the Chairman who liked the idea but thought the plot was restricted to a rather small and obscure area of hospital life and suggested that it may be better fitted into a wider picture. And indeed, so it did.

Molly and Sam went home the next weekend to collect the remainder of the props. Their arrival was greeted with a full-scale afternoon tea and supper banquet – best china, silver cutlery and napkins, nothing spared! True to form Rose had sorted out one or two adornments for the Morris-men's white outfits on loan from Theatres, and Wills had a collection of sturdy stalks of corn and wheat.

Molly was eager to find out if Rose had any further thoughts on her outfit but before she could ask the question, Kate burst in the room … "Da De Da," with a flourish of THE dress! Everyone gasped. Rose and Kate had produced the most fantastic creation adorned with every sewing room and haberdashery item you could think of. Molly dressed up and twirled around, "Wonderful," said Sam, "You will steal the show!" Rose smiled rather knowingly, or hopefully!

Wills came through from the kitchen heralded by his usual 'Hum, Hum!" He had his hands behind his back to bring forth, with a rare flourish from the performing arts, a large pair of silver painted cardboard scissors. "I thought you might like this as your hat, Nitto." The scissors were open and Wills demonstrated how he thought Molly might wear the hat with the scissor points tilted over one eye, the long satin ribbons adorning the handles could hang down the back of her head, and the ribbons fixed to the hinges tied in a bow under her chin to hold the hat in place. Molly was absolutely speechless; she flew into her father's arms to hug and kiss him. "You are a genius, Dad," she said. "Wait a minute though, I also had an idea that you might like these." And he presented two cardboard casings painted black and resembling a flat iron to fix onto her shoes! "You are a miracle worker, Dad," she said with tears streaming down her face. "That's OK Nitto, have fun," he twinkled. Sam pondered on this moving spectacle of Molly's transformation and the love and pride that beamed out from the face of her father – a privileged insight indeed!

Out came the leather holdall, normally used to transport Molly's laundry, and the costume was carefully packed away to take to the hospital. The remainder of the evening was spent chatting around the fire – needless to say Sam took centre stage!

After breakfast the following morning, Wills took Sam a walk around his terrain which involved a few odd jobs on the farm. Sam returned beaming from ear to ear, his face flushed and his eyes sparkling, "I think I may need to change course in my career," he said "What a fantastic life-style!" Molly and Sam left to catch the bus back to the hospital with Molly's family still basking in Sam's charisma!

Returning to the hospital, Sam and Molly sat on the bus noisily planning Molly's routine. "What kind of dance?" "What music?" "Where will I fit in?" "What will Bertie say?" By the time they arrived they had a jumble of ideas but no solutions!

Sam was in a quiet, ponderous mood as they walked through the hospital grounds. He stopped suddenly and looking intently at Molly asked, "Do you think I would I fit in with your family, Molly?" Molly just knew he would be perfect but as usual in their tender moments she played the joker saying, "I don't know, Sam. You would have to earn your corn!" They said, "Goodnight," and parted.

Putting the unresolved Pantomime issues to the 'cocoa gang' later that night was a different story. A dance was invented that resembled a cross between the 'Highland Fling' and the 'Sailors Hornpipe'. With sudden inspiration Petal revealed her hidden talent of being able to play the Recorder – "Sure, I'll do that for you Mol – how about we call the dance 'the Cotton Reel'?"

Petal's play on words sent the gang rolling about in fits of laughter!

The idea was presented to Bertie at the next rehearsal. "Wow!" he said, "It is too good to be part of a sketch, we will have it as the 'Grand Finale'. The Morris Dancers can join with the group of Sewing Room Girls to form a backing group." And so that's how it was.

In the run up to the show, the Sewing Room Girls rehearsed their routines in the Nurses' Home dancing up and down the corridors, in and out of the lounge and gradually all the residents began to join in with the jaunty music and fleeting steps. Finally, they rehearsed in the ballroom once they had formed a troupe of ex-Sewing Room sub-pros. They looked a mischievous bunch dressed in sheet-tunics tied at the waist with tape measures and mad hatter-type pillowcase hats – with hospital logo in full view, of course!

Sam and his fellow thespians were well pleased with their straw hats and stylish costumes as they clapped and stamped to the Morris dance rhythm. The sketch of hospital life and its personalities, including Miss Goad's Sandy, was a novel experience for both staff and patients. Molly swirled around in her gorgeous costume to the singing and clapping of the 'backing group'; and Mr Shepherd as 'Bubbles' stole the show. The applause said it all. Finally, accompanied by Petal on the piano and the rhythmical clappers of the Morris Men, the singing of Christmas Carols rounded off the performance to perfection.

Bubbles could be seen hovering at the back of the hall at every performance clapping, humming and thoroughly enjoying the show. During the second performance the sewing room sub-pros were delighted to see Mrs F and Miss Goad sitting on the front row. They all sat and chatted together after the performance and it suddenly seemed that the ice had melted away ... and once again, Molly thought of Sam's words, "It's amazing what you find when you scratch the surface."

CHRISTMAS AND PARTINGS:

After the final curtain it was all hands-on deck to restore order. Molly noticed Sam hovering and excused herself from the group. "What's next?" said Sam, "Have we time to pop up and see Tommy before Christmas?" Molly agreed that was a must and they arranged to meet next Wednesday at 5pm.

Wednesday came and they were hopping on the tram. Both of them still flushed with the success of the Christmas Show but Sam had another cause for feeling good. The informal interview at the Paediatric Hospital had impressed Sam and it seemed that he too went down well with the staff he met during the visit. So far, so good: now a look at Manchester.

Sam had his own special Christmas present for Tommy and his family - a progress report from the hospital, which was said to look promising. "I think we might see the beginning of a change in Tommy," predicted Sam. But before visiting Tommy, they popped into the shop with flowers and chocolates wishing them all a "Happy Christmas". They were curious to hear about Sam's interview and wished him well – whatever his decision. After a quick toast to the festive season, they left to visit Tommy.

Tommy was delighted to see them; he certainly looked brighter and more optimistic tucked up in a cosy blanket sitting in a chair by the fire. Although he still suffered from extreme tiredness, Tommy explained he was able to move short distances around the house with his walking aids and join in family life. But they were agog to hear about the Panto! Miss Goode's Sandy was the source of much mirth, particularly when they heard about the improvisation! Then Sam took his costume from his rucksack and to their delight demonstrated his performance as a Morris dancer. Meanwhile, Molly changed into her sewing room costume in the kitchen and after Sam's performance she appeared swirling around in full splendour – Sam seemed to find Molly irresistible and they swirled around together before finally collapsing in a rather prolonged cuddle in an armchair. Tommy just stared in disbelief. Sam promised to let him have a selection of photographs when they were developed.

After all the excitement, Tommy's mother served them with tea and Christmas cake ... "Now, if this is your first taste of Christmas cake you must close your eyes and make a wish when you take your first bite." So they did, afterwards to be reminded, "for a wish to come true it must never be told!" Sam and Molly looked at each other with something akin to a plea in their eyes, which didn't pass unnoticed by Tommy.

Christmas presents were exchanged and they decided to open them whilst they could share the spirit of Christmas. To Molly's delight she received some lace trimmed handkerchiefs and Sam a blue woollen scarf, which he immediately wrapped round his neck and enjoyed its softness and warmth. Molly gave Tommy a book on the History of Art and as he flicked through the pages his face flushed with pleasure as he recognized Lowry's 'matchstick men' and discovered a selection of early cave drawings and their meanings in time. Sam had chosen a colourful jumper in the hope that Tommy could wear it to accompany Lizzy to the Citadel on Christmas Day – both Tommy and his mother were moved to tears. Next came the present for Tommy's mother. Sam delved into the bottom of his rucksack to retrieve a package wrapped in sparkling paper and adorned with gold-coloured bows. "It looks too lovely to open," she said as she gently looked inside to find a powder blue cashmere jumper. "Oh! I have never had anything so beautiful in my life," adding dreamily, "it's so soft!" Sam clasped Molly's, and Tommy's mother's hands and they joined up with Tommy to sing 'Auld Lang Synge'. Tears of joy all round and another pot of tea.

Then, as if triggered by the old Scottish tradition, Tommy suddenly remembered the Christmas card and letter he had received from Vin. His mother took the card down from the mantelpiece to pass around and Tommy gave the gist of Vin's news, which included April, the satisfaction they were experiencing in their studies at Edinburgh University, and the interests their new home offered. For a brief moment the light flickered on Molly's Christmas but quickly rekindled in Sam's presence and his enthusiasm for the future – their future, wondered Molly as she momentarily became lost in thought? She realised Sam was recounting the London experience and sharing his intention to visit the 'Gynae' team in Manchester before making the final decision.

"Why go to Manchester?" Tommy's mother asked, "We have an excellent Women's Hospital here? Sam explained not only the advantages of a dual opportunity to link women's health with cancer treatment in Manchester, but the need to spread his wings, "and get known!" Seeing the hint of a crest-fallen look on Tommy's face, Sam affectionately reassured Tommy that he would never forget him. Wherever he went Sam promised he would write to him often, and visit as the opportunity arose. Tommy said he would never forget Sam and thanked him for giving him hope.

Molly, not wanting to leave on a sad note briefly told Tommy about Dominik's letter and because time was short she left the letter for him to read later. Tommy said he would use the Atlas to help him follow the story as he read the letter. Time to leave with more hugs and happy Christmas's and they parted.

On the tram returning to the hospital Sam asked Molly when she was going home for Christmas. "At the end of next week, I shall catch the usual Friday bus. What about you?" Molly asked. "I am on duty over Christmas and into the New Year, then I have some holiday due, so I shall finally depart late February, possibly early March, depending on when I start the new job – but we'll meet up well before then – won't we?" "Oh, yes," said Molly with a reminder of the supper date at the shop! As they walked to the hospital Sam fished in his rucksack once more and gave Molly a little parcel with instructions, "Not to be opened until Christmas morning." Molly, also prepared, pulled a parcel from her bag and saying "the same to you!"

They hugged each other and for the first time Sam kissed Molly with lover's kisses and Molly responded with the realisation – 'I do love you, Sam – but as a lover?'

As Molly walked to the Gate House on Friday to catch the bus home for Christmas, she was surprised to find just how sad she felt about the prospect of Sam not being around anymore. On Christmas morning Molly opened Sam's present – an ornate bottle of expensive perfume with the words ... "Because you are special." Clipped inside Sam's Christmas card was a Fob watch with the engraving, "Time will tell?" In the midst of such joy Molly was heartbroken, what was it that constrained the wonderful love they had for each other but could not share? Molly hoped Sam appreciated her rather more practical gift of one of the new biro pens with three different coloured inks for his ward charts. How she wished she had been able to choose a more intimate token of her feelings.

Christmas was over. Sam and Molly met up as soon as she returned to the hospital – each delighted with their Christmas pressies. Sam thought Molly very clever to be so far-sighted and practical – "and what is more important," added Sam, "the pen will be with me every waking hour!"

The evening they joined Pru and her guests for a meal at the corner shop Molly felt a real sense of celebration. In addition to Sam and Molly both furthering their careers, Pru and Reg were planning to marry in the foreseeable future and move to the coast to set up a Guest House. Maisey excitedly explained that when her fiancé graduated in June, they would pursue the idea of moving to Canada as their permanent home. Paul and Connie were not thinking of "rushing into anything at the moment", they were doing well at work and Paul was happy to run the shop with his very able assistant, Geoff, who had now progressed from 'errand boy' to trainee manager. The announcement of Geoff's advancement and commitment to the family firm provoked a rousing cheer in Geoff's direction and glasses were raised with a toast, "To the future – each and every one of us!" The party gathered round the large oval dining table to enjoy a sumptuous meal in the subdued lighting of the dining room, with Pru's favourite classical music quietly playing in the background. It was a wonderful time of companionship and celebration, but one which felt like a 'grand finale' as they were all set to pursue their different destinies – exciting in many ways but laced with uncertainty and loss in others.

In due course Molly was asked to visit the linen stores to meet Home Sister where she would be issued with her student nurse uniform in preparation for PTS Spring intake – she was about to wave her white coat and butterfly cap goodbye to re-enter as probationer 'Nurse Molly Lange.'

When she told Sam about her day he said, "Oh Molly, I was so looking forward to seeing you tripping around the wards in your nurse's uniform before I left – you have worked so hard to get this far – well done." The following evening after supper they had planned to play table tennis in the recreation room. As a surprise, Molly quickly changed into her uniform, complete with fob watch, for Sam's approval. But before she could gather herself, he had swept her off her feet with a wild 'WHOOP' and kissed her. Molly looked mock-shocked and said, "Not in uniform please, doctor!" So Sam daringly repeated the embrace and as they leaned together laughing, Gwen sensed that the world felt good for them – 'go on, make the commitment,' she silently urged.

Molly broke away to change but Sam clutched her arm, "Don't run away, Molly, please," he pleaded. Seeing the look on Sam's face she said. "OK. Promise." And so Sam continued his heart-felt supplication. "You must know how I feel about you, Molly. Long before you were aware I saw you on the Orthopaedic Ward - your first week in Physiotherapy I was told. You were manoeuvring an awkward wheelchair whilst trying to keep that unruly cap on your head! But it was the smile you exchanged with the patient that blew me away! Then when you came into theatre, I just couldn't believe my luck!" Molly was overwhelmed but she also realised they had been playing, 'cat and mouse'. "Well," she said, "I have rather enjoyed your company too, and to be selfish, I am sorry you have to move on." Sam made an attempt to speak. "No, Sam hear me out. You are way ahead of me in your career and I have not yet started mine and who knows, I may not be as successful as you have been. You will need a partner who can complement and even enhance your success. "Oh! Molly this is not a job interview, you know!" Suddenly, they clung to each other laughing at the absurdity of Sam's remark! After their laughter was spent Sam said, "you could be that person – just give me some hope." But Molly was insistent, "love does not conquer all, but time will tell Sam! For now then, best friends for life?" Sam quietly said, "Yes, best friends for life, dearest Molly."

CHAPTER 5

ON THE WARDS

THE DAY ARRIVED:

The hospital's PTS new set of some fifteen student nurses were told to report to Sister Adams, Junior Sister Tutor, in the dining room at 8.30am.

Molly had been up and dressed in her new uniform since 6 o'clock making sure the seams of her black stockings were straight and her petticoat did not show beneath the lilac-coloured uniform dress. The collar felt uncomfortably tight and seemed to grow tighter – it seemed all right when she practised with Home Sister! Now for the apron, not to be worn except on the ward of course, the bib held on one side by a tiepin and the other by Sam's Fob watch! Finally, to fit the royal blue cape with red lining which was surprisingly cumbersome and difficult to manoeuvre. However, when in place and fastened at the neck with the decorative hook and eye it looked very smart. Next, to collect the PTS folder containing a note pad and pen and 'Here we go,' thought Molly, 'on the next leg – the start of a three-year training commitment!' Molly began to hear doors along the corridor opening and closing as the new recruits gathered to walk over to breakfast; Sister Adams joined them to walk to the School of Nursing.

Once seated in the classroom, Sister Adams positioned herself at a desk on a raised platform at the front of the class. Almost immediately a door behind her opened and a tall lady entered. She was regal in demeanour, good looking with her dark hair piled in a chignon on top of her head, blue sparkling eyes and a roguish smile. Similar to Sister Adam's grey uniform, she wore a navy-blue dress with a lace collar and the long sleeves were edged with lace cuffs. Sister Adams introduced her as Sister Sparrow, Principal Nurse Tutor. Sister Sparrow; she bid the group "Good morning," as they stood in response. From that day on Sister Sparrow became Molly's hero and life model; she only ever met one other such person during her career but she turned out to have feet of clay! Molly was as putty in her Tutor's hands and from that day Molly strived for perfection. Sister Sparrow was a fun person who always seemed to have a battle with her weight, she would sit behind her high desk at the front of the class, roll her eyes and bemoan the fact that she only had to look at a cream bun for several extra pounds to appear on the scales.

Molly's PTS set was composed of an interesting mixture of personalities and cultural diversity. Five students lived locally, notably Hetty, the older woman from sub-pro days who had been here, there and everywhere! A number came from various other parts of the UK and Ireland, together with several overseas students, including three ladies from Germany. Rosetta, one of the students from Germany was particularly friendly, she had blonde curly hair, round pink cheeks and an enchanting smile – one could imagine her in the Austrian mountains yodelling and tending the goats just like 'The Sound of Music'. Molly and Hetty were the only ones to know the hospital so they were nominated to 'show the others the ropes'.

GETTING STARTED – PRACTICE MAKES PERFECT:

Sister Sparrow gave out the timetable for the Monday to Friday, 8am – 5pm Induction period and the dates for the regular study programme for the first year. High on the Induction syllabus was the History and Ethics of Nursing, Anatomy and Physiology, and the practical tasks of nursing, "starting with one of the most straightforward," said Sister Adams, "bed making." The first few sessions were rather jolly but they all said, "If this is the most straightforward of tasks then heaven help us when we come to the more complicated." There were just so many different kinds of beds - admission, post-operative, and divided beds and in addition numerous gadgets were used! Say, a pulley suspended over the top of the bed to help a patient move more independently, or a bed-cradle to take the weight of the bedclothes off painful limbs, not forgetting the 'donkey', a device placed under the thighs to prevent a patient from slipping down the bed. The 'donkey' looked like a Christmas cracker and was made by wrapping a pillow in the centre of a draw sheet with the ends of the sheet tucked underneath the mattress to keep it in place.

Needless to say, clean linen needed to be at hand together with a receptacle for soiled items. Two chairs set back-to-back were placed at the foot of the bed on to which the bedclothes were folded - which under no circumstances must touch the floor! Finally, the bed making procedures were governed by a very strict discipline. First and foremost, preservation of a patient's dignity at all times. Other important rules included accurately mitred corners at the foot of the bed, a fingertip to elbow depth of top sheet folded over the bedding, pillows arranged exactly according to the patient's prescribed needs and with the open end facing down the ward, and a final check that the bed wheels were lined up straight and turned inwards.

The initial 'run through' of making an occupied bed in the classroom involved three students, each of them taking it in turns to be the 'patient'. Without exception, all of them found the rolling back and forth a rather queasy experience and one they never forgot when doing the real thing – Molly's 'patient' took a few minutes to recover from feeling seasick! Needless to say, they had rolled their 'patient' over far more times than was necessary.

During the lunch break Molly found a note from Sam in her post box saying he was on his way to Manchester for an informal interview. "Wish me luck!" Adding, "and don't get lost in all the classroom paraphernalia before I get back!"

The afternoon was spent on the wards helping to 'tidy the beds' and settling the patients after lunch. It was not as daunting as expected, the nurses were helpful and some patients winked at the students conspiratorially, one man said to Molly, "You'll soon be a dab hand at this nurse."

Returning to the practice and procedures of nursing, Sister Sparrow demonstrated some of the tray and trolley settings with which they needed to become familiar. The first exercise was presenting food to a patient and once again they all took it in turn to be the patient who required assistance to eat breakfast cereal. "First and foremost," Sister cautioned, "remember mealtimes are usually social occasions, so always position yourselves at eye level with the patient and communicate as appropriate." When unpacked like this, assisting a patient at mealtimes became an art form – which, of course, it was!

The first part of the Induction period concluded with dressing and undressing a patient: another everyday task, which suddenly presented such unimaginable complexity.

At 5pm Molly left to catch the 6pm bus home. Needless to say, on this first visit home after joining her 'set' Rose was keen to know all about Molly's fellow students and the 'ins' and 'outs' of hospital life. As Rose listened, Molly could sense her relating, 'how things should be done' to the experience of attending patients in the 'sick bay' at her own home!

Molly's fellow students were duly placed under scrutiny. So, seated in front of the fire with father in his usual chair, she proceeded to give an account of her colleagues. Rose responded, "It must be nice to have some local girls in the group, you will be able to support each other." However, Molly's parents expressed some disquiet on learning that three German girls were in her set - memories of the war were never far from the surface. Apart from family tragedies, the press had been emblazoned with graphic accounts of the horrors of flattened, burning towns and cities, the traumas of prisoner of war camps and eventually the holocaust. "Do be careful," Rose warned, "you don't really know them. Are they all right with the patients, I guess they are well supervised?" Tutting from father prompted the usual ... "I told you no good would come of all this but you would have your way."

The Induction period continued with '20 questions' on the previous teaching. Sister Sparrow made the session quite light-hearted, although there were some glazed looks and silences to which Sister would roll her eyes and respond, "I know what you are thinking, 'never 'eerrd of it,' but when you look at your notes you will discover otherwise." 'Never 'eerrd of it,' became very familiar to them as they progressed through training! When Sister sensed that the class felt they had achieved a respectable result she cautioned, "the proof of the pudding will be in the eating, ladies!" Molly later learned that Sister Sparrow's father was a policeman. If that was the case, she had certainly acquired the direct delivery approach laced with an unusual sense of humour and persuasion!

The following two afternoons were spent on the wards relating nursing skills to body functions, such as sitting a patient on a bedpan through to the end task of operating the wheezing, spluttering sluice room bedpan sterilizer. They also found that bed making was not quite the daunting exercise carried out in the classroom, and feeding a patient whilst sitting at eye level seemed awkward but not impossible. So the exercise ended on a more positive note, or so they thought.

As Molly was dashing to catch the bus home, Sam waved from the end of the corridor and hurried towards her bursting to say he had an interesting time at Manchester and like London, it had ticked all the boxes but he had decided to apply to London – perhaps Manchester in the longer term. Pausing he said, "You've been a bit elusive, I wondered where on earth you had disappeared!" Molly briefly told Sam about her new regime, explaining that she was leaving for a weekend at home. "How about you join me sometime?" she asked Sam. "Absolutely, I have been waiting for the opportunity to thank your folks and return the props." Meanwhile, they agreed to meet on

Wednesday evening. "I have lots of news; OK if we visit Tommy?"

The weekend passed all too quickly with Rose delighted by the prospect of Sam's forth-coming visit. Soon it was Monday and the first session focused on an evaluation (usually referred to as a post-mortem!) of the ward experience! "Not bad, on the whole" said Sister Sparrow, "some unsightly sheets trailed on the floor, a few unfortunate patients were left with crusty food debris on their mouths, and some rather unsightly and precarious bedpan handling to be smartened up." Sister presented each student with the GNC Practical Training Schedule with clear instructions to keep it clean, safe, and up-to-date. Sister reminded them it was a legal document to be presented as part of the State Examinations for admission to the Register of General Nurses. The Schedule listed all the practical nursing procedures, which a Ward Sister marked with a 'tick' when demonstrated to the student, the 'tick' was converted to 'X' when the Ward Sister adjudged the student to be proficient.

Sister Sparrow opened the history books to show how nursing, as the profession of today was founded from the early 1800's by determined visionaries. A College of Nursing (later conferred 'Royal') (RCN) was created to set up a Register of trained nurses, promote nursing education and practice, and to safeguard the employment nurses – strictly not a Trade Union at this time! Florence Nightingale paved the way towards this day by establishing the St Thomas' Hospital Nurse Training School in London as far back as 1860 – a standard emulated in other large towns and cities with the support of the 'City Fathers' and the well-heeled business community.

Legislation enacted in 1917 formalised the profession by establishing three General Nursing Councils (England and Wales, Scotland and Northern Ireland) and remitting to Councils' the statutory responsibility of setting up and regulating a Register of Trained Nurses. Sister Sparrow spent time discussing the implications of their accountability to the profession as students and subsequently for as long as their names remained on the Register. Furthermore, she stressed the importance of belonging to the RCN, their professional organisation and distributed Membership Application Forms to show she meant business when the time came. It all seemed rather daunting and there was so much to learn to reach that stage when lo and behold a life size skeleton and his friend appeared!

RUPERT AND SADIE:

Rupert, the skeleton, was brought out of his hidey-hole to confront the class as the focal point of the week; along with Sadie presented on a colourful wall-mounted chart showing the muscles and other soft tissues that adorned the skeleton ... Anatomy and Physiology (A&P) the basis of all understanding they were told! The names and purposes of the notches, protuberances, fosses, sockets, hinges and digits on Rupert's frame with the overlay of muscles and other soft tissue became like finding their way through a maze - Molly was thankful for her Sub-pro's College Course. Sister prepared a simplified graphic for immediate reference but she warned the class that this was no substitute for the regulation textbooks such as, *"Anatomy and Physiology'* written by Evelyn Pearce an esteemed Sister Tutor and member of the GNC; *'Gray's Anatomy'* was also commended as a more advanced textbook. They all groaned at the thought of 'the heavy stuff' – "No gains without pains ladies, you will remember A&P all your life!" said Sister Sparrow with a wide grin on her face. Molly was glad she had chosen Evelyn Pearce's textbook as a night school prize in anticipation of this day.

With Rupert and Sadie as their mentors in mind, the afternoon was spent practising bandaging and the application of slings. The capelin head bandage was included in the session with each of them practising on the other. One of the students almost passed out because the bandage had been put on too tight ... "Lesson learned, nurses!" admonished their Tutor. But other forms of bandaging also presented challenges, such as the Figure of 8 for the elbow and the Spica shoulder bandages where the end result resembled untidy window drapes - Will's scarecrows flashed before Molly's eyes! Sister suggested they took a collection of bandages to practise in the Nurses' Home!

The subjects of hygiene and safety, which threaded through the training, brought some relief! One afternoon they spent packing drums with various sorts of dressings, protective sheets and clothing. Molly was well versed in the procedure from her experience in Theatres and the admonishment by Sister, which she would never forget! On another occasion they practised operating the long-lever ward tap, a technique in which elbows held out like wings replaced their hands prior to an aseptic procedure - Molly's technique had been rehearsed in Theatres as she watched and learned from theatre staff!

The sessions were followed up by ward experiences where they practised setting up various trays and trolleys to perform a nursing procedure. A senior Nurse first demonstrated the procedure to the students on a willing patient, which on completion was followed by dismantling and preparing the used equipment for sterilisation. Such preparation was critical. The serrations at the end of the forceps and the hinges of the instruments were scrubbed free of any debris and packed in the sterilizer according to a set pattern. Preparation of the sterilizer demanded the exact height of the water to which the sterilizer must be filled, the right amount of soda bicarbonate (soda-bic) to raise the boiling point of the water to ensure optimum sterility and finally to set the timer. Many uncomfortable lessons were learnt by the fledgling nurses but the most embarrassing was to add too much soda-bic which caused the sterilizer to boil over like the incoming tide to flood the sluice floor and probably out into the corridor if not spotted in time! Most student nurses fell into such traps; but only once - thankfully, Molly had picked up some 'know-how' in Theatres! The completed procedures earned the students their first ticks on their GNC Schedules.

Sister Sparrow was beginning to interlace an elementary understanding of pharmacology into the scheme of things:

Poisons and how to store and use them, the safeguarding of drugs prescribed for individual patients including the special legal requirements governing controlled drugs, the position of the Nurse in law and his/her accountability to the GNC. In these days the administration of controlled drugs was a teasing task. For example, morphine was dispensed in tablet form of various strengths. So, to say administer a dose of one-sixth grain of morphine from a one-quarter grain tablet, the nurse placed the tablet, together with a measured quantity of sterile water in a special china spoon, heated it over a Bunsen burner until the tablet dissolved and then withdrew the prescribed dose of morphine! It was a nightmare; but times changed and the day came when the exact dose was prescribed in liquid form in individual glass phials.

The nurse's accountability for the administration, safekeeping and recording of drugs administered to a patient was taken very seriously and subjected to detailed teaching, demonstration and supervision throughout training. Unfortunately, on very rare occasions a nurse might be tempted to take prescribed drugs for their own use, say a headache, or to help him/her sleep during the day whilst on night duty; sadly, for a small minority it was the slippery slope to addiction. There were however, some breaches of protocol from which all nurses learned a lesson, such as the story about a male nurse who had sore eyes due to late night revising before taking his practical Prelim Exams. A colleague offered to bring some soothing eye drops from the ward at break time. She did as she promised, and administered them but they were the wrong drops - a substance used to dilate the pupils! When the male nurse later attended the practical examination to be handed a long bone with a request to describe its characteristics, he could not immediately identify the bone and experienced even greater difficulty in identifying the fine details for the examiner. The story was a salutary lesson to the whole set and hopefully one that would never be forgotten. But these were serious offences for which a nurse could be dismissed, required to attend the GNC Disciplinary Committee with the prospect of being 'Struck off' the Register, and possibly proceed to a criminal charge.

Before one week of chaperoned experience on the wards, the PTS set was given an appreciation of the services that supported patient care. Their first visit was the hospital autoclave department where the drums and various pieces of equipment were sterilized. What went on behind the scenes in this foundry-like environment truly amazed them. The unsterile drums with the vents open were packed into the autoclave in a systematic arrangement to allow the heat to penetrate and do its job of sterilising the contents. When the operation was complete, the autoclaves were unpacked and the vents of the drums closed immediately to maintain sterility before being dispatched back to the wards and departments.

Monday morning dawned and Molly reported to the male surgical ward for her chaperoned experience. The PTS students were allocated a designated mentor with whom they worked the same duties – including a midweek day off, which was a novelty! The week was pretty intensive and exhausting, not least due to the good-humoured teasing by the younger patients. Molly set up and dismantled various trays and trolleys for surgical dressings and made umpteen beds! Her GNC Schedule gathered a number of 'ticks' and two were converted into 'crosses'!

Wednesday evening arrived and Sam was waiting for Molly at the lodge for their evening together. Molly sensed that Sam was bursting with news, so once settled on the tram she said, "OK, you first." Sam told of the short notice given to attend the hospital interview for his next Paediatric Houseman placement; thankfully he had made it and was accepted. Sam was enthused by the spirit in which his interview had proceeded; he found the clinical landscape impressive, as too was the programme of medical education and personal development. Sam hugged her saying, "It will not only be a good career move Molly but we shall be able to spend REAL time together, perhaps see a West End show, or go to a Gallery." Molly was pleased for him but knew she would miss Sam's close friendship and good humour.

Gwen, the silent observer, suppressed her foreboding as she thought of the tears that had yet to be shed.

News of Tommy was encouraging. Molly listened intently as Sam outlined the details of the proposal about which the Consultant rheumatologist had consulted Tommy, his family and the family doctor. The proposal would involve Tommy in a research programme trialling a regime that combined immunology, pharmacology and physiotherapy. Some treatments would be home based and others undertaken at the hospital. The Consultant had sensed that Tommy's parents were encouraged but cautious and needed lots of reassurance that the programme would do Tommy no harm. On the other hand, Tommy himself had seemed more optimistic. "So far, so good!" Sam pronounced.

Arriving at their stop, they walked up the street to the corner shop – the 'ting-ting' of the shop bell was as dear to Molly's heart as ever. Pru welcomed them looking very well and happy as she told of the satisfaction she was experiencing helping Geoff in the shop during the daytime until the children took over in the evenings and weekends. She also told of her enjoyment at the ballroom dancing classes and the continuing relationship with Eric. Yes, things were looking promising for Pru. Molly explained that they were visiting Tommy and briefly mentioned the optimistic changes in his treatment. Pru had already heard the good news by 'shop gossip' and from her cleaning lady who lived in the street. Molly had hoped that Maisey and Paul would arrive home from work before they left but it was getting late and Pru decided to close the shop with Sam's usual helping hand. And they left to visit Tommy.

Tommy was in good spirits and wanting to know all about Sam's new job. Molly left Sam to explain whilst she went into the kitchen to talk to Tommy's mother. Yes, his mother was cautious about her son's new treatment but she seemed reassured that it would all be carefully monitored and Tommy would be safeguarded from harm. Everyone had tea and homemade cake in Tommy's room whilst Sam and Molly shared their news. Tommy was sad that Sam would be leaving but Sam promised to keep in touch saying, "Who knows one day you might come to see me!" Molly gave an update on the latest news from her Hungarian pen friend, Dominik and Tommy was eager to get out the Atlas and show Molly how he had traced Dominik's terrain. Molly also told of her exploits in the nurse training school – not forgetting to mention Rupert and Sadie and Sister Sparrow's frequent ... "Never 'eerrd of it."

Sam and Molly left 'on a high' by seeing the difference that hope had brought to Tommy and his family. They called in the 'chippy' and ate their supper as they walked back to the hospital. Suddenly, Sam started to talk about Dominik and the information he had shared about his homeland and its chequered history. Sam was interesting to talk to having studied Eastern European history and politics as an optional subject at school; he asked if he could read Dominik's letters sometime. Needless to say, Molly was delighted to have the opportunity to gain more insight into Dominik's background and life-style.

Nearing the hospital, they sat on a park bench and Sam enfolded Molly in a bear hug. "I'm so thrilled to be moving to do 'Paeds' but my goodness, I shall miss you, Molly. You have been such a good friend and, in a way, my mentor." Sam took a deep breath and with the slow release came the almost inaudible whisper, "I had so much wanted it to be more." Molly leaned into Sam's warm embrace and as the tears choked her, she whispered, "Yes, well perhaps there is more – 'time will tell', she quoted from the inscription on her Fob watch. "But we've been good for each other, haven't we?"

However, time now seemed to be of the essence as Sam asked Molly to help him to organise his move; one case for his short holiday at home, another for his London apartment in the hospital complex; and a create for Sam's books and medical equipment be sent on in advance. There was no immediate hurry to pack but it was a good excuse to spend time together sorting out and planning what needed to go where, eventually rounding off the evening with a meal followed by either a game of table tennis in the recreation room, competing on a crossword, or just sitting and talking.

Sam spent a weekend at Molly's home where Rose greeted him with her best impression of Mrs Bouquet! Sam was relieved of the returned props saying how much they had all enjoyed wearing the costumes and appreciated the interest and help Rose and Wills had taken to make their act a success. Sam presented 'thank you' gifts from the 'Morris Men', Rose and Wills were clearly touched by their thoughtfulness. Supper was ready for serving, Kate joined them at the last minute and the meal was a jolly affair. Sam told about his new appointment at the London Paediatric hospital, he described the sick children and the kinds of treatments they received. Rose was full of questions having experienced Molly's febrile childhood.

Sunday morning arrived and they all attended church, the service was an uplifting experience with Kate note perfect on the organ! After lunch whilst Molly spent time with Rose, Wills introduced Sam to two recently born calves and demonstrated his technique to encourage the 'suckie-mullies' to suckle. Wills laughed and said, "There you are, Sam you will have a trick up your sleeve for your new job!" They took the long route through the village back home; it was wonderful to see the developing bond between them. Not for the first time Molly thought, "What a shame Dad didn't have a boy, Mum had all the fun with two girls!"

Teatime and fond farewells sent Molly and Sam on their way to catch the bus back to the hospital. It was a quiet journey each knowing that in a few days, time life would have changed ... possibly forever. Passing the gatehouse, Stan called, "Goodnight, you two." Sam waved and continued to walk with Molly back to the nurses' home. "Gosh Molly, I don't know how to end tonight, I do so want to tell you, "I love you" but I sense for you the time is still not right." "We both have so much to do, Sam," said Molly with more conviction than she felt, "and this isn't 'Goodbye', but a temporary change of direction." A quick bear hug and Sam left.

LIFE IN THE NURSES' HOME:

In addition to revising during the evening, Molly continued the routine of one hour's study each morning. She was usually awake with her head in a book before a rap on the door herald, "Good morning nurse, 6am," and so on down each corridor. Molly's buddies became aware of this routine and asked her to give them a second call to enjoy an extra snooze time before breakfast at 7.30am!

The curriculum was progressing with increasing complexity and diversity. Time spent on the wards related theory and practice, interspersed by regular assessments to ensure the new knowledge was being assimilated – and applied! Light relief was essential. The PTS set shared a remarkable camaraderie. Hetty was the joker of the group and the three students from Germany came into their own. The 'cocoa gang' in the Nurses' Home was a real bonus and one, which their colleagues from Germany also seemed to enjoy. Rosetta, in particular, became quite friendly with Molly, seeking her company in the dining room and sometimes joining in her early morning studies!

Hetty, who lived in the room next to Molly, had a quirky, spontaneous sense of humour that was always ready to burst forth – often in the most unhelpful of circumstances! She seemed to transcend the 'set' hierarchy and made friends with everyone. She was quite a stylish dresser but when Hetty slipped her feet into her high-heeled shoes, she would laughingly remark … "I just look like a pig in court-shoes," such quips lifted the mood after a hard day. Hetty seemed to have a continual problem with her 'roll-ons', a small version of today's 'body stocking'. For instance, if they were in town she would frequently groan, "My 'roll-ons' are just killing me, I shall have to take them off," and so they would head for the nearest 'Ladies'! One night, however, whilst they were clearing away the debris of the 'cocoa gang', Hetty came bursting in after an evening with her latest beau saying, "Bloomin' heck! I've left my 'roll-ons' in the back of his car." Hetty's 'roll-ons' were legion, so that evening they sniggered, not really knowing whether to sympathise or laugh when she said, "Don't blooming laugh, his mother will use the car first thing tomorrow morning to go to the WRVS." There were no mobile phones in those days to alert the lad, so they could only hope he tidied up the car after his evening with Hetty!

Hetty was not alone in her amorous activities. One night a third-year student unexpectedly joined the gang for cocoa when suddenly she jumped up saying, "Oh no!" They looked at her as she became over-wrought and panic stricken and waited until she eventually said, "we've left the condom at the side of the sofa!" Ah well, again there seemed no answer to that and an uncomfortable silence descended this time. The details were perhaps a bit of a mystery to some but it just didn't seem right! Sometimes there was talk of 'having a fumble', which Molly thought of as Sam's hug – obviously not! Looking back Molly wondered if Paul was 'fumbling' when they sat on the sofa after the Mission on Sunday night. Well, if so she didn't like it, it didn't feel right and made her feel uncomfortable – Vin didn't do it. Molly could only recall her mother's maxim, "I've always taught you right from wrong, so don't let me down." One's body was seen as one's private space and its functions such as dressing and undressing, bathing and toileting were conducted discretely and in private – hence Molly's shock by the experience of the school showers which violated Rose's rule of modesty. Suddenly inspired she thought, 'I will talk to Petal, she has a regular boyfriend!'

Regular weekends at home were soon to be a thing of the past as the prospect of one day off each week became the norm and a whole weekend would be a luxury. However, Molly continued to enthral Rose with details as her training advanced and her experience on the wards assumed more responsibilities. Rose was always fascinated whilst expressing the hope that "all that 'squatting' (meaning swotting) will not overtask you." One such weekend, Molly carefully broached the subject of bringing Rosetta, the German girl home on her next weekend off. Molly and Rosetta had become quite friendly; they both came from country families and Molly wanted to give her a taste of home comforts. The suggestion was met with polite acknowledgement and "we'll see." The next day as Molly was preparing to leave, Rose said, "I can see it is important to you, so do bring Rosetta home for the weekend." Kate quipped, "Yes do, I have never met a German in real life!" Molly was disappointed that her request had not been greeted more enthusiastically but knowing of the prejudice within the family she was at least glad to have their assent.

And so, on the appointed weekend Molly and Rosetta arrived home on Friday night to find Rose waiting to welcome them to a warm and friendly atmosphere. The fire sparkled in the grate, the smell of food most appetizing, and Wills appeared dressed in his Sunday best to greet his guest. The weekend went very well. On Saturday Wills proudly showed Rosetta around his garden and Rose was interested to hear about Germany and Rosetta's way of life. Rosetta mentioned she played the piano accordion in a Country Dance Band. By a happy co-incidence Rosetta and Rose both knew the song 'Lilli Marlene' which prompted Rose to move to the piano saying, "Shall we have a go?" It was a strange cacophony of sound but they played and sang along together and quite enjoyed themselves.

Kate returned home as the duet drew to a close. Introducing herself, Kate apologised for her late arrival by explaining that a young couple, for whose forth-coming wedding she was playing the organ, wanted to check the music. Rosetta showed interest in Kate's musical talents and responded enthusiastically to Kate's invitation to join her on the 'organ bench' to turn the pages on Sunday morning. 'Do you go to church, Rosetta?" asked Rose. "Yes, I am a Lutheran." Seeing Rose frown, Rosetta explained, "we are a Protestant denomination too." Gwen silently shared Molly's feelings that Rose was not entirely convinced but the fact that the girl had a faith seemed to count for something!

When seen together Rosetta and Kate had a striking resemblance to each other – rosy cheeks, blue eyes, blonde curly hair and a winsome smile. Molly could quite see why Wills and Rose might take to Rosetta fairly easily, albeit cautiously!

The final stages of PTS flowed into the study blocks with an introduction to 'Public Health', which included visits to a sewage station – not exactly for the faint hearted! The visit endorsed the importance of infection prevention and control, which began and ended with personal and environmental hygiene. And, much to their surprise, they discovered the by-products of waste was not 'waste' at all but valuable recyclable substances!

The students were embarking on more complex nursing duties, such as bereavement in its widest sense to include not only loss of life but loss of limb, loss of hope, and the shock of 'bad news' such as a diagnosis of a life limiting condition. The Marie Curie Foundation was leading new insights into the end-of-life care that were taken on board. The Mortuary, as a resting place for the deceased was an important part of end-of-life care. Nathan, the Mortuary attendant hosted the students' visit and although a perfect host, he was regarded with a degree of apprehension. Explaining his role, Nathan talked about the approach he adopted to preserve the dignity of the deceased, with the reminder … "the deceased have lived a life like the rest of us; they have made their contribution to the world we live in today; and they are loved and cared about - or have been - by someone." Nathan provided a useful conclusion to the nursing care given on the wards … and also prepared them for their post-mortem observation.

DAY DUTY AND NEW ROUTINES:

With their programme of study blocks for the forthcoming year underway, the fledgling nurses were given their permanent ward allocation of three months duration. Molly was to report to Women's Medical at 8am the following Monday. So the forthcoming weekend at home was the last one she would have for a while and once again, Rosetta accompanied her.

Rosetta was received with an enthusiastic welcome, perhaps due to Rose's surreptitious investigation into the Lutherans at the town library one market day! Wills took Rosetta to see the animals and introduced her to his 'suckie-mullies' and the old sow recovering from Swine Fever. They viewed the state of play on the land, which Rosetta observed to be rather flat compared with her beloved Bavaria. As usual Wills was fascinated to discover new aspects and secrets of 'Mother Nature' and to his delight he found Rosetta well informed about its healing power.

They all went to morning service at church on Sunday and once again Rosetta accompanied Kate on the organ bench! Rose now understood there would be parts of the service in which Rosetta felt she could not participate. Sunday lunch was a jolly affair and before leaving to return to the hospital Rosetta was invited to "come over whenever you are free, with or without Molly." Rosetta was genuinely touched by the invitation and said she would very much like that.

Rosetta and Molly arrived back in the Nurses' Home to be welcomed by the 'cocoa gang' and share the gossip. Suddenly, a knock on the door and Molly was called to the telephone – what a shock, she couldn't think whom it could possibly be! Well, of course most of the gang guessed and yes, it was Sam! Sam wanted to know all about Molly's comings and goings; and news of Tommy. Having satisfied Sam's interest Molly said it was her turn to know about his new life. Apparently, it was all going well, "I have a nice room overlooking a courtyard with shrubs and tubs of various plants in flower." Sam laughed when he told how strange it seemed to be working in this miniature world of children and of their instant and open reaction to his attentions. He seemed clearly moved by the plight of some of his young patients and the stoicism of their worried parents. Molly asked about the 'big bad City' and whether he had sampled the highlights yet! "Well, yes," he replied, "A group of us went to a concert at the Royal Albert Hall last night followed by supper at an Indian Restaurant. And if it's nice at the weekend we plan to take a boat up the Thames - just sampling ready for when you come down, you see, Molly!" It was great to hear Sam's voice and to feel included in his new life but the time came for them to say, "Goodbye," with promises to "talk again soon." Molly returned to the 'cocoa gang' with everyone waiting for the news. Some rolled their eyes, "Oh, we knew it wouldn't be long before Sam got in touch, he'll be missing you like crazy." Molly laughed saying, "Come off it, it's not like that." To which the whole room exploded saying, "Oooooh, No?"

Women's Medical was a busy thirty-bedded ward with very ill patients to be cared for. In these times the hospital wards were segregated by gender and clinical categories and not the more defined 'clinical specialties' that were gradually introduced. For instance, anything that required an operation was 'Surgical'; non-surgical wards were classed as 'Medical'; 'Paediatrics' for children aged up to 14 years; 'Orthopaedics' catered for bone, joint and ligament conditions; and 'Gynaecology' for irregularities of female reproductive systems.

Although most of the nursing routines had been practised in the classroom, on the wards some of the once familiar routines felt strangely different. As the junior nurse, Molly's main duties included toileting rounds, bed making and cleaning the lockers. The ward cleaners did not work at the weekend and Molly was told that would be her job. Immediately her father's words of concern came to mind, "They will have you scrubbing the floors until your hands are red raw." However, it was not like that at all. Wet tealeaves, collected from the ward teapots by the night staff, were left for Molly to scatter on the ward floor to settle the dust before sweeping. And when she had finished, woe betides Molly if Sister found a few odd tealeaves lurking in some unsuspecting corner of the ward!

One very poorly elderly lady was nursed in a side ward and Molly was often assigned to care for her under the supervision of a more senior nurse. The lady died but Molly always recalls the vase of Mimosa flowers on the lady's locker she moved every day in the process of wet-dusting. To this day a bunch of Mimosa brings back the memory.

A death on the ward was always treated with great dignity and respect. Molly was taught the process of 'laying out' by a senior nurse and she was often surprised by the peace that descended on a face that had been racked with pain. The Mortuary Porter came with the trolley to collect the deceased. Once on the trolley, the body was protected by a cage draped over with a large purple velvet cover decorated with gold braid. All the screens would be drawn to shield other patients from the view and on this particular ward the stately Ward Sister walked ahead of the trolley like the funeral official at a burial service. When the cortège had left, life on the ward immediately returned to normal, although Molly did not always adjust so easily in these early days. Looking back Molly appreciated the compassion of Sister who did not object to the nurses giving time to talk to the patients, whereas some Ward Sisters regarded talking as idling and a nurse would be admonished and told, "When in doubt, dust."

But Molly had other worries – her poor feet were throbbing, swollen and painful from walking up and down the ward with under floor heating. Molly's weekly letter to Rose explained the difficulties she was experiencing. Almost by return of post Molly received a parcel containing Monica Dickens' novel 'One pair of feet' as a little frivolity but of greater value, two tubes of 'Foot Balm' with the chemist's strict instructions accompanied the ointment. Family gossip claimed that Rose and the Chemist had once been sweethearts but when Molly had asked Rose she had shrugged off the idea saying, "We've been good friends for a long time!" The foot balm worked miracles and most of Molly's set had a tube by their bedside. Rosetta had been one of the grateful recipients and towards the end of the week she wrote to thank Rose and to ask if they might meet in the town one market day – Rosetta explained she did not feel confident enough to negotiate the journey to the village!

Time to move on and the next allocation, which would include Christmas, was to the Children's Ward. The management of ill children was quite challenging for the young nursing students, thankfully Molly was able to draw from her experiences as a sub-pro in the Physiotherapy Department. In Molly's time the 'good child' on the Children's Ward was the one who sat in his/her bed/cot without a murmur, whilst the 'difficult children' were those who screamed incessantly and were inconsolable when their parents left. Research had not yet shown the error of such assumptions but many years later in Molly's career she would watch the teaching film, 'A two-year old goes to hospital' which demonstrated otherwise. In fact, the 'good children', namely those sitting quietly and unnoticed with the blank stare of 'frozen watchfulness', were the ones who were 'grieving' and psychologically distraught; whilst the children who screamed and received attention however, were thought to be far less traumatised by their experience. To show tenderness and encouragement to these little people in distress was an important and very demanding part of Molly's role on the Children's Ward. The Ward Sister was superb, she spent so much time teaching and supporting her nurses (and the medics) and the children would often lift their arms for a cuddle as she passed – a gesture that she never ignored.

The ward was a mixture of boys and girls with a wide variety of conditions from small babies who lacked the energy to suck on a bottle teat and needed to be tube fed, to the more robust school aged child almost well enough to be discharged. Molly found it strange to see the sub-pro collect children for physiotherapy, it was a stage that seemed such a long time ago and now here she was attending revision studies in preparation for the State Preliminary Examinations (Prelims)!

As time went by, Molly began to notice a young boy aged around 14 named Sydney appear on the ward most weekends. Sydney was an ex-patient who came to play board games or read with some of the children; he also helped with tasks such as clearing away the crockery after mealtimes – Sidney must have been one of the pioneers of hospital volunteering schemes!

One Saturday morning Sister arranged a meeting between the nurses, medics and patients to decide on a theme for the Christmas decorations. A wide variety of suggestions came forth from Bible stories, fairy tales and story lines from the children's comics. Cinderella won and ideas began to flow – garlands, slippers, mice, clocks, ragged Cinders, the ugly sisters and ball gowns. Sister must have left the meeting with her head buzzing! In no time at all coloured paper, scissors, glue, tinsel and sparkles of every description appeared for the nurses to work on with the children – even the parents and other visitors joined in!

The day eventually arrived for the ward to be decorated. Two porters appeared with long stepladders to a cacophony of instructions and squeals of delight from all corners of the ward as the transformation began. Then, 'Hey Presto', and the decorations were completed as if by magic. It was the usual custom for the nursing staff to visit each other's ward when the decorations were finished – the ingenuity of some wards was quite unbelievable. It was on one such visit that Molly met Rosetta. Rosetta told of her meeting with Rose on Market Day last week and she bubbled over with enthusiasm for the quaint old town and its traditions. Rose had shown Rosetta the memorial kiosk commemorating Dr Samuel Johnson and told her the story of this famous eighteenth century son of the County. They stopped for a coffee at a vantage point overlooking the memorial whilst Rose dipped in and out of Johnson's life. She told Rosetta about his contribution to literature, including the first English dictionary. Rose shared what she knew of Dr Johnson's rather troubled life and his ultimate act of altruism when on his death he left most of his wealth to a Jamaican slave he had befriended. It was clear that Rose with her flare of storytelling made this a memorable coffee break for Rosetta! Wills took time out from the cattle market and met them for lunch at the White Horse Inn.

After lunch Rose asked if Rosetta had time to visit Kate's workshop, explaining that a tentative arrangement had been made with the tailor if time permitted. "Oh, yes I would love to. My grandfather was a tailor," said Rosetta with sad tenderness. The tailor was delighted to welcome them and to hear of Rosetta's association with the Guild. He took them to the workshops where Kate had been working on the buttonholes of a fine riding jacket – now on display awaiting the tailor's approval. Rosetta's eyes danced as she looked around and took in a deep breath saying, "This looks, feels and smells just like Gramp's workshops," and Kate's handiwork was admired with a knowing eye. Rosetta was brimming over with stories about the day she had spent with Rose but now was not the time or place so she went on her way saying, "So much to tell, see you tonight over cocoa."

One week before Christmas, the Consultant Paediatrician arrived to switch on the Christmas tree lights in preparation for the carol singers. He arrived dressed as Prince Charming bearing a slipper for Sister to try on. Needless to say the fit was perfect and everyone cheered and shouted, "It fits!"

The carol singers arrived on Sunday afternoon with the Salvation Army Band and choir. The sea of Salvation Army uniforms and their glistening wind instruments made a spectacular sight as the musicians gathered in the centre of the ward. Molly, who had just returned from the late lunch break, could not believe her eyes when she spotted Tommy gingerly stepping out of his wheelchair to give Lizzy a hand to distribute the song sheets. Time was short for too much conversation but Lizzy proudly showed off her sparkling engagement ring which just could not be ignored and Tommy was bursting to tell of the part-time job in the hospital library he was due to start in the New Year. It was just all too wonderful for Molly to take in but before she left to sit with the children and sing carols, a date was set for them to meet after Christmas.

Sam and Molly had exchanged Christmas greetings, news of their advancing careers, and Tommy's achievements. Sam sounded very happy in London and showed considerable interest in Paediatrics – there was also mention of fellow housemen, Sarah, James and Edward whose company Sam seemed to enjoy. Sam invited Molly to visit London on her next weekend off. "I could arrange for you to stay in hospital accommodation and we could see a show – it would be just great." A weekend off was few and far between but Molly replied with enthusiasm asking Sam for a convenient weekend date and she would negotiate with Sister. Almost by return Molly received the information and arranged time off after she had taken her 'Prelims'.

The weekend arrived and Molly set forth by train to alight at St Pancras station midmorning. Sam met her with his usual 'Whoooop', swinging her round and kissing her with such joy. A quick journey on the underground during which Sam was eager to know how 'Prelims' had been and following a brief discussion on the question paper Molly's confidence increased. They arrived at the hospital where Molly was shown to her room – a quick freshen up and they were off again. During lunch at a Lyons Corner House, Sam told Molly of the evening arrangement to see a show … "Surprise, surprise!" he teased. Then supper with Sarah and Edward – James was home for the weekend and others had cancelled due to staff shortages. "I do so want to show you off," said Sam with a protective hug. After lunch they walked by the river hardly noticing where they were walking as they each talked about their life and interests. Sam asked a passer-by to take a photograph of the two of them with Big Ben in the background showing 4pm – "to give to Tommy, with my love," he said … "and for you to remember me by," he added. Molly smiled and kissed Sam on the cheek saying, "I do not need a photograph, Sam." Sam gripped Molly by the shoulders and looked into her eyes, "is there a hint of a commitment, dear Molly?" Molly smiled and leant into Sam.

Returning to the hospital to change for the theatre they met Sarah who was briefly introduced as she sped off saying, "See you both later – have fun." The show was indeed a surprise and Molly was most amused when she realized they were going to see 'Kiss me Kate'– they held hands and Sam softy crooned 'So in love …" in Molly's ear. As they emerged from the theatre the romance stayed on and Molly playfully rebuked, "Why can't you behave?" The streets of London were flooded with people when they came out of the theatre; a taxi was like gold dust but eventually their turn came and they were on their way to meet Sarah and Edward for supper.

Sam's colleagues were pleasant and easy to talk with and there was clearly a good rapport between Sarah and the boys. Molly silently speculated, 'Sarah's just the sort for Sam; what a very, very lucky girl she could be!' They returned to the hospital for a drink in the common room – Molly could not help but smile as she thought of the similarity across hospital life and wondered what the 'cocoa gang' was talking about!

Sunday morning came and the friends left for a visit to Petticoat Lane Market after which they planned a lunch-stop before returning Molly to St Pancras to catch the 4pm train back home. The weather was just right - the market and its treasures waiting to be discovered was fascinating. The 'auctioneers' with their Cockney speak and humour made for great entertainment, whilst the amazing feats of the unicyclists and contortionists gave much delight to their audiences, although the medics watched with an air of clinical caution! Molly went on her way from St Pancras station with a warm farewell from Sarah and a great hug and kisses from Sam, both waving as the steam train puffed out of the station shouting, "See you soon". Molly sat on the train, closed her eyes and savoured her weekend with Sam. Whilst Gwen wondered about their mixed messages, she was only too well aware of Molly's turmoil. Yes, she loved Sam … but as a soul-mate, the brother she never had, or lover? Whatever … strong emotions bound them together.

NIGHT DUTY AND BERTIE:

The time arrived for the new duty rota to be posted – night duty the next stop! Full of excitement tinged with apprehension Molly visited Tommy and the corner shop as planned.

When she arrived at the shop everyone was spilling over with his and her personal ambitions. Pru and Eric were planning for their wedding and a future together. Starry-eyed Maisey was also in the throes of change as she anticipated emigration to Canada with her fiancé later in the year. Paul, who always felt he had a calling for the Ministry, told Molly of his application to train as a 'lay preacher' and his intension to continue to work in the railway offices and oversee the corner shop – Geoff was proving to be a very capable manager. It all sounded so promising. Molly updated them on Sam's Paediatric experience and of their time in London, she was also brimming over with stories from her ward placements and the 'cocoa gang'! Molly said her 'goodbyes' and left amidst peals of laughter to visit Tommy.

Tommy was aglow with his engagement to Lizzy. They did not have immediate plans to marry. When they finally decided to make a home together, Lizzy's father's carpet shop on the outskirts of the City had a ground floor storeroom, which could be converted into a flat for them.

Tommy, who was enjoying his work in the hospital library, told of the course of intensive rehabilitation, he had been offered at a local spa centre. Tommy explained that he would engage in a variety of physical activities such as exercise and massage, swimming and cycling with the prospect of driving lessons! Also included were occupational rehabilitation skills involving typewriting, use of the Gestetner, a mechanical calculating machine of the day, and office management. Tommy's mother was so pleased that her son's life was being turned around, and "Lizzy is like a daughter," she said.

So, Molly began to tell of her weekend with Sam and his friends. Tommy and his mother listened intently to the account of Molly and Sam's visit to the theatre and wanted to know what the ornate West End theatre looked like. Both Tommy and his mother had heard of 'Kiss me Kate' and were intrigued to have a copy of the programme. Whilst Tommy and Molly were talking through the programme and humming the familiar songs, tea was prepared and the family gathered to hear Molly's description of Petticoat Lane Market. Her account of the busy Market with its vast array of stalls, acrobats and auctioneering was greeted with wide-eyed amusement, almost as if they had all been there! But the photograph of Sam and Molly with Big Ben in the background was the icing on the cake!

Tommy asked, "Is Sam happy?" "Yes," said Molly and reassured Tommy of Sam's pride in the hospital and interest in the work he was doing with the children. Molly told about having a night drink in the doctors' common room, which she described as "rather plush but informal and comfortable," and of how Sam seemed to enjoy Sarah's company... mischievously adding, "perhaps a budding romance?" Tommy looked pleased and then turned to Molly asking, "are you sad, do you miss him?" Molly did not quite know how to answer – yes, she was sad and yes, she did miss him - but from the depth of her heart Molly honestly said to Tommy, "Of course I miss Sam but I am very happy that he finds his work really fulfilling and has made such interesting friends."

After snacking on the leftover Christmas cake and toasting the engagement of Lizzy and Tommy with a glass of Sherry, Molly left with more reassurances to 'keep in touch'.

The next morning the post arrived with the letter from the GNC confirming Molly's success in Parts One and Two of the 'Prelims'. Now to exchange her white first year belt for a mauve second year one – and a quick note to Sam! All but one of their set had passed – which was somewhat anticipated because almost immediately after the examination Daisy, one of the local students, had realized she had misread a question on Tuberculosis and given an answer for the nursing care of Tonsillitis!

The second year of training, during which Rupert and Sadie re-emerged continued to progress through an understanding of the structure and normal functioning of the body to ill health, medical and surgical interventions and nursing responses. It would be a challenge supported by classroom and practical teaching sessions, some of which were likely to occur during precious off duty times! And, for Molly her first spell of night duty was due to commence.

Night duty was an adventure because few of them had ever seen that part of the day before. It was exciting to know you were awake whilst the rest of the City slept; to hear the first birdcalls of the morning; and the sound of the first trams into the City ... and on New Year's Eve the City would resound with a cacophony of noise created by the sounding of the factory hooters and the trains as they let off plumes of steam and shrill whistles to herald the New Year – magical!

However, they were all to yet discover a new way of life, not to mention a rare condition known as 'Night nurses' paralysis' – a condition about which Petal had forewarned Molly. During the night the nurses on duty sat beneath a shaded table lamp in the middle of the long, 30+ bedded 'Nightingale' ward. When night sister entered the ward door, it was the tradition for the nurses to rise to their feet – the most senior nurse proceeding respectfully to greet night sister and the second nurse stood in waiting. However, under the rare influence of 'night nurse's paralysis' a nurse would know what was happening around her but could not respond. An inexperienced night sister could mistakenly think the nurse was sleeping until she came closer and saw the glazed staring eyes. It was a frightening experience. Sleeping on duty was a dereliction of duty beyond reproach – certainly Matron's office the next morning!!

The well-established routines of night duty included reporting for duty to the day Sister for the Ward Report. First, the nurses were subjected to a top-toe appraisal of their appearance. If it didn't present to the required standard, the nurse was sent to "tidy up before taking Report." Following Report, a ward round was conducted to introduce each patient, discuss his or her clinical condition, treatment and special needs during the night.

Molly's first night duty assignment was to a male surgical ward. Her duties began by serving the patients their night drinks followed by a toileting round and assisting the senior nurse with the medicines before 'tuck-down' and light's out.

The medical staff arrived for final checks and to make the necessary adjustments to treatments. Night sister was the next to appear and the senior nurse, usually a third-year probationer, escorted her on a ward round. The nurse was expected to know the names of all the patients, 35 or more if the ward had a balcony, their diagnosis, treatment and the effect of any intervention carried out during the day – quite daunting really! Night Sister returned about 2am and 7am for the next ward rounds.

At 8am the following morning, time to hand over to the day staff and the procedure was repeated – this time by the senior night nurse. Most Ward Sisters were generally encouraging and thanked the nurses for their efforts during the night but a few were just awful. They would nit-pick on the presentation of the written report; double-check a patient's chart and question unexplained gaps with the scrutiny of a barrister. Seemingly in collaboration, intra-venous (IV) drips stopped in sheer devilment after running to schedule all night and drainage equipment blocked for no reason. The bed wheels would have a mind of their own and suddenly slipped out of line to stand like a guard's boots at 'ten to two'. Whilst the neatly mitred corners of the bedclothes, so painstakingly placed by the night nurses would rebel and look untidy, and the top of the sheet turn over (always fingertip to elbow deep) would seem to deliberately violate the rule. Some Sisters went to such lengths as requiring the night nurse to re-write the Report, redraft the charts, or strip and remake the non-conforming bed(s) before being allowed off duty.

Even the patients seemed to be inclined towards bizarre behaviour. For instance, patients confined to bed would go to the toilet and those 'Nil by Mouth', might be about to crunch an apple or devour a bar of chocolate!

The kitchen was another focus of inspection following the night nurses' routines of buttering the bread for breakfast, laying the breakfast trolley and preparing the large teapots ready to make the breakfast tea; likewise, the sluice and bathroom. If those areas did not pass muster, then that was another job for the nurses to do before they were allowed to go off duty. Hey ho! As they gathered for their meal in the dining room the atmosphere was always a mixture of quiet despondency, a resounding state of hysteria, and genteel anarchy!!

Hetty was one on her own - her student days were a series of catastrophes and adventures. For example, having almost completed one of her first night duties on a surgical ward, the domain of Sister Starlight, a renowned dragon, Hetty lost a draw sheet down the sluice! A quick ring round her friends on other wards for advice produced lots of sympathy - and mirth when the phone was put down - but no solutions. The nurse on duty with Hetty when the Night Report was given told of Sister's reaction of absolute shock, horror and having recovered from her rare speechless state, suggested the nurses went off duty to be contacted later. They came to the dining room in a state of misplaced hysteria because Hetty knew that the proverbial 'sword of Damocles' was hanging over her head!

It was on night duty that Molly met Bertie Connel, one of a number of qualified Psychiatric nurses regularly seconded from the local Psychiatric hospital to complete a shortened form of General Nurse Training. Bertie was an old Romeo and his attentions lighted upon Molly. "Do be careful, Molly," Petal would caution – "he's a rogue – a delightful one maybe!" Bertie would sneak onto Molly's ward during the night, ostensibly to borrow a cup of sugar, and as he met her in the corridor, he would softly sing his version of the wartime song, "This is the story of a starry night … "Two lovers met to kiss goodbye; two lips meeting; two hearts a beating …" Molly was intrigued by this vivacious, blond haired man with rosy cheeks and such lovely dancing eyes! Much to Petal's concern they frequently went out together whilst off duty. However, the old Romeo lost his footing when it was rumoured he was married, possibly divorced. Petal was greatly perturbed, "How on earth can you take a man like that home to your parents?" Sound words indeed!

Molly and Petal, although with two sets of seniority between them, developed a close friendship and there were many times when they bailed each other out. For instance, Petal helped Molly to perfect the equivalence of a magician's sleight of hand using sterile forceps to manipulate the small cotton wool balls when cleansing a wound. Then Petal needed a sympathetic ear to recover from her experience of performing 'last offices' - attending to deceased patient. Petal described how as Sister rolled the patient over towards her the man groaned: "I nearly let the patient roll off the edge of the bed in sheer fright, Mol! But Sister looked up at me with a gentle smile saying, "just wind, nurse."

STUMBLING BLOCKS:

Then joy of all joys, Petal and Molly were both allocated to a male medical ward and the placement included Christmas! It was a magical time; they worked together in such harmony – bed bathing, monitoring blood transfusions and saline drips, collecting sputum mugs and cleaning the sluice, not to forget the seemingly never-ending bedpan and bottle rounds! Petal's bubbly personality cheered up the faces, and for sure the hearts, of the most desolate patients. The relatives would chat with her and because she was 'local' Petal always knew where they were coming from and the challenges they would probably be facing. However, the most illuminating experiences were the reactions of the young doctors but Petal never even noticed; Timothy, her boyfriend from school days was the apple of her eye.

When Molly and Petal's off duty coincided, particularly after payday (£4 each month), they would join forces with their buddies on a trip into town for coffee, or afternoon tea at Boots café. One such day it was raining and they folded their umbrellas to alight the tram. As they climbed the stairs to the top deck Molly's umbrella poked Petal's leg. "Oh! I am so sorry," she said, "Did you feel it?" Quick as a flash Petal turned round and said, "Felt it? I tasted it, my dear." How Molly climbed the rest of the stairs for laughing was a mystery, Petal really was a very funny and quick-witted person.

Then, disaster – big time!! Christmas was approaching and as usual the wards were making secret plans to decorate with some magical theme. It was a wonderful time as one might imagine. Then, three weeks before Christmas Molly was transferred to Sister Starlight's ward – the dragon! Petal and Molly were both distraught and tried to console each other. Petal was particularly concerned how Molly would fare with 'Starlight' at Christmas. It was worse than ever they could have imagined. On Christmas day when nurses were taking turns to visit each other's ward and 'party' (with decorum), Starlight set Molly the task of cleaning the fluff from the bed and locker wheels. Sister was cross and critical and put the fear of death into Molly. At coffee break, Molly went to her room ready to pack her bags for off. Petal found her and was resolute, "Don't be so silly, Mol, it will pass; we've got the Pantomime and there will be other Christmastimes to enjoy, show her you don't care and make believe you are enjoying it!" Petal looked for the best in all situations, and people, and usually found it. She was a good friend and an inspiration.

Almost by telepathy Sam telephoned Molly to suggest she came to London to see the Christmas Lights! Her next day off was due in five days' time, so she hastily made arrangements and was off! Molly caught the early morning train and was met by Sam for a late breakfast. They roamed around Hamleys (Molly's favourite Christmas treat), popped out to Knightsbridge for a taste of luxury at Harrods and back again to Regent Street for a late lunch at Fortnum and Masons. Sam reclined back in his chair and said, "Phew, that was a bit of a 'Cook's Tour', don't you think?" They sat for a long time talking about their work and life in general – Sam saying, "Sarah hopes to join us for supper, so she can tell you more news!" Late afternoon, with darkness beginning to descend they made their way to find an open top bus to 'do the Lights'. As usual the Christmas Lights were spectacular and Molly felt she and Sam were in their own fairyland! Returning to their place of departure, Sarah was waiting and off they went to China Town for supper. Supper was a chatty affair as they revelled in 'shop-talk'. Sam and Sarah were deeply involved with a joint Paediatric/Maternity and Child Welfare (M&CW) study and the conversation sparkled with their intellectual sparing; they were clearly very close and enjoyed their common interests at work. After the meal they took one last look up Oxford Street and descended the Underground to see Molly on her train back home. As usual Molly was swamped by Sam's bear hug and kisses with his "See you soon, very soon dear Molly." As Sarah and Sam stood together waving her off into the night ... Molly wondered?

It was with a spring in her step and resolve in her heart that Molly returned to duty. Molly reflected on how strange she found Sister Starlight's behaviour when she had seen a very different side to her personality. Earlier in the year the ward was cleaned and disinfected before reopening to admit children for 'Tonsil and Adenoids' (T's & A's) operations, Sister was like a mother hen clucking round her little flock and making every effort to calm their fears. After the operation Sister Starlight worked with her nurses to wipe the sorrowful faces of the children with a damp towel, give them sips of water to soothe their sore throats – ice lollies and ice cream came later.

Whilst Molly was working with Sister at the bedside of one little boy, he said, "Miss, I saw God in the theatre." "Oh did you dear, how do you know that?" asked Sister. "Yes, I did," said the child. "A man with a bright light shining on me said, "Oh my god, just look at these tonsils! Then God came over and I saw his face in the bright light looking down at me." Sister looked thoughtfully at the child, "Well, how interesting, dear. Now you have a little sleep to rest your throat and we will hear all about it later," and the pacified child drifted off to sleep. Before the boy went home, Sister was heard talking to the child about his experience in theatre, explaining what might have happened. "When the surgeon came to see you after the operation, he told me how large your tonsils had grown and that you would feel much better without them. At your operation, the Surgeon knew his junior doctor would be interested to see your rather large tonsils. So, yes, I suppose he said those words of surprise when he called the young doctor to have a look." The young boy smiled with a sense of pride that he had been a star attraction, although Sister sensed he would have liked to think God had been there too! So, she asked, "do you know about, God?" "Oh, yes," said the boy, "We learn about Jesus and his Father, God, at Sunday School." Sister smiled lovingly at the boy saying, "Well then you will know God is present wherever you are because he loves you." "Oh, yes," answered the child, "that is why I just know God was there and as interested in my tonsils as were the doctors."

CHAPTER 6

WHOOPS! NEW TIMES AHEAD

PANTOMIMES AND FRIVOLITIES:

Petal was right, the experience was eased by the Pantomime and there were other Christmastimes. Both Petal and Molly were involved with the hospital concert party and the Christmas Pantomime event for the patients this year was to be stage managed by Bertie!

Molly discovered that Petal had the most beautiful singing voice; she was also a very accomplished performer. However, Petal was always conscious that her rather upper-class boyfriend, Timothy, now her fiancé, had told her, "The Stanley's do not perform on stage" ... nevertheless Petal reconciled her dilemma by cautioning, "Oh well, he won't know if you don't tell him, Mol." Molly performed in song and dance routines ... and so they auditioned for a part in the show.

On the night of the performance, Petal dressed in a long midnight-blue velvet gown stood confidently on the stage and sang like a nightingale – hands clasped lightly in front of her and her head gracefully motioned from side to side to give emphasis to the moving love song from 'Madam Butterfly'. Bertie moved onto the stage to escort Petal taking her bow – the applause rang out to a standing ovation. Then much to Petal's surprise Bertie began to sing, 'This is the story of a starry night ....' and Petal, who was always a good sport, joined in the duet to the delight of both the cast and the audience. When Bertie came off the stage he whispered in Molly's ear, "I sang that for you, my lovely Molly."

Molly's heart was already pounding as she waited in the wings for her turn to perform and Gwen knew that the feel of Bertie's familiar closeness was a distraction Molly did not need at that time. Molly had auditioned as a member of the Can-Can troupe, expertly led by a professional dancer who had just entered PTS! The dancers each made their own costume – a length of 'black out' curtain with strips of crepe paper stitched like frills to the underside of the skirt and on their knickers. A terrible disaster was averted on the night when at the dress rehearsal, after one almighty kick the stitching on Molly's interlock knickers snapped and the frills dangled like tassels around her knees! A pair of black uniform stockings held in place by decorated suspenders and a large plume of black feathers as a headdress completed the costume. Their photograph hit the local newspaper with the caption "The 'Follies Bergère' comes to our hospital." Molly delighted in sending Sam a copy of the photograph and reciting the exhilarating experience! Sam's prompt reply told of the heart-stopping moment he opened the letter at the breakfast table – a moment shared with everyone present who unanimously agreed you looked fantastic; "I told them you are!" he wrote.

On the last night of the performance whilst Molly was helping to dismantle the stage and collect up the props, Bertie crept behind her in the storeroom cupboard. Like a magician he whipped out his hand from behind his back to present her with a Christmas present, saying "For you my lovely, Molly" and during her moment of surprise he kissed her as never before; and much to her amazement she did not resist. "Can we start again?" asked Bertie but Molly was 'saved by the bell' as other helpers came into the room and the moment was lost.

Later, as Molly and Petal shared their cocoa time, Molly told of the encounter and the present, which still lay unwrapped on her bed. "Do be careful, Mol," cautioned Petal and then with a twinkle in her eye she said, "but let's have a look at the present." The present was a small reproduction painting of the 'Blue Boy' by Gainsborough. "Well, I never," said Petal "He is a one, guess he fancies himself as the Blue Boy you will never forget and he is making sure you don't!" The end of Panto Party lived up to expectations fuelled by the relief it was all over whilst basking in its success. There seemed to be little doubt by their tentative togetherness that Molly and Bertie's relationship could be going somewhere this time! However, as time wore on it all came to naught – how much Molly will owe to Gwen, she will never know as her better judgement prevailed!

The hospital was gradually becoming a more multi-cultural community. The least favoured were the Germans but the Irish were always regarded with humorous affection. The West Indians were embraced largely because of the soft almost haunting sound of their voices, their colourful nature and exuberance. Whilst the Asian's held the mystique and fascination of a world only discovered in books or at the cinema. Three Asian medics had joined the medical staff and one year they decided to provide entertainment followed by a curry supper in the Nurses' Home's magnificent ballroom. No one had ever encountered curry, so murmurings laced with excitement were widespread. "What would it taste like?" "Would we like it?" "What would we do if it was too hot – we couldn't leave it?" And of course, "what should we wear?" The evening arrived and the Nurses' Home for the first time in its history was invaded by the smell of curry. Everyone assembled in their brightest and best frocks; Matron, dressed Indian-style, seated on a colourfully decorated mattress was carried in on the shoulders of the medics! It was a wonderful evening; the cuisine quite intriguing and surprisingly appetizing; the party danced the night away to Asian music provided by instruments introduced as the Sitar, Tambura, Indian drum and the Violin.

The next and last time Petal and Molly worked together was on a general Obstetrics/Gynaecology Ward. They seemed so young for such huge responsibilities, particularly on night duty. Their one source of support was the dear Yorkshire born and bred night sister who would be in attendance at a flash if needed and sometimes appeared as if by telepathy in anticipation of a pending difficulty. The ward included women who had been admitted with 'threatened abortions' (term miscarriage was used because it did not carry the same criminal intent as 'abortion'). The majority of patients were on bed rest and definitely not to go to the toilet! One young patient did just that, her labour pains started and she was made comfortable awaiting the arrival of Night Sister – it seemed quite a wait being on the top floor at the far end of the hospital!!

Petal and Molly dealt with numerous hair-raising experiences but none so strange as when threatened by the gypsies. As usual, they commenced their duty by receiving the 'Day Report' from Sister. On this particular evening they were informed that a gipsy girl had been admitted with a threatened miscarriage. Some members of the Romany family were unhappy about this and had threatened to break in during the night and take the girl home. The windows were secured leaving only the ward door as possible access – thankfully morning came and all was well.

In addition to nursing the Mums; there were also the newly born babies who needed attention. Petal was a natural with the babies. Molly always recalled one little fellow who would not settle; he had been changed, fed, winded, and loved but all to no avail, that is until Petal gently waltzed him up and down the corridor singing, the 1939 Tommy Trinder rendition of "Oh Nicholas don't be so ridiculous ..." Molly gave Sam an update on her experiences ... saying she understood now why he was so taken with the specialty; in fact, a colleague was tempting her towards an 'Obs and Gynae' work experience in South Africa after they qualified!

ALMOST THERE:

As time progressed Molly's PTS set prepared for their pre-final year mock theory and practical examinations. It was an important time and no room for any slip-ups! The results were announced by Sister Sparrow – "tested your metal did it then ladies?" They all groaned, fearing the worst. "You did well," she commented and announced they had all passed. "Now this year is going to be tough as it leads up to your finals. It will stretch your clinical knowledge and its application on the wards. There will be an emphasis on teaching and management together with the legal and professional accountability of a Registered Nurse. She proceeded to explain that study days would continue together with two study blocks, one at the beginning and another just before finals. "Don't forget to keep your GNC Schedules up to date Ladies, and in respectable condition!" Armed with good results and a Schedule near completion Molly commenced her placement in theatres. Molly thrived in 'theatres' – there was a lesser sense of hierarchy, they worked as a team with each person's role seamlessly slotting into another's. The daytime rota was staffed by a full team but at night the two City hospitals alternated on a weekly 'on-call emergencies rota'. At each hospital, the rota included one theatre sister and a minimum of four senior student nurses.

One night, theatre sister on call with Molly as one of the 'on call' nursing team, was prevented from reaching the hospital by the unexpected descent of a heavy freezing fog. An emergency arrived and Molly was asked to 'take the list' i.e., to take full charge of the theatre. As Molly described after the event, "the whole team seemed to go on automatic pilot, everything slotted in like clockwork and the list was successfully completed by the time Sister arrived … we were so relieved to have risen to the challenge" When Molly was summoned to Matron's office, she collected the accolade for them all – any one of them could have done what Molly did … that's theatre; everyone at the top of their game! Needless to say, Sam was the first to know about her achievement and his response was filled with admiration.

Now, what is happening thought Molly when two weeks later her left leg began to hurt and she was gradually limping her way around theatre. Off she went to be 'Warded' suffering with a deep vein thrombosis. Whilst the condition was a concern, Molly achieved a good outcome and discharged home for a period of convalescence. Rose provided superb care and encouragement and both parents enjoyed the unexpected bonus of time with Molly. Time passed quickly, and she was welcomed back to theatres to complete her span of duty ... and prepare for the hospital pantomime!

The Concert Party was robust and once again under Bertie's direction. The frivolity of the 'Sewing Room Girls' was replaced by an even more daring performance by six male nurses dressed in ballet tutus performing to the 'Dance of the Cygnets' from Swan Lake Ballet. Near the end of their routine, they attempted a rather ambitious ballet leap with arms in the air, three of them fell off the back of the stage. Undaunted the 'ballerinas' climbed back on the stage, reassembled to complete the dance and take their bows. The applause brought the house down.

Petal once again gave a stunning solo performance of 'People will say we're in Love," from the film Oklahoma, and being recently engaged to Timothy, she provoked an uproar of clapping and cheering! Petal was always referred to as "our bit of class!" Molly, dressed in nurse's uniform danced around a male nurse seated in pyjamas as a patient and sang, "When you're nursing ..." *(replacing 'smiling' with 'nursing')*. The Grand Finale was kept secret until the night when the curtain was opened to reveal the Salvation Army Band in all its glory! The band played a selection of Christmas music bringing the evening to a close with Christmas Carols. And guess who was sitting in the audience? Lizzy, Tommy and his family!

HANDS OFF! STAFF NURSE'S BEAU:

And so the years passed and the syllabus covering the numerous systems of the human body, their dysfunctions related to nursing practices and legal framework was drawing to a close. Each new nursing experience left a tale to be told and each 'season' relived its traditional festivals.

The climax of each year was the Christmas Ball held in the magnificent setting of the Nurses' Home ballroom. This year, one of the third-year nurses, who had a very desirable brother named Ian, arranged to introduce him to the senior Staff Nurse on her ward. The grapevine had made sure that the message was passed around – "hands off." But Ian seemed like a bee drawn to a honey pot in his attention to Molly. They danced together and at the interval when Ian was supposed to go to the Sisters' Lounge for refreshments with Staff Nurse, he insisted on joining Molly in the general common room. Molly was relieved from this embarrassing situation when she saw Ian's sister approaching to guide him to where he was expected.

When the dancing re-commenced Molly joined another group of colleagues and found Bertie eager to dance with her – lovely Bertie, it was a shame he was out of bounds. Ian, however determinedly made his way across the room to ask Molly for the last dance. The evening closed with the traditional 'Hospital Gallop' a rumbustious item in which a core of dancers formed the hub of a wheel to which others latched on to resemble the spokes. The music speeded and the gyrations gathered momentum! Ian seemed reluctant to leave and Molly found herself strolling down the main drive with him when much to her surprise he asked if she would like to go to meet him next week but she declined.

Bertie was just leaving as Molly returned to the Nurses' Home. In true Fred Astaire style, he stepped back on tiptoe, flung open his arms and tripped across the tarmac towards her. "Saved the last dance for me then my lovely Molly?" Taking her in his arms to dance he sang the old familiar refrain ... "This is the story of a starry night ..." Bertie gave Molly a hug, kissed her tenderly and danced off into the night. Smiling, she watched him disappear thinking, 'dear Bertie, never lose your joie de vivre!'

Living in the Nurses' Home was a once in a lifetime's experience – joys and sorrows shared, secrets and confidences told, and clothes borrowed for special occasions. But, one can imagine the confusion Molly, quite unintentionally, created when she seemed to steal the prize that night!

The usual 'post-mortem' on the evening was in full flow with a degree of caution. How would Staff Nurse react? How would Molly fare, not to mention the position of Ian's sister? But Petal was well pleased this time – "if it goes anywhere, he's a lovely, sensible chap, Mol." However, Joy, a senior colleague, was less impressed because she could see their South Africa dream coming to nought!

However, Ian was a persistent suitor, soon they were meeting about once a week when he offered to take her home on his motorbike for her day off. Much to Molly's disappointment, her parents were quietly cautious about Ian; they thought him too old for her and the motorbike, as a means of transport most unseemly. As time unfolded and they met Ian's parents, Lily and Harry, their reservations grew. Rose called them 'townies' and disliked their seemingly intrusive manner, not the type of 'polite conversation' to which she was accustomed. Molly wrote to Sam to tell him about Ian; although not swept off her feet – there was something about him. Sam replied by return of post to say he understood because he and Sarah had reached that stage. Before signing off, Sam reminded her that he would always love her and although she wouldn't admit it, he knew she felt just the same! Once again Molly was caught on the back foot thinking, 'well only time will tell.'

Ian's father's forebears originated from Sussex with a family name that was regularly mistaken for a French name - the spelling probably distorted over time. When it seemed that Molly could be around to stay, his sister Joan warned her that if she married Ian she would spend the rest of her life spelling the name for people! Harry's forebears, coming from Sussex, had possible connections with the French Protestant Huguenots who fled France in the seventeenth/eighteenth centuries to avoid persecution by the Roman Catholic government. The name certainly had strong similarities with Huguenot family names listed in the Huguenot Directory – maybe in the generations to come, someone will research the family history?

Harry, a kind and gentle man, married Lily after serving in the First World War and they made their home in her hometown in the Midlands. Lily was a feisty woman, diminutive in stature; she had lost her teeth to pyorrhoea a common gum disease in these times, probably due in part to poor dental hygiene and diet. Much to Harry's disappointment, Lily refused to wear her dentures, which found a permanent home in the top drawer of the dresser. Lily coiffured her short grey hair with the help of curling tongs, which she heated in the coal fire – a rather hit and miss procedure, against which the family tried to dissuade her but to no avail. Lilly was proud of her family and fiercely defensive of Ian and Joan. Gwen always had a strong suspicion that Lily secretly hoped that Joan's best friend, Marion, would one day be her daughter-in-law!

Ian was a clever lad who won a scholarship to the Grammar School but because the family could not meet whatever financial contribution was required at the time, he was unable to take up the place. Harry always regretted they could not afford Ian's education and "give the lad the chance he deserved." However, all was not lost. Ian was awarded a place at the Technical School where he met a schoolmaster who proved to be his inspiration in so many ways, not least by introducing Ian to the local rowing club at which he held membership. The club was very successful and over the years Ian had many stories to tell about the various Regattas and boat races they entered. Ian's collection of trophies some seven or so, were a testament to his skill as a Cox. Much later in life, Ian proudly presented one of his most ornate cups to his granddaughter when she was awarded a Law Degree and became a Member of the Law Society.

By the time Molly met Ian, his father had changed employment from a platelayer on the railway to that of a school caretaker. Their new home, the schoolhouse, was a well-appointed and impressive looking dwelling. Harry and Lily worked together in the school like two turtledoves, and they both had retirement pensions. Harry would often stand and look into the sky with tears rolling down his face remembering the hard times and saying to Ian, "Eh, lad I never thought our day would come!"

Molly's new love affair was the talk of the 'cocoa gang' but one night they all seemed to feel the need to share the ups and downs of their romances. Suddenly the tension was relieved by one of the nurses from the Paediatric Ward bursting in to tell of a case of suspected scarlet fever on the ward. It seemed a child had been admitted the previous evening with a severe chest infection and by the morning the tell-tale 'strawberry tongue' and the typical 'scarlatina' rash began to appear. The child had been transferred to the Isolation Hospital and the public health model of Test – Trace – Treat was now in full swing in anticipation that the infection would been contained before other patients and members of staff were affected.

The high drama was then disturbed by a knock on the door and Molly was called for a telephone call! "Oooooh, lover boy," they chorused whilst some cautioned, "You can't have two Mol!" Sam was on the phone desperate to tell Molly of a secondment he had been granted to the local Public Health Department's M&CW section. "The secondment will be guided by the Medical Officer of Health and include a programme of experience with specialist medics, midwives, health visitors and district nurses – perhaps I shall not need to go to Manchester! Any chance of you coming down for a day, Molly?" Without any hesitation, "sure thing," she responded enthusiastically. "Just give me a couple of dates to choose from." That done and Sam wanted to know how Molly was faring. She told him about the case of Scarlet Fever on the Children's Ward, which immediately engaged his clinical know-how, or perhaps revealed the lack of it! "Come on," Molly challenged, "There you are with the Broad Street pump virtually on your doorstep, its historical association with the 1800's cholera epidemic and Dr John Snow's contribution to public health! Shame on you!" Sam laughed saying, "OK, I shall have done my homework by the time we next meet, Molly."

Changing the subject, Sam asked, "How are things going with Ian?" "I wish I could say steadily," laughed Molly "but things are moving a bit too fast and there is dissention at home." Molly shared her disappointment that her parents were not too taken with Ian because he was older and they seemed to see her childhood dream and their ambitions melting like butter in the sun. "Only you can make the decision, dear Molly. I do wish it were easier for you but remember, enjoy the moment! Ian obviously makes you happy; he does, doesn't he Molly?" Running away as usual, Molly retorted, "How do you define happiness, Sam?" They were silent for a while until Sam said, "Goodnight, dear Molly, sleep well."

Yes, Ian did make Molly feel happy; she admired his logic, his caring, and his sense of adventure. A whole new world, outside the Nurses' Home seemed to have opened before her! A different social network of Ian's family and friends, summer evenings walking in the local park, travelling to the seaside on Ian's motor bike for her day off, double seats on the back row of the Odeon cinema, and evenings gliding around the ornate ballroom of the local 'Palais'! Gwen quietly feared it might be window dressing.

Molly spent a day in London with Sam who, as they walked the familiar path beside the Thames, sensed her inner turmoil. Sam listened compassionately before commenting. "Well! I don't need to ask if you are OK with Ian because I sense you share with him something you couldn't share with me. But do you trust him? Trust him with your love and your future?" Molly hesitated, "That's a tall order, Sam. How can one predict the future?" They continued to walk with their own silent thoughts and eventually Sam cautioned, "However right it might seem, don't be rushed Molly. I know your long-standing goal is to build a family but be careful it doesn't override all others – like, your life's dream to be a nurse! Why not put everything on hold until after your finals and think afresh?" Molly reiterated her sense of satisfaction in having been a nurse and went on to say that for her, family life would be a fulltime commitment, "so why delay for the sake of a qualification I will never use?" As he listened, Sam's silence seemed to continue for a long time when he eventually said, "Don't say you are thinking of giving up all you have ever worked for, dearest Molly? The future is unknown to us my precious ... Think hard."

The breeze off the river was blowing cold when they suddenly realized it was way past lunchtime. They found a pub where they could eat over-looking the river at a table on the patio against a brazier. Now it was Sam's turn. He talked enthusiastically about his experience in the various M&CW departments and his expectation the study would produce some interesting recommendations. He was excited by the anticipation that the experience would complement his work as a Paediatrician. Sam shared his aspiration to possibly specialize in 'Paeds' – probably think about preparing for a Registrar's post quite soon! It was good to see Sam so upbeat with the prospect of such a bright future before him.

By the time Molly arrived back at St Pancras station to catch the train home, she knew Sam had pinpointed the issues to be confronted and probably the answers she was seeking were looking her in the face? The solidarity and strange oneness she enjoyed with Sam made Molly feel quite emotional; could it be as her soul mate and lover? Time was running out; and she sensed Sam had decisions to face too.

DECISION TIME:

Petal's fiancé completed his engineering apprenticeship and they knew Timothy would soon be recruited for his obligatory two-year National Service. When Timothy received his 'call-up' and knowing he was likely to be posted away – probably abroad - it was time to take stock. Petal told Molly they had decided to get married before she sat her State Finals. Shock, horror, thought Molly – no one did that! Bravely, Petal faced Matron in an interrogation becoming of MI5 but she survived and received Matron's approval to marry Timothy, to continue her training and take her finals. Unheard of!!!

When Petal returned from her Honeymoon it was rather a novelty – married nurses were not accepted in these days. Bubbles, the strange, rather racy cleaner could not resist asking Petal, "You survived then, did you Nurse?" Nathan, the mortuary porter was another such character, winked and nodded knowingly when he met Petal and took great delight in seeing her blush.

The friendship between Petal and Molly deepened following Petal's marriage: they talked about everything – their hopes and fears; their dreams and nightmares. Molly impishly recalled, "Petal taught me all I knew about birth control." Petal successfully completed her finals and moved away with Timothy to his posting; the first one, a short stay in the Home Counties and then a move to Germany.

Ian and Molly's romance blossomed and they received Sam's blessing when he heard of their forthcoming engagement. In due course Ian and Molly visited the corner shop to share their news and it soon became evident that 'Congratulations' were due all round. Pru, was full of excitement as she gave Molly an invitation to her wedding and described the Guest House on the Isle of Wight to which they would be moving. Maisey's fiancé had graduated with a 'First' amidst great celebrations and with the hope that they would be leaving to make their home in Canada as soon as all the formalities were complete. Paul had received an enhanced promotion at work and he was due to commence his lay ministry training shortly. Meanwhile, Paul intended to run the shop with plans to marry Connie in the longer term.

When Ian and Molly eventually left the shop to visit Tommy and tell him of their decision, he wished them well. But really Tommy was too full of excitement about his experience at the Spa rehabilitation centre to concentrate on Ian and Molly's celebration. Tommy who looked fit described the Spa as a "life changing time" and one from which he had developed skills and confidence that he would never have thought possible. One of the most unexpected experiences had been the optional art appreciation class. The talents Tommy's charcoal artwork demonstrated had impressed the art tutor who offered to keep in touch and further his interests ... "How about that, Molly?" he said triumphantly.

However, the all-important issue of 'earning a living' was uppermost in Tommy's mind. On completion of the rehabilitation course, he had been offered employment at the local Remploy factory but after meeting with the Hospital Secretary, Tommy had decided to take advantage of the opportunities open to him in hospital administration. Marriage to Lizzy was on the cards, not immediately but hopefully in the foreseeable future. The smell of toast began to float into the room as tea and toasted buns arrived to divert their attention!

Whilst Ian helped Tommy's mother to take the empty crockery back to the kitchen, Tommy now looked hard at Molly and said, "Is it alright with Ian? He is rather different to Sam." Molly assured Tommy that she loved Ian ... "OK he was older and perhaps not so much of a people's person as Sam but Ian is good to be with." Tommy frowned, "But you and Sam were such a pair!" Molly smiled, "Yes, we still are," she tried to reassure him. Ian returned from his domestic chores and they prepared to take their leave in anticipation of meeting again at Pru's wedding.

After Ian had said "Goodnight", Molly strolled into the Nurses Home and up to her room. It was late and the 'cocoa gang' had retired to bed. Molly surprised herself by the feeling of relief at having a breathing space - how life had changed since she met Ian!

MOLLY'S CHOSEN PATH:

Rose and Wills gradually became accustomed to Ian and his 'townie ways' and as time went by he began to win a place in their hearts as well as their home – well, in truth, Wills was not quite so enthusiastic. Rose, however, was fascinated by Ian's

DIY skills and she began to welcome him with the greeting "Oh! Whilst you are here Ian, could you look at 'so and so' for me please?" But there were times when Rose seemed to feel left out as Molly spent more time on her days off with Ian. The weekly letter would either include a gentle admonishment, or a request for Ian when he next came over to "just look at ... for me please." When Rose felt really peeved, she would remind Molly to bring her nail clippers because her toe nails were becoming painfully long!

Rose began to join in with Ian on various DIY projects and an amazing bond developed between them. Knowing of Rose's delight in the radio programme featuring Horace Hotplate with his stuttering speech, Ian nicknamed her 'Hottie'. Much to everyone's surprise, instead of feeling Ian had overstepped the mark she revelled in this distinction almost as a term of endearment!

Kate didn't escape Ian's delight in nicknaming, as she became known as Duke. Molly, of course was 'Wifey' from the day they met. In fact on the night of the hospital dance Ian wrote to his father, 'Tonight I have met the girl I shall marry.' He sealed the letter and gave it to his father with the instructions not to open it until Ian gave him the word. The word came on the eve of their wedding day!

And so the day came when Ian formally asked Wills for Molly's hand in marriage. Wills, having preceded his consent with the usual 'hum, hum' cough, he turned to Rose with mock accusation in his voice, "Did you know about this?" With a twinkle, Rose bantered, "I rather suspected it, why didn't you?"

Molly and Ian became engaged. The romantic occasion was shared as they walked across the local Golf Course with Ian teasingly circumventing the moment when he tenderly placed the ring on Molly's finger and pledged a love that would last a lifetime ... And it did. Molly shyly began to call Ian 'Hub' in response to his 'Wifey'!

Shortly after Molly and Ian's engagement, Pru and Eric were married at a quiet Registry Office event with Paul and Maisey present as witnesses. The following day, a special blessing was included in the morning service at the Mission and the Reverend, still enthusiastically romping around on the platform with his mop of hair in disarray, did them proud. The wedding breakfast, a wedding gift from Paul and Maisey, was a lavish celebration enjoyed in the company of family and friends. It was particularly good to meet Maisey's fiancé and to see Tommy taking part with such confidence and happiness. Sam and Sarah were even able to get up for the day and stayed on for supper with Ian and Molly.

Molly's next move was to the Orthopaedic Ward. Here, many of the patients were long-stay with their limbs suspended in traction supported by a trapeze of ropes and pulleys. The elderly with fractured femurs were particularly vulnerable to the risk of developing pressure sores, which required considerable diligence and nursing skill to keep the skin intact and the patients in good spirits. Visiting times, at one hour each day, was just not enough to boost their flagging morale.

Other patients suffered from various forms of arthritis. They were often feverish, debilitated and in considerable pain and the nursing care was equally intensive but presented in different forms. By contrast, there were the young men who had been admitted following an accident, or sports injury – the surgeon would sigh and say, "Ah, the impetuosity of youth!" The balcony housed patients with different forms of tuberculosis affecting their bones. Once stabilised, the balcony patients were renowned for their exuberance and the nurses were always at risk from some unsuspecting prank. Nursing care was a fine balance between keeping them rested and their energetic minds occupied – the occupational therapists worked wonders.

Molly found Orthopaedics an interesting and challenging nursing environment in which the camaraderie between the patients was quite inspirational. Patients with plaster-clad limbs and approaching the convalescent stage would hop around the ward with the aid of walking sticks or crutches helping to serve teas and clear away the crockery after mealtimes. During the quiet times on the ward these lively young men displayed their talents on the ward piano, organised board games, or simply sat and talked and maybe read to the more frail and bedbound patients.

Her self-allotted 6am study time had never been more important to Molly. Although the ward experience was interspersed with study periods, the classroom work and self-directed studies increased in intensity and complexity during a period when she wanted to spend more and more time with Ian. In one way 'finals' seemed to loom ever closer but in another, next spring seemed a long way off. Towards the end of her time on the Orthopaedic Ward, Molly and Ian planned a holiday, which very nearly came to naught when Molly was 'warded' in the sick bay suffering from suspected cerebral irritation. Whatever the cause, it was most unpleasant and Ian felt helpless as he witnessed Molly's discomfort from headache, neck stiffness and light sensitive eyes. Molly was well cared for by her colleagues and eventually regained a level of fitness, which allowed her to go on holiday. The recuperative holiday seemed to cement their relationship as they walked along the beautiful Northumbrian coast sharing thoughts and making preparations for their life together. Ian was besotted by Molly, once he had found his perfect 'wifey' there seemed no shadow of a doubt in fixing the day.

State finals seemed a lifetime away when in reality it was only a few months but Molly had made up her mind to leave. However, she was a star student and her decision was a great disappointment to Matron and her Tutors. A surgeon with whom Molly had worked in theatres exploded on hearing the news, "What a waste!" he exclaimed. But such was the esteem within which Molly was held that special concession was given for her to continue to attend for revision classes and take her final examinations after her marriage.

So, Molly and her family were soon abuzz with activity preparing for the great day. Wills organised local produce for the wedding breakfast. Rose preserved fruit from Wills' garden, created delicate pastries and a three-tier wedding cake for a local master chef to decorate. But after all Rose's planning, the decoration of the cakes was not completed until the eve of the wedding day when Ian took Molly on his motorbike to collect them from the Chef's home. The Chef waved a cautious goodbye as he watched his work of art transported away on the back of a motorbike!

Kate worked with great flare and precision to complete a young cousin's gold satin dress and 'Bo-Peep' bonnet; she made Joan's white bridesmaid dress to match the dress Kate had worn only a few months before at her crowning as the village 'Rose Queen'. Meanwhile, Molly nipped into town with Joan one off-duty to buy her wedding dress. The decision was made surprisingly quickly once Molly had spied the glistening long white satin dress embossed with small sprigs of white matt flowers. The 'borrowed' item, a headdress on loan from a sister of the 'cocoa gang', the 'blue' a nifty suspender relic of the 'Can-Can' outfit - job done!

The glorious autumn day dawned. As Molly stood in a quiet sense of togetherness with her father waiting for the wedding car, Wills gently squeezed her hand and tenderly beseeched Molly, "You are OK about this Nitto? You do not have to go through with it if there are any doubts at all you know." But there were none and Molly and Ian were married in the picturesque Norman village church entered by a steep path lined with Yew trees.

Leaving the church after the ceremony Molly will never forget the sight that greeted them. The church path was lined with village people mingled with nursing colleagues and Mrs F; the Dolman girls were there in full force too! As Molly and Ian walked down the country lane to the Village Hall their path was strewn with bunting, confetti and happiness.

Rose and Wills catered for the 'Wedding Breakfast' in its entirety; their talented hands and know-how created a feast to behold. After the formalities of the wedding breakfast and speeches were concluded, Molly looked around at the 'snapshots' that would remain in her memory. Her father sitting quietly smiling with pride on all he surveyed.

Seeing Sam and Sarah together at the wedding it was clear they were beginning to move towards a closer relationship. When Molly asked "what's next for you then?" Sam explained he was being drawn to the wider picture of 'Paeds' and he had made an application to a Missionary Society. It seemed that Sarah was developing her interest in medical research and the pull of a return to academia. They smiled at Molly, and Sam rather wistfully said, "So it could be quite a time yet before we think of tying the knot."

Tommy and Lizzy were a joy to behold but it was Tommy who Molly looked at as he stood beside Lizzy and his mother as 'his own person!' Molly felt such pride in his tenacity and achievements.

Rose felt she knew the guests well, but had never actually met many of Molly's hospital colleagues and friends. So it was a great delight for Molly to see her mother chatting away with Mrs F as they sat with Tommy and his family. The Dolman girls were in full flow with Jane and her husband looking proudly at their little daughter who had performed her role as the 'golden bridesmaid' to perfection. Sam and Wills talked together animatedly, whilst Ian was deep in conversation with his best man, Robert. Robert, Ian's long-standing friend, his old school chum from the 'tech' days, and fellow novice at ballroom dancing lessons was now a building inspector with a local council. Molly smiled as she guessed Ian was getting some guidance on the forthcoming project of remodelling their terraced house. The 'cocoa gang' occupied the noisy corner with peals of hilarious laughter and conspiratorial silences. Kate and Ian's sister Joan, were perfect hosts as they wafted around in their long flowing white bridesmaid dresses.

Molly and Ian left for to honeymoon in London, staying at the Strand Palace Hotel. "Hey", said Sam as he nipped out to their retreating taxi, "how about we meet up for Evensong at St Paul's Cathedral tomorrow followed by supper?" "Done," said Ian "6 pm prompt ... and don't forget to put the clocks back; British Summertime ends at midnight on Saturday!" Molly and Ian felt they were part of history as they travelled to London on the 5.45pm - one of the first diesel trains. Their arrival at the Strand Palace Hotel entrance was a wonderful greeting and the hotel lived up to all it was reputed to be. On Sunday morning, Ian and Molly made their way to Petticoat Lane Market where Molly bought a pair of pink glass swans as a keepsake.

Sunday night and they joined Sam and Sarah for Evensong at St Paul's Cathedral. Ian had been to a service in the Cathedral but the others had only seen its glory on the tourist trail, so the impact of the music and atmosphere of worship was all the more poignant for Molly, Sam and Sarah. Supper was enjoyed at the Strand Palace. It was such a special occasion with everyone seemingly on the brink of a new period in his or her life. Molly and Ian talked about their new house and plans to start a family as soon as 'everything was straight'. Sam seemed beset by conflict and less certain of the future. On the one hand he had a vision of practicing medicine and making a contribution to the pastoral care of sick and disadvantaged peoples in other countries, whilst on the other his love for Sarah was beginning to blossom. Sarah also faced conflicting choices – sacrifice her career, or Sam! They parted at the end of the evening with all four of them in a rather reflective mood but vowing to keep in touch. "Often!" added Sam looking wistfully at Molly.

The week sped by. Ian knew London like the proverbial 'back of his hand' having served in the Royal Corps of Signals during the war based in the War Office teleprinter section. Molly and Ian had a wonderful time in the autumn sunshine. They took a trip on the river to Kew, visited the Tower of London; and spent an evening at the London Palladium where they enjoyed the latest musical, 'South Pacific', featuring Mary Martin. It was all too good to end but there was a future to be built together and 'One Enchanted Evening ...' became their signature song throughout their married life.

Molly reached her 21st birthday but the celebrations were postponed until after her Finals. She returned to the hospital for revision classes and in due course sat her examinations with the rest of her set. Ian famously tells of the day he met Molly off the bus returning from a visit to her parents and of presenting her with an unopened letter. Knowing the likely contents and fearing the worst Molly said, "Let's wait until we get home, Hub." Molly opened the letter announcing the results of her State Final Examination – "I've passed!" she squealed. Then Ian announced, "There is a second letter, Wifey." Molly took the unassuming brown envelope and reading the contents on the familiar hospital headed paper she was speechless – Molly had been awarded the Hospital Gold Medal with an invitation to the 'Prize Award Ceremony'. Molly felt so humbled... and yes, unworthy.

The large 'Awards Board' with the names of 'the best' i.e., gold and silver medallists inscribed in gold writing was fixed on the wall directly opposite the front door in the Nurses' Home. It was difficult not to miss, and quite naturally during their student days they had often speculated on next year's award winner – little did Molly ever dream that one day it would be her!

Rose was thrilled with the news; she was proud but maybe disappointed that Molly had left before realizing her full professional potential. Wills quietly smiled and said, "Well done Nitto, but remember that is for what you have done – to own it you have to continue to earn it."

The 'Awards Ceremony' was a wonderful time of celebration and reunion. Molly's PTS set and many other old colleagues were reunited. Rosetta had met a German medical student, a Lutheran from her hometown and they were planning to work in obstetrics at Cambridge. Hetty was to be married, two other members of the PTS set had places to train as Midwives; and Molly's friend pursued her South Africa dream.

This was the first time Molly and Petal had met since their weddings and it would be half a century later that they paid a nostalgic visit to their old training ground to find the Nurses' Home demolished and the hospital transformed beyond belief.

CHAPTER 7

FAMILY AND FUN

FAMILY AND NEIGHBOURING:

So, Molly gained her SRN qualification and a bonus prize! But from the inner sanctum of Molly's being Gwen feared Molly might always chide herself for disappointing her mother and the ambitions she harboured for her. But perhaps most hurtful of all, would be for Molly to live with the regret of not proving to her father that she could truly claim ownership of the Gold Medal. So had it all been in vain, or was it just the tip of an iceberg? Perhaps only Gwen knew the full extent of the turmoil in Molly's life: her aspirations, joys, and doubts in the years to come.

Following their whirlwind romance and subsequent marriage, Molly and Ian lived in a terraced house in Ian's hometown, situated halfway between the training hospital and Molly's village. It was with some reservations that Gwen noticed the true extent of the attention needed to turn the old terraced house into a home. Nevertheless, she drew reassurance from Ian's passion for problem solving and the support of friends from engineering backgrounds: Robert, his school chum, for advice on the structural technicalities; and Ian's long-time work friend, Ray, who shared Ian's enthusiasm for DIY.

Ian and Ray laboured on the house after work every night and through the weekends - often until the early hours of the morning. The house resounded with their voices carousing in imperfect harmony, laughing at their own wisecracks, interspersed with the quieter more contemplative times of sorting out problems and decision-making. They were like a music hall double act as one sparked off the other – they assigned themselves the same nickname, 'Chizz'. The two 'Chizzes' enjoyed a close relationship through work, their love of motorbikes, and dancing, as well as the rather bizarre proclivity for sharing a pair of pyjamas - one wore the coat and the other the trousers! Approaching Christmas, it became a family joke to hear them say in unison, "Can we have a pair of pyjamas, please?"

Meanwhile, Molly worked in the local geriatric hospital. It was a new experience to nurse the elderly all collected in the confines of a 'Geriatric Ward', previously she had nursed the patients according to their clinical needs and not their age. In the fullness of time, probably the 1960's, 'Geriatric Medicine' became a specialty headed by a Consultant Geriatrician.

As work at the house progressed Rose also became a stakeholder in the enterprise! Ian knew nothing about wall papering and decorating to the extent that when he arrived at that stage he simply went to the shop and asked for a tin of red paint. "What kind of paint, Sir?" came the response. "Red," replied Ian. "But what for?" ... "The house," said Ian. The shopkeeper must rarely have met such a novice as he proceeded to explain to Ian about the different types of paint, other than colour.

When the time arrived, Rose gave Ian both moral and practical support. She travelled the twenty-mile journey from the village by bicycle and bus to spend the day with Ian and returned home in the evening. 'Decorate a room in a day' remained her motto. On one occasion they over-ran their allotted time but Rose fully prepared to miss her bus said, "We must get the border on before I go;" they did and she missed her bus. "OK, Hottie, I will take you home on my motorbike." And unbelievably Rose agreed. It was a sight to behold to see this dignified matron sailing off into the sunset astride a motorbike!

Molly did not shy away from her contribution to home-making either! Using the Singer Sewing Machine presented to her by Ian in celebration of her 21st birthday; she made curtains, cushion covers and table linen as well as clothes for herself and the children. Ian often gave Molly a hand with the difficult jobs but one night he must have lost concentration because whilst feeding some heavy material into the machine the needle went straight through his finger!

Eventually Molly became the proud owner of a new gadget on the market – a knitting machine. With this new toy Molly made some amazing garments for the family. Sadly, as the carriage travelled across the needles it was a rather noisy process and certainly not one for an evening by the fireside. The knitting machine was soon consigned to a new home!

Needless to say, Sam was kept up-to-date with Molly's enterprising home management skills, her professional success, and recent pregnant status. Sam just could not contain his delight in the forthcoming baby. Eventually, Molly and Ian prepared to celebrate the transformation of their little house. The garden was ship-shape with a sunken lawn and the sloping banks emblazoned with flowers; a healthy-looking vegetable plot was also in preparation. In addition, plans were in hand to build a wooden storage-cum-summer house adorned with flowering hanging baskets at the far end of a sunken lawn. At their house-warming party the little terraced house bulged at the seams, thankfully it was a nice day and the overflow easily accommodated in the garden.

Sam and Sarah came to the party, along with Tommy and Lizzy. Paul, now the owner of the corner shop, and his fiancé Connie arrived during the afternoon and that was a wonderful surprise. The guests toasted Molly and Ian's achievement and in return they acknowledged the inspiration and practical support received from family and friends. Rose's contribution was affectionately acknowledged, to which Rose added a few of her own stories, including the daring rides back home on the motorbike! From this time and throughout their married life,

Ian and Molly took great pleasure in celebrating each other and sharing their success and happiness by 'partying' with friends and family in their own home. No event was more important than Ian's strawberry tea birthday party, a ritual celebrated from birth when on that memorable summer Sunday morning a strawberry seller was trading her wares beneath the bedroom window!

As the time came to prepare for and to welcome the 'pitter-patter' of tiny feet, Sam and Sarah visited to share their news. Sam's application to a Missionary Society had been successful and he would be leaving for Africa by the end of August. Sarah then explained she had received the most unexpected piece of good fortune when her Professor suggested she considered incorporating an international element to her research and naturally, she had chosen Africa! Sam and Sarah were over the moon that they would be able to continue to share their lives and professional interest: "You just couldn't have written the script," Sam exclaimed. So, it was with joy and sorrow mixed that they wished each other, "Goodbye for now, see you soon." Sam added, "And promise to send lots of pictures of your new baby - please!"

It was a real joy to see Ian and Molly settle so contentedly into their new home, albeit with limited creature comforts such as a bathroom and inside toilet. Without hot water and a bathroom, Friday night, bath night, was always a special time of contentment. Ian would bring in the long tin bath from the shed, set in front of the kitchen fire and fill it with hot water from the back boiler of the fire. After their weekly bath they cuddled up on the large sofa to listen to the Friday night play on the radio. One Friday night, the play featured the character of a girl who had a spirited but sweet and endearing nature; the girl's name was Joy. "I say, Wifey, wouldn't that be a nice name for our baby if it is a girl?" said Ian.

After Joan, Ian's sister, gained her SRN qualification she continued at their training hospital as a theatre staff nurse and brought home all the gossip. It was heart-warming for Gwen to sense Molly's feeling of 'inclusion' in the old days as she giggled and the dancing eyes of carefree youth reappeared. On one such visit, early in September when Joan was about to embark on her midwifery training, she and Molly decided to go into town together to buy Joan a new fob watch. Molly had been up very early that morning with backache and feeling increasingly restless, which did not escape Gwen's antennae – well; the baby was due for heaven's sake! On the way to town, Joan's new watch was forgotten in the race to the Maternity home where daughter, Joy, was born in undue haste. Post-natal care was very different at that time and Molly stayed in the Nursing Home for ten days – mainly in bed. The day she was discharged Ian's parents invited them to lunch but before Molly entered their home, Ian's mother had insisted she was 'Churched'. *Churching is a service of blessing and cleansing attended by the mother following the birth of a child.*

Arrangements were made by Ian with the local Church of England vicar to hold the service after Matins. It was a very reverent and prayerful thanksgiving for the safe delivery of a child and although Molly was a bit shaky, she felt richly blessed. Although Ian's parents were not 'church people' there was considerable superstition about allowing a recently delivered woman over the threshold of your home until she was 'Churched' – cleansed! Gwen silently reflected on the hypocrisy.

Family life took on a new meaning and serious responsibilities. For instance, Ian's day now began about 5am when Joy awoke to be fed. Having settled Molly with baby Joy and taken a pot of tea to bed, Ian switched on the electric copper to heat the water, assembled the dolly-tub and wooden dolly-pegs in readiness to pound the nappies and other soiled clothes. Ian always aimed to peg out the washing before he left for work.

However, Ian's work entailed regular attendance at the firm's residential engineering and management schools for various courses, some up to one-month duration. Such an assignment arrived whilst Joy was a small baby and Chizz No. 2 popped round most evenings to keep Molly company and address any domestic issues until Ian came home for the weekend. This was only one of many such occasions when Chizz 2 kept a 'watching brief' ... "Well, it's all in the family," he would chuckle.

Then one winter Molly discovered the joys of the television dancing competition programme, 'Come Dancing' (the forerunner of 'Strictly'). One night each week during the series, Molly took a bicycle ride across town to watch the programme with Edith one of Joan's school friends – Joan would join them if she were off duty. The 'Girls' night out' was fun and the magical setting of the sparkling ballroom, the fairy-tale ankle-length crinoline-type dresses, and the elegant men in evening suits, was pure escapism – a feast for Molly's eyes, heart and soul!

Two years after Joy was born, a brother arrived one Sunday morning in late August. The new baby, named Gavin, was delivered at home in the comfort of Molly's bed under the strict supervision of Mrs Plant, the district midwife. And for Ian, it was time to pick up his old routines - but a solution was soon found this time in the form of a Hoover washing machine!

Rose was a regular visitor, helping here, there and everywhere. She accompanied Molly on the afternoon walks with the babies in the pram and continued to entertain them in her novel way. Joy loved Nannan-Rose and Granddad-Wills dearly and before she was very old Joy would pack her little pink suitcase and be waiting to leave with Nannan when she caught the bus home in the late afternoon. At first Joy stayed with Nannan overnight and Ian collected her the next day but the visits gradually extended; and when Gavin was born it wasn't long before he had his little suitcase ready to join them.

Rose was once again in her element as history repeated itself with visits to Benjamin Bunny's burrow under the bedclothes! Their afternoon walks through the village invariably included 'Church Farm' to say, "hello" to Granddad Bull in his stall.

Granddad Bull was a fearsome animal. If Joy and Gavin called out to him when he was in the wrong mood he would bellow, and snort, and scrape his feet on the concrete floor. When they arrived home after a walk through the village Joy and Gavin would be set the task of drawing a picture whilst the meal was prepared. The judge was the pet cat who when called was deemed to have chosen the winner by the first drawing on which he placed his paw! The 'winner' and the 'tryer' both earned a piece of Nannan-Rose's famous treacle toffee. The treacle toffee was known throughout the family and when later in her life Joy went to University Nannan would send her a box of toffee – together with the recipe should she care to make some for herself!! The recipe is a family heirloom and the product much better than the Palm Toffee from Miss Goodwin's shop!!

Ingredients: 1/4lb butter 2lb sugar 2 teaspoons vinegar 2 tablespoons treacle
Method: Grease and warm a saucepan with the thick base. Add all ingredients
Boil slowly for ¼ hour on low heat; turn up heat and boil until the mixture starts to discolour.
Test: Drop a spot of the mixture into a cup of cold water; if it hardens it's done.
Nuts, raisins or sultanas may be added at this stage – stir in thoroughly.
Final: Pour toffee onto a greased tin; on the brink of setting cut it into pieces. Yummy Yum!

Wills at last had the boy he had probably missed not having the first time round! From the time his Grandson, Gavin could toddle they would walk hand in hand to go fishing in the nearby brook using a jam-jar on a string with Wills always teaching the little lad to understand and respect the wonders of 'Mother Nature'. Kate married and lived in the next village to her parents, she had given birth to her first son and eventually two more followed. Wills was overwhelmed with his boys who he taught to fish, respect 'Mother Nature', to mend punctures in their bicycle tyres, and clean their boots ready for the next day's adventures.

Back at home, life in the close-knit street community of terraced houses provided some interesting encounters for Molly and Ian – and absorbed by Gwen too! A very large three-generation family lived on the opposite side of the street where, it was rumoured, they boiled the potatoes in a bucket because a saucepan was not large enough! The little grand-daughter in the household named Hilary, was Joy's age and they would sit on the front doorstep with their dolly-prams chatting away like two old ladies. Unfortunately, Hilary used words that were a novelty to Joy and one day when Molly called her in for lunch Joy looked at her and said, "You little buggar." Molly was speechless and explained to Joy that there were some words that were not nice and quite unnecessary to use and 'buggar' was one of them. Forbidden fruits are always the nicest, mused Gwen and Joy, true to form, seemed to delight in saying the word. After repeated warnings of what would happen if Joy continued to say the word, one day regardless of the cost Joy confidently announced that the doll was "an awkward old buggar" for slipping down the pram. On this occasion Molly put the threatened spot of mustard on Joy's tongue; but Joy's distress was far more punishment to Molly than it was to Joy and such draconian measures were abandoned for gentle persuasion until the novelty wore off.

Elderly neighbours in the street were kind and helpful and doted on Molly's children. In particular, one married couple of near retirement age whose familiar genteel ways attracted Molly became good friends. Sadly, the husband fell ill and after a short illness, he died. His wife came to Molly and Ian and knowing Molly was a nurse, asked if she would "put him tidy before the undertakers came?" Molly and Ian washed and shaved her husband and dressed him in a clean nightshirt. For some strange reason, the next day Ian parcelled up the clothes he had worn and taking them to the dry-cleaners he advised the assistant of the purpose for which they had been worn. That evening Ian responded to a knock on the door to find a police detective asking what it was all about!

There seemed never to be a dull moment in the street. Another family with young children became friends and frequent visitors, especially the eldest son Graham, who when preparing for school examinations found Ian's help a great asset. Gradually, Graham appeared more often particularly, during the school holidays when he would feed Joy as she sat in her highchair and accompany Molly on her afternoon walks. Graham, who realized his ambition and joined the Royal Air Force, became a friend for life.

Molly walked with the children around the neighbouring countryside every day – wet, or fine. In the springtime, the children delighted in watching the frolicking newly born lambs; they learned to imitate the sound of the cuckoo's call and the staccato tapping of the woodpecker.

In the summer they watched the hay making and mighty harvesting machines travelling up and down the fields and heard the late afternoon call of the cowmen reminding the cows it was time to return home for milking. Sometimes Molly, remembering the picnics with her father in the hay fields, took a few sandwiches and drinks for them to enjoy on the headland. When the pram tyres wore thin and Ian took them into the shop to be repaired the shopkeeper was amazed, "Well, in all my life, I have never known a set of pram tyres to wear out. Wherever does your wife go?"

By the time Joy and Gavin had grown into sturdy toddlers, Ian bought seats for his and Molly's bicycles. Gavin sat in a chair-seat fixed behind Molly's seat and Joy on a seat attached to Ian's crossbar. It was great fun to whizz through the air up hill and down dale with the bicycle wheels doing most of the work! An opportunity for a picnic was rarely missed, and the bicycle rides were no exception!

Molly attended the family meeting at her local church every Tuesday afternoon. It was always a chance decision of who to get ready first – herself, then baby Gavin and lastly, Joy, or the other way around? One Tuesday, Joy was the first to be made ready in a white dress and bonnet embroidered with strawberries. Molly thought Joy was being exceptionally good whilst she prepared baby Gavin and placed him in his pram. Eventually, Joy was given the signal that it was nearly time to leave but when she came through the door her face was covered with smuts and her lovely white dress streaked with black marks. Molly was not amused - well only a bit because Joy made such a comical sight swishing her little chubby hands on the skirt of her dress saying, "there Mummy, all done." Molly had forgotten the early morning delivery from the coalman and Joy had helpfully picked up the few bits of coal he had dropped in the yard and put them in the coalhouse. They were rather late for the Tuesday service that afternoon!

It was not long before the family experienced a setback when Molly suffered an acute flare-up of an old knee injury. The Consultant prescribed medication, immobilization of the limb, and rest. "Phew! That's a tall order," exclaimed Molly thinking of Gavin and Joy. Once again, Rose came to the rescue and Molly, Joy and Gavin went to stay with her and Wills. Molly was in considerable pain, her leg had been immobilized by a plastic casing, she walked with the aid of crutches to avoid weight bearing and twice a week an ambulance came to collect her to attend hospital appointments. Ian stayed at home and went to work as usual but mid-week he would cycle some 20 miles after work to see his family and return the following morning. It was a very difficult time for them all but they got through it and Molly returned home with the children and gradually resumed her old routines.

FAMILY, FRIENDS AND AMBITIONS:

Petal, Molly's old friend from nursing days, who had two boys about the same age, was just the boost from the domestic times that they both needed! They corresponded regularly and visited each other in turn about every month. Gwen always enjoyed eavesdropping as they gossiped about family life, shared confidences and laughed about the times they had been through together. During one such visit, Petal was brimming over with news - she had returned to their training hospital on part-time duties! Molly could not believe what she was hearing – "Married nurses!" said Molly. "Come off it Mol, this is the dawn of the 60s," joked Petal and proceeded to say how she worked a night duty on Friday and Saturday so she was able to sleep the following day with husband, Timothy at home to look after the boys. Molly was pleased for Petal but she certainly did not imagine herself as a 'working mum'. However, 'the best laid plans of mice and men ...' as Molly discovered!

Then surprise, surprise, Petal became pregnant with number three! But she had particular problems to be taken into consideration and this time a hospital delivery was planned. Preparing for the family during her absence naturally concerned Petal and without hesitation Molly offered to stay with Timothy and help to look after the family during Petal's absence. With Ian's help and the loan of his friend's car, Molly, with Joy and Gavin, moved in to look after Petal's two boys and her husband, it was a very full house but such a jolly time. Petal came home with son number three and their close friendship continued. Molly returned home feeling 'broody' for the family of four children she had always hoped to have. But now it was Ian's turn to shine!

Ian had obtained further qualifications and gained promotion to a more advanced position in a neighbouring city. This time he found a brand-new house on a good-sized plot in the suburbs into which they sunk all their savings. "Nothing needs doing to it at all, Wifey!" Ian beamed and they moved in one week before Christmas. Ruth, the next-door neighbour greeted them with coffee and mince pies - Ruth and Molly became lifelong friends and confidantes. All the neighbours were friendly and most of them had small children who attended the nearby school. However, it was not long before Ian's itchy DIY fingers were re-arranging the central heating system and drawing up plans to enlarge the garage to house their newly acquired Austin 30 car, which they named 'Bessie'. Bessie was great fun, she rattled and bounced around on the road, the windscreen wipers fell off in a heavy downpour of rain, the roof also leaked and the back-seat passengers sat beneath an umbrella.

In 1960 Molly learned to drive Bessie. It was quite a challenge given Bessie's peculiarities, not to mention the required skill of double-declutching! A three-point turn was a particular 'blind-spot' for Molly but it was Gavin who showed her the knack as he patiently demonstrated the manoeuvre to her time and time again in his little pedal car. Her first attempt at the driving test was a disaster –thankfully, second time lucky!

After the Easter holidays, family life continued its course as daughter Joy started at the Infant School whilst son, Gavin waited to enter Nursery School. Gavin missed having big sister around and thought he would like a pet. So off to the pet shop they went: a mouse? A hamster? A kitten? A bird? Nothing took Gavin's eye until he spotted the tortoises and he came home with 'Joey' having first asked the rather bemused shop assistant, "Is it a mother or a father?" Ian helped Gavin to make a nest for Joey and a secure pen in the garden. The little animal quickly became Gavin's pride and joy. Towards the end of autumn, Ian taught Gavin how to prepare Joey for hibernation during the winter with the reward of seeing Joey's little head poke through the box in the spring ready and raring to go after his long winter sleep. Sadly Joey did not survive a third winter and a tearful funeral took place on a bright early spring day with a resting place Gavin prepared for Joey waiting in a corner of the back garden.

Molly's mind was in turmoil. On the one hand there was a certain excitement about returning to nursing whilst on the other, she felt guilty and deeply disturbed at the thought of reneging on the very reason for terminating her training prematurely and for the distress she had caused so many people. Full of doubt she wrote to Sam who shared her conflict at the time. Molly received a letter from Sam the next day - obviously their letters had crossed in the post; or was it telepathy? Sure enough, Sam's letter opened with thoughts of concern for Molly and how life was working out for her. He then went on to announce his and Sarah's wedding in two months' time at Sarah's family church in a small market town in Hampshire. Molly replied with congratulations and delight in accepting the invitation. A second letter from Sam arrived with his usual wise counsel and advice. "We all made rather profound decisions in the past, decisions that perhaps we wouldn't make now. It's the future that matters, you can't change the past only learn from it." He ended with the cautionary advice, "but think carefully, dear Molly ... Good luck!" Sam continued to say he felt in the same boat; the Mission field was his Calling but realised he might need to think again when he and Sarah were married with a family life to nurture.

However, Petal's idea of returning to nursing was germinating at the back of Molly's mind but Ian was most reluctant. Nevertheless, in the fullness of time Molly convinced Ian that it would be possible, with his help. So off she went, like her friend Petal, to work Friday and Saturday night duties. But, unlike her friend who was returning to her old stomping ground, Molly was disillusioned by the experience. After eight years absence, a strange hospital and unknown colleagues Molly felt 'all at sea' – no induction programmes or back-to-nursing courses in these days! She disliked the relief night duties to which part-time nurses were assigned and longed for a permanent area of responsibility where she could get to know the patients and ward routines. When Gavin went to Nursery School Molly changed to 9.30am to 3pm duties, she enjoyed the continuity of patient contact but the feeling of being a 'spare part' continued – part-time nurses were often seen as less committed and only there to earn 'pin money'.

However, in time she enjoyed working with her new colleagues, particularly mature students often embarking on a second career who were always willing to point her in the right direction and keep her afloat. One such friendship was Vera, a mature student who lived with her Psychiatrist boyfriend in an imposing house in a neighbouring village. These 'posh' friends, as they were teasingly known, frequently held gatherings in their country retreat for hospital colleagues – 'something like the 'cocoa gang' of days gone by', thought Molly! Molly and Ian were always invited but Ian was never enthusiastic and preferred to stay at home rather than, "be bored out of my mind by talking 'shop' all night!"

One group of third year students were particularly friendly and when one dropped out of a caravan holiday in Wales, Molly was asked if she would join them. "We need her share of the expenses," they said laughingly when Molly declined. "I have two children and a husband to be at home for." Molly reminded them. To which the immediate reply was, "Bring the kids with you and surely husband can look after himself for one week!" Ian was not easily persuaded that they would be OK, although agreed that he would have no trouble in coping for one week. But it was with a heavy heart that Ian waved them off from home.

But Ian's family returned home safe and sound having had a wonderful time. The little Morris Minor had bounced along to their singing – Lonnie Donegan's, late sixties song was a particular favourite:

Does your chewing gum lose its flavour on the bedpost over night?
When your mother says, "Don't chew it", do you swallow it in spite?
Do you swing it round your tonsillitis and heave it left to right?
Ohhh! Does your chewing-gum lose its flavour on the bedpost overnight?"

The sun shone all week and the caravan was spacious with cosy sleeping arrangements. Molly and the car driver, a mature second career person, slept in a double bed arrangement at the far end of the caravan with Joy and Gavin, whilst the other two tucked up in bunk beds towards the front. They took turns in cooking the meals; washed in water from a nearby spring and with the farmhouse close at hand for toileting and a supply of fresh milk and eggs, it was a very convenient arrangement. They spent all day at the seaside. One time at Shell Island, the blustery sea carried in swathes of seaweed. Great fun was had chasing each other up and down the beach with streamers of seaweed flying in the wind and the adults became kids again!

However, that night Gavin, whose vivid imagination was either expressed in his noisy dreams or creative storytelling, jumped up in his sleep shouting repeatedly, "He's coming after us!" Because Gavin slept at the end of the row of four his movements banged on the side of the caravan and frightened everyone out of their wits. The two bunk sleepers rolled off and crashed onto the floor – it was 'Bedlam'! The holiday lives in everyone's memory as if it were only last summer!

Happy to be reunited, Ian heard all about their adventures as Joy and Gavin jumped up and down waiting to top each other's stories!

A quick turn around and it was time to leave for Sam's wedding. Dressed in their finery they set off with the early morning mist foretelling a lovely sunny day ahead. Sam, dressed elegantly in a grey morning suit greeted them with his parents; he was a younger mirror image of his father combined with his mother's graciousness. Tommy and Lizzy arrived and as they all gathered around the table for a quick lunch it seemed like old times. Tommy and Lizzy announced they were planning to marry in the autumn when their new apartment in the carpet shop would be ready. "Thanks for the warning – we'll be there," smiled Sam. Family and friends were gathering in the little church as they arrived and they were escorted to a good vantage point. The bride attended by her three sisters looked radiant. Her ivory and gold trimmed brocade wedding dress teamed up with the ivory satin dresses worn by her three bridesmaids; they each carried a posy of deep yellow roses. Sarah's parents were a tall regal couple whose joy beamed from out of their every pour. During the late afternoon wedding breakfast, Molly and Ian chatted easily with the previously unknown family – Sarah's sisters were bubbly bundles of fun! All too soon the day was drawing to a close and the bride and groom left for a working honeymoon in Africa, which Sam announced could be one of their last trips – "watch this space!"

Molly was finding it increasingly difficult to resolve the disillusionment of returning to nursing. When, quite coincidentally, a new health visitor called to introduce herself. She talked about the children's health and welfare and showed a general interest in family life. Molly mentioned her part-time hospital work and the disenchantment she felt. The health visitor seemed to understand, saying "What about Health Visiting?" ... and the germ of an idea was planted.

Molly and Ian settled into their friendly community. The mothers socialised with each other at coffee mornings, they took it in turns to baby-sit, and gave a helping hand in times of need. Molly was surprised to discover the interest they all expressed in returning to work once their children settled into school and she began to test the water about their thoughts on Health Visiting. But Ruth had a much bigger decision to make. Her accountant husband wanted the family to emigrate to Australia on the '£10 Pom' package! Ruth made her difficult decision and they left for a new life in Australia. It was a painful parting – the two friends thinking they would never meet again ... but life is full of surprises!

Molly decision, as yet unmade suddenly thought, 'who better to test the idea with than Petal?' But it was not the right time. Petal's world had crumbled when Timothy returned home one night to announce he had attended an auction and bought a run-down Manor House, situated in rather isolated rural terrain further North. With Petal happily ensconced in her modern, stylish suburban home, and her nursing career kick-started as a district nurse she was propelled into a state of shock. "I am not moving," she declared, "Timothy can go himself and I shall stay here with the boys." But of course, it didn't work out that way and the family moved into the cold, drafty, neglected Manor that was as far from a family home as one could imagine. But the family knuckled down to make a go of things and Petal continued with her nursing career.

Her friend's desolation seemed to seep all the joy out of Molly's new venture. Nevertheless, rather cautiously and with an open mind, Molly wrote a letter of inquiry to the Medical Officer of Health (MOH) at the local Health Department. A prompt and full reply arrived enclosing literature on Health Visiting, together with an invitation to attend an informal interview. After the interview Molly felt much better informed but she was concerned about the fulltime obligations of the mandatory Midwifery Course and the shift duties involved. Molly pondered on the idea; sometimes dismissing it completely only for the possibility to re-emerge in her mind when she least expected. Eventually, Ian asked, "Is something troubling you, Wifey?" With a great sense of relief, she told him about Health Visiting and what it would entail – "but if we could manage the training, we would be OK."

Ian was never one for snap answers, so they took a break. Having been to Butlin's Holiday Camp with the children the previous year, he suggested a repeat holiday to "talk it over." So off they went. Molly remembering there would be a variety of competitions went prepared for Joy and Gavin to enter as the fancy took them. They had a lovely time; Joy learned to swim with Ian well on the way by the time they went home. With reservations, Ian began to accept that perhaps Molly would always be drawn back to nursing. Joy and Gavin thought it was a grand idea because their best friend's mother had offered to collect them all from school to play together at her house.

CHAPTER 8

NURSING BECKONS

PASSING MUSTER:

But this time the new dimension of Public Health Nursing engaged Molly's ambitions as she applied for a place on the Midwifery Course at the local hospital and Health Visiting Course located in the Public Health Department of the City Council headed by the Medical Officer of Health (MOH). The interview for the Midwifery Course went well but the Health Visitor experience was quite daunting. Molly responded to rather probing questions about her motivation, her family circumstances and professional background. It all seemed to be going well when the MOH asked her thoughts on a mother's role in family life and its influence on emotional stability? She felt she gave a reasoned reply to be confronted by, "Well, what would you say to the mothers? Do as I do, or do as I say?" Molly's composure in answering the question belied the guilt she had buried and that was less easy to deal with. She was offered a place conditional on gaining the Midwifery qualification!

MIDWIFERY AND HEALTH VISITING:

Molly was bowled over by her midwifery experiences. Whilst nothing would replace the sheer joy and wonder of seeing Joy and Gavin at birth, to witness a baby being born was nothing short of a miracle. When first the wet shiny top of the baby's head appeared, almost spontaneously a little face turned upwards and gazed straight into Molly's eyes and her love affair with midwifery was sealed. Molly conducted her first delivery on 8th August and every year since she celebrates, with 'her baby', the joy of this miracle of life in which she participated! Molly's midwifery training was to be a powerful experience, and one she always said was the most rewarding time of her career. In 1960 Molly was awarded the Midwifery prize on the successful completion of her training; she longed to develop a career as a district midwife but knew it would be a step too far for family life, as she wanted it to be.

Next it was Tommy's turn to step forth into married life. One cool autumn day towards the end of September, the old gang including Paul and his fiancé, celebrated the wedding of Tommy and Lizzy at the Citadel. Sam was Tommy's Best Man and Sarah, Lizzie's Matron of Honour.

Lizzy's father gave his speech in which he reflected on the joy that Lizzy had always given to them; their pride in her achievements; and now the gift of a new member of the family, Tommy and turning to Tommy's parents said, "and indeed a whole new family as well!"

Then the bridegroom's turn came with a resounding cheer as he rose to his feet. Tommy's speech was thoughtful and moving as he thanked Sam for providing the key that opened the door to his future and to his beautiful bride Lizzy, who had guided him over the threshold. Then to, "dear Molly, the great architect behind this wonderful master plan" The band started to play 'Molly Malone' and Molly thought back to all the ups and downs. Ian looked and listened with pride. Sam's speech gave due appreciation to the loveliness of the Matron of Honour, his pride in her sincerity and trust, and the dignity in which she had performed her duties that day. Sam concluded with a few jokes at the expense of the bridegroom and finally, admiration for all Tommy and Lizzy had achieved. The guests rose to their feet to sing and clap as the band started to play 'For he's a jolly good fellow …'

During chat-time following the formalities, Molly enthused about her midwifery experience and the surprise of being awarded the Midwifery Prize. As usual, Sam was overjoyed and gave her a long, loving hug. "Now," Sam exploded, "We have news for you!" Sam looked at Sarah who shared their news of a baby due next spring with the necessity of changing their lifestyle significantly. Sam's contract with the Missionary Society terminated at the end of November when they would return to live permanently in the UK. Sam planned to return to Paediatrics to achieve his former ambition and Sarah to a combined local Health Department/University appointment following the interest created by her research. They would live in hospital accommodation until they found an easy commute, say somewhere in the Home Counties. "Wow," said Molly, eyes sparkling, "all change and so soon. I am so very pleased for you both." Tommy and Lizzy were given the gist of their news before setting off on honeymoon to warmer climes. Everyone left the wedding with a real feel-good factor.

With the pressure of the midwifery course behind her Molly arranged to visit Petal in her new surroundings. To Molly's delight, Petal sounded a little more upbeat, "Bring the family at the weekend, Mol," she said. Ian mapped out the route to Petal's rather isolated spot and off they set. From the road the Manor House, looked magnificent positioned on a hill and surrounded by parkland. The estate was accessed through lodge gates and at the end of the long drive Petal stood excitedly waving her arms in the air and as Molly stepped out of the car they embraced with great affection. "Wow! Petal" said Molly, "it seems unreal." "Oh no, it's real all right" replied Petal with an unfathomable look on her face.

Petal welcomed them towards the house, Ian not quite believing what greeted him, whilst Joy and Gavin looked through wide-open, unblinking eyes. "Come in," invited Petal and they entered through a door into a place that looked as if it was part of a spooky film set. As Molly grew accustomed to the gloom, she could see evidence of Petal's 'home-making' with cushions, potted plants and a cheery fire in the grate. After refreshments,

Petal gave them a conducted tour of her 'establishment'. First, into a kind of vestibule from which rose a magnificent staircase, then down a long dark corridor giving access to the larders and storerooms terminating in a rather derelict area. By this stage, Petal was eager to tell them about some of the historical features of the Manor and its association with the 1817 Pentrich Revolution. The derelict area, through which entrance was gained at the end of the corridor, was indeed the cottage in which a workman was shot having been mistaken for an absconding revolutionist. It was all so eerie in the cobweb festooned darkness and quite frightening to the extent that Joy and Gavin stood at the door wide eyed and barely breathing!

Petal's tour eventually continued into an impressive courtyard surrounded by stables and covered parking for the carriages (now Petal's car). On top of the stables stood a clock tower – it was Timothy's priority to repair the clock and get it chiming again! But Petal was enthralled by the thought of the swallows that returned to nest in the rafters each spring. The courtyard was enclosed at either end by impressive wooden gates.

Retracing their steps back along the dark corridor they were shown the ancient bathroom and toilet facilities with Petal proudly directing attention to the ornate toilet with its impressive wooden seat, high ornate cistern and chain with a magnificent delft-like china handle. Next, on to the ballroom where this magnificent expanse was adorned by a high ceiling decorated with exquisite plaster designs from which chandeliers hung gracefully. The windows were enormous, they seemed as if they would have filled a wall of Molly's house from the ground level to rooftop! The curtains were faded and slightly worn – Molly shuddered thinking it felt almost like entering Miss Haversham's parlour! Only, the shining wooden floor gave testimony to Petal's pride and hard work. The hearthrug in front of a fireplace of enormous proportions had once been the fitted carpet in Petal's former lounge; and the dining room suite arranged in a corner looked like doll's house furniture.

They were then given the thrilling experience of climbing the vast wooden staircase to the first floor where they glanced at the bedrooms, toilet and bathroom facilities as they walked through this surreal setting. Two more floors had yet to be discovered but Petal gave a resigned sigh, "All in the fullness of time, Mol!"

Timothy joined them for lunch and afterwards he escorted Ian and the children on a tour of the estate leaving Petal and Molly time to talk. It was then that Petal looked Molly straight in the eyes saying, "Hey, Ho! I'm pregnant!" When their hugging, laughing and crying was spent a look of concern settled on Petal's face, "but how am I going to rear the little soul in this inhospitable place, Mol?" Molly hugged her dear friend whilst they sat in silence. Then, with sudden resolution, almost like an electric shock, Petal sat up declaring, "I'm a country girl – perhaps not from parts as wild as these but I know the challenges and we shall be OK. The little soul will come along and snuggle in as one of the brood, duckie-darling" - another of Petal's whimsical endearments!

Timothy and his admiring visitors returned for tea. Molly left her dear friend with a heavy heart but Joy and Gavin were astounded by what they had seen and talked about their adventure all the way home and long afterwards. Ian thought it was a DIY nightmare – but he did not have Timothy's vision!

The next stop for Molly was Health Visiting and family life returned to something like normal. The essence of health visiting is within its title with emphasis on 'health' and 'visiting'. Health visitors visit to advise and teach in environments, such as the home and school, where the health values of individuals are formed and reinforced.

But first the challenge of the Health Visitor Course! Held in a large cavernous classroom, Molly shared the experience with students from a range of backgrounds. Some had worked both at home and abroad in combined posts as district nurse–midwives, or in triple duty posts, which included health visiting; others had worked in management or with special health promoting projects. Three fellow students came from the Mission field so, just like Sam, Molly knew they would have some valuable experiences to share. Molly's thoughts often turned to Sam as she wondered how the monumental changes in their lives were progressing. Their Christmas card arrived with the sad news that Sarah's pregnancy had not continued but they had found a lovely home in Hampshire and were looking forward to starting their new appointments in the New Year. "See you soon, Molly," he ended. Molly received the Christmas greeting and their news with mixed feelings: so sad Sarah's pregnancy had not continued but glad that their relocation had gone smoothly. She longed to share her health visiting experience with them, including the MOH's rebuff at the interview but now was not the time.

When the Health Visitor Course was completed, Molly found it impossible to describe the experience ... "In a nutshell," she enthused, "It is one I shall never forget. I felt it dismantled my world, re-constructed it and left me with the power of a new pair of eyes." Thinking of the domain into which Miss Smith the English teacher had first shed light and fired her with the desire to unlock the many facets of poverty – not only financial. Molly felt she had been given a second chance to attend the 'Scholarship Class' at her senior school – an opportunity so carelessly rejected. The experience so impressed Molly that on qualifying as a health visitor she enrolled on the University's extra mural Social Studies Diploma Course!

Interspersed with the classroom sessions and as an introduction to her first caseload, an experienced fieldwork teacher moulded theory into the reality of the health visitor role. And so, dressed in her navy-blue suit and pillbox hat she eventually set forth to discover the area to which she had been assigned.

Molly's first visit was to a new baby. The midwife had completed her contact and the baby was 11 days old. Molly found the young mother confidently breast feeding her angel-faced child; dad and granny were in the kitchen washing up and doing a few household chores. They all joined together with a cup of coffee to talk through their queries and Molly prompted attention to the Child Health Clinic. They were well versed in the facility – the midwife has done a good job here, Molly thought! There was a feel-good factor about the home but as Molly left she hoped she had not missed anything as she reflected on her tutor's warning, "never underestimate the complexity of apparent simplicity!" Molly knew that a climate of trust was essential because unless the family moved out of the area, she would continue her contact until the child, or any future children reached school age. Long-serving health visitors often followed through to the next generation when these babies married and had children!

The weekly Child Health Clinic backed up home visits. The Clinic managed by Molly was held in a church hall at the centre of her area. At the Clinic, Molly worked harmoniously with an experienced colleague from the adjoining area who brought with her considerably well-informed know-how. The Clinic offered medical checks and immunisation programmes by a specialist child health doctor; developmental checks by the health visitor, and eight-month-old hearing checks by specialist health visitors. The Clinic also provided a space for mothers to socialise; some organised tea and biscuits, or a play area for toddlers whilst a mother took the new baby for various appointments. It was the hub of the community!

In addition to Molly's activities as the family health visitor, she developed links with specialist health visitors assigned to various hospital specialties and public health departments. For instance, it was important that sexually transmitted diseases were detected early, contacts traced and treated promptly in the best interests of the baby, its parents and the community at large. These were extremely sensitive situations which needed to be dealt with discretion and understanding

Health screening of all kinds were an essential part of antenatal care. Sometimes, however efficient a mother's antenatal care, babies were born with disabilities which required special techniques and facilities. This was a distressing time for the family; often causing the mother to berate herself for simple things she felt she had done, or not done. Molly worked alongside the parents to enable the needs of the baby and the rest of the family to be met and, in turn, Molly often learned so much from a family's creative and almost intuitive responses. She recalled one little fellow with a congenital disability and the remarkable capacity of his parents to cope. His mother was marvellous in the way she learned to nurse her son on a soft pillow and handle the child without causing injury; her reward was his smile and his bright blue eyes looking into her face.

Infancy is a vulnerable time in many ways and family life equally so. Present-day health visiting, as a means by which to respond to some of the pitfalls, stems back to the 1860's initiatives of the Manchester and Salford Sanitary Reform Society. By the turn of the century Florence Nightingale challenged health visiting to create a new area of work and a new profession for women (men were not accepted until the 1970's). And so, it has flourished to become the cornerstone of health promotion ... and without the legal powers of social work.

A number of sad events were identified in these early days and probably before. For instance, a condition known as Cot Death (now renamed Sudden Infant Death) to which children under the age of one year were particularly prone. Health visitors, working at the interface of family life, could play a critical role in prevention although all too often the cause was unknown. Times and understanding changed but it was a dreadful experience when this happened in a family, the parents were often consumed with guilt, or sensed they were blamed for negligence. Whereas, the primary need was for comfort and reassurance.

By the nineteenth century a potentially abusive childcare arrangement known as 'Baby Farming' was exposed by the activities of Margaret Walters, a baby farmer, sentenced to death for the murder/manslaughter of children and infants placed in her care. These times focused a concern from which a raft of present-day legislation was introduced and refined to protect children cared for away from their natural home.

But it soon became apparent that children needed to be safeguarded in their own homes too. By the time Molly embarked on her Health Visiting career in the 1960s, intentional injury to children within their own homes was being identified as 'Battered Baby Syndrome' (now known as 'Non-accidental Injury'). At first there was a sense of caution or even disbelief that this could happen but a pattern became apparent which helped to identify the risk factors to which health visiting and other agencies were alerted. Molly intuitively reflected back to her training days on the Children's Ward and the 'frozen watchfulness' she had begun to observe in children who were uncertain, insecure and afraid.

On the rare occasions when a cot death, or a non-accidental death occurred the repercussions for the family were dire and it's ripple across the immediate community prompted varied emotions of grief, anger, guilt, and blame as neighbours asked of themselves, "Should I have noticed?" "Could I have done something more?" The health visitor, together with other agencies was left to rebuild this shattered world notwithstanding the personally disturbing effects they too might experience. Molly remembered one Non-accidental Injury fatality in particular, where the effect on the family health visitor was palpable and she required all the support and understanding her colleagues and manager could muster. When these cases eventually appeared in the professional and national press the debate inevitably widened to include the greater society, a challenging but healthy debate that caused the professions to re-examine their practice. Sadly, on occasions the 'jig saw' phenomenon would be highlighted as different professions and agencies each held a piece of the jigsaw that was never shared and pieced together as a whole.

Inevitably, staff training and personal development was examined and new initiatives were often forthcoming. Molly recalls one Non-Accidental Injury Conference where the background effect as delegates assembled was that of a crying baby. When the first speaker was ready to begin, she stood up and switched off the tape. There was an audible sound of relief from the delegates; a resounding "Phew!" Sensing the tension in the hall, the speaker made the opening remark, "I rest my case!"

Having exposed Non-Accidental Injury and abuse, critical enquiry began to reveal the extent to which other groups such as the elderly and handicapped might also become victims. Indeed, it seemed that anyone who lacked the power to control his or her environment was at risk. As a consequence, a range of other health and social care professions became involved with health visitors and their work integrated through the Case Conference mechanism.

Rather typical of most health visiting areas, Molly's included people and families from a wide spectrum of society who were confronted with difficult choices and challenges. She began to appreciate that all families could share similar experiences to herself as a young mother – unsure, apprehensive and proud to the point of self-isolating themselves from the health visitor. In addition, under-developed parenting skills, the consequences of anti-social behaviour, poor health and poverty could compound the demands of parenthood.

Molly admired the sense of achievement experienced by mothers who came through these difficult times as confident and competent parents to become meaningful neighbours and members of their local community.

To achieve such parental maturity, support from within the family network was invaluable but there were situations when a mother may not have access to such support, or need extra help and encouragement. On such occasions the Home Help, or a Home Start volunteer might be assigned as a kind of 'home-tutor' to help develop parenting skills, family and domestic routines, and to promote the parents' understanding of their own health needs. But Molly found introducing and co-ordinating outside resources often very tricky; it was essential to preserve the dignity and build the self-esteem of the mother and her family whilst safeguarding its vulnerable members.

Clearly, family life and relationships within the community could be complex and require specialised support alongside health visiting. For example, the School Attendance Officer made a difference for children whose schooling was at risk; the Probation Officer contributed to the rehabilitation of offenders where the law had been infringed; or the National Society for the Prevention of Cruelty to Children (NSPCC) Officer where the likelihood of neglect, or cruelty became an issue. Molly, like all health visitors, was trained to attend Court when necessary but it was the one duty that the majority hoped would never be theirs to fulfil. On the other hand, Case Conferences were seen in a different light as the means by which interagency working could be monitored and strengthened according to changing circumstances. Molly found such gatherings to be generally very helpful and enlightening. Each agency seemed to hold a different part of the jigsaw and when they were all put together a very different picture could emerge.

As the children in her area grew older Molly maintained links with her families through the local Infant and Junior schools where she worked as the school nurse (traditionally nick-named 'Nitty Nora'). It was a joy to meet the children who were often spilling over with news of a new baby, or Granny who had taken them to the pictures, or 'Miss' who was getting married. But Molly's favourite school activity was the Minor Ailment Clinic. It was here that she attended to a variety of conditions from sticking plasters to more serious dressings, treating cases of infestation, and sadly, on occasions, she might detect signs of Non-accidental Injury. Molly always said it gave her a sense of being back on the Children's Ward!

No stranger to the local senior school, Molly taught on a curriculum described as 'Interpersonal relationships' – previously known as 'Sex Education' until an enlightened

Health Education Officer came into post! The sessions began by looking at the human body and the social context within which human beings live and thrive, or struggle to survive. The sessions included interpersonal relationships between friends at school, within the family, the Street community, and in the workplace. They were usually very lively sessions with most girls willing to draw on some aspect of their relationships to bring to the group – the television and radio 'Soaps' usually produced interesting issues for discussion!

A teacher was often involved in these sessions. In one sense it was a useful arrangement to contain the more boisterous pupils but in another, it could be an intimidating presence. Occasionally a girl would stay behind on the pretext of, "help you to clear up Miss?" This usually indicated the girl was troubled and Molly needed to create time and privacy to listen to and counsel the girl who may need to share distressing experiences. There were also occasions when Molly found herself in a similar position with a teacher in distress.

The problems faced by some individuals and possibly the family were complex and testing and it was at such times that Molly appreciated her nursing background, the advice of specialist health visitors who may be familiar with the situation from hospital appointments, and the support of her more experienced peers. A central base, where the health visitors usually started and sometimes ended their day promoted the importance of such networking. It was here, where health visitors received new referrals; made contact with other agencies; and benefitted from the opportunity to consult with more experienced colleagues.

Clearly, health visiting was a demanding profession and Molly appreciated the time to 'come up for air' with her own family. Outside work, whilst family activities kept Molly's feet on the ground, they were also an essential part of maintaining a strong work/family balance and for keeping in tune with each other's needs and interests. Bessie's replacement by a modern car was a great asset, which together with Ian's love of adventure provided them with access to a wide range of activities across the country. A firm favourite was the visit to the Derbyshire Peak District where they experienced the joys of riding on the open top deck of the trams at Crich Tram Museum; the exhilaration of climbing Abraham Heights (no cable cars in these times!); and spooky explorations of the disused mines and caverns. Their favourite sites included the Great Masson Cavern through which they walked and climbed with the help of a Guide and a miner's lamp to hold to light their way; Speedwell Cavern where they travelled by boat with a Guide on the underground lakes was an intriguing experience; and the Blue John Mine usually followed by a visit to the shop where Molly could never resist a little purchase of an article made from the Blue John Stone.

On occasions Gavin's schoolwork became the focus of their adventures with such projects as 'Dry Stone Walling', an attractive and functional feature of the Derbyshire countryside. Eyam, the 'Derbyshire Plague Village' was always a source of somewhat macabre fascination. Here in the mid 1600's, the Rector closed the village to contain an outbreak of the Bubonic Plague. The gruesome but heroic story presented in great detail by the Eyam Museum, and the 'Plague Register' in the village church serve as a grim reminder of Eyam's death toll and suffering. Visitors were also reminded of the symbolism of the song "Ring a ring of roses' in association with the plague! Finally, the little car left the village to wend its way home passing the defining landmark of the 'boundary stone' where supplies were left for the villagers to collect during the outbreak – no one left, or entered the village.

The weather always seemed to be just perfect on these outings, which would inevitably include a picnic on a hillside, or sometimes a rather complicated detour to visit Petal. Life had returned to a new normal for Petal. Her fourth son arrived, sound in wind and limb, the family seemed secure and complete, and gradually the Hall was refurbished and became 'home'!

Molly and Ian had many other friends, some with whom they not only kept in touch regularly but were also each other's houseguests from time to time. Molly's 'posh' friend, Vera from part-time hospital nursing days, who now lived in a small village in Hampshire, provided the most excitement for long weekends and summer holidays! The avant-garde couple were delightful hosts and their little Hampshire village was rather special with its close access to the seaside. The local self-pick strawberry fields were an added attraction for Joy and Gavin who, when presenting their basket to be weighed did so with a broad smile and strawberry stained mouths!

During these holidays, Molly and Vera played with the children, read a book, or just sunbathed with the protection of Katie Boyle's purported recommended concoction of olive oil and vinegar – their skin must have fried but it certainly kept away the flies! The children played on the beach and in the receding tide they dug up lugworms for Gavin's fishing expeditions. A local shopkeeper gave them free use of his beach hut where tea was always on tap and when Vera's mother came to stay, teatime was embellished with her Lardy cake! Ian loved Lardy cake! Sometimes, he stayed on with the family and their days on the beach were interspersed with visits to the Zoo and trips on the Watercress Line steam railway with Vera telling of its historical commercial function.

Looking back, they were the kind of holidays that dreams were made of – even the disasters, which were indelibly marked in their memories, provided a strange kind of amusement in retrospect. Gavin seemed particularly vulnerable! For instance, one breezy day with an off-shore wind saw the children running up and down the beach delighting in the swirls and turns of their kites when a sudden unexpected sharp gust whipped the bobbin out of Gavin's hand and the kite flew off out to sea with Gavin left in dire distress after his unsuccessful chase. But the kite was gone forever.

And so their holidays would unfold with seemingly innocent pastimes that sometimes turned into near disaster, such as the fishing exploits that Gavin and his father enjoyed. One day whilst fishing from the headland Gavin felt a mighty tug on the line and with their combined efforts, they hauled in the writhing mass to find they had caught a large energetic conger eel. The eel was strong and wriggled around uncontrollably eventually wrapping itself around Gavin's legs – it was a miracle that Gavin was not pulled over the cliff edge. The incident brought back a similar memory of a family holiday in a cottage at the water's edge in Salcombe - when the tide came in the water came up to the windows! On that particular holiday a neighbour had lent Ian an inflatable dingy in which he and Gavin sat happily fishing almost within reach of the window. Suddenly the boat rapidly disappeared across the water with Ian frantically shouting, "Let go of the line" - Gavin had caught a conger eel and they were in danger of being taken out to sea!

Oh! The thrills and spills of their family life and Gavin seemed to be fearless. Having long outgrown the little pedal car, Ian and Gavin embarked on a project to build a Go-cart. It turned out to be a splendid contraption with a wooden platform set on a front and rear axle to support four wheels and the steering manoeuvre was undertaken with a piece of fine rope used like the harness of a horse. The driver had a nicely appointed seat with a pad of carpet near the front platform for his feet. Ian fixed a 'Registration Plate' front and rear with the number 'ZZV1' – from memory, it had a link with 'Z Cars' the popular TV serial of the day. Gavin perfected the skill of racing quite fearlessly down the streets on his Go-Cart. Joy caught the bus to her Grammar School from the main road each morning and Gavin was always a willing taxi service if she was running short of time; and late afternoon he patiently waited at the bus stop for her return.

As time went by, after the untimely death of Joey the tortoise, Molly encouraged the children to have other pets. Joy chose a rabbit she named 'Bun'. Bun was a cheeky and self-willed chappie. To attract attention whilst in his cage he would bang his back paws on the floor, which made the children think of 'Thumper'. Ian often took Bun out of his cage to be with him whilst he worked in the garage; Ian talked to the rabbit who ran around with Ian like his shadow. But Bun had a mind of his own, and when Ian came to the end of his work saying, "Come along, time to go back home," Bun stood on his hind legs and 'boxed' Ian with his front paws!

Needless to say, there were occasions when the interests of Molly's family life came into conflict with her work commitments, such as times of sickness and the long school holidays when her holiday entitlement had expired! At these times the support given by Molly's parents was inestimable and the children always welcomed any excuse to stay with Nannan-Rose and Granddad. Joy was no problem; she was so engrossed in school that whilst staying with her grandparents she attended the village school until their term closed and as a consequence, she developed friendships with the local children that were to last for life! Gavin was less enthusiastic about school; he couldn't wait to join Kate's boys in their rough and tumbles.

Interspersed with all these adventures Molly, like the children returning to school, she too needed to refocus on the task ahead - health visiting. On one occasion Molly's return coincided with a staff meeting to discuss the pros and cons of operating from satellite bases adjacent to their health visiting areas. Whilst there were mixed feelings about the loss of a central workplace the decision seemed inevitable. Molly was transferred to a satellite base on the outskirts of town where she worked with a group of six other health visitors and the local district nurses. The two groups had little opportunity to mix because they occupied separate parts of the building and their duties rarely coincided. When Molly did happen to meet with the district nurses, she found them to be a friendly group and intensely enthusiastic about their work.

As time passed, Molly began to make time to spend with the nurses; she was becoming curious about their work, their duty rota and training. This seems to be more than a passing interest, mused Gwen! And, sure enough after several years as a health visitor Molly began to think about a career in District Nursing.

However, this time Ian was involved from a very early stage, which was inevitable because Molly made friends with one of the nurses who always had problems with her car and sought Ian's help on a regular basis! Joy and Gavin were older, established at school, and beginning to develop their individual interests and ambitions. Molly could hardly contain herself with optimism about her newly found interest, which unfortunately would not be the 9am – 5pm weekday commitment that had been so convenient for family life.

Once again, the family took a break on the East coast, this time inviting Rose to join them. Whilst Rose and the children competed in building the best sandcastle, finding the most unusual shells and catching crabs, Ian and Molly just talked. It was a lovely relaxing holiday and on the last day Rose and Molly visited the hairdresser for a 'tidy-up' before they returned home. Rose had pure white hair and the stylist suggested a colour rinse. Rose was apprehensive but the stylist was persuasive and a pale blue rinse applied. Rose might well have been apprehensive because when Wills saw the result he was most put out, saying she looked like a 'fallen woman'. The rinse was washed out immediately and never to be repeated!

A letter from Sam and Sarah telling of the challenges of their new posts and the joy of finding their ideal home was clouded by a suggestion the Sam had not been as well as he might have been. Molly responded wanting to know more and sharing her interest in district nursing. Sarah's reply awaited their return to say that Sam had just been discharged from a spell in hospital suffering from a viral infection, which has left behind complications that are proving difficult to resolve… "but seems to be on the mend – prospects look hopeful," she wrote.

As the children grew older, Molly's career needed to accommodate new interests. First and foremost, came the need to encourage their schoolwork, out of school activities, and family times together. Gavin joined a Scout Group and Ian was drawn to support various activities. Joy joined a ballet class – well, it was not surprising that she exhibited a gift for the performing arts given Nannan-Rose and Molly's undisputed flare! Joy was a dedicated pupil who needed little encouragement to practice her exercises or prepare for a stage performance. Kate, having three boys, also took an interest in Joy's activities and made creative contributions to her dance-costumes. A 'Little Drummer Boy' outfit in red silk, edged with gold braid and a black silk top hat; a huntsman's bold red waistcoat and peak cap, (granddad Wills provided the riding crop), and an elaborate tutu for one of Joy's ballet examinations were perhaps the most spectacular! Throughout her life Joy was destined to be a bit of a 'Diva'; a 'mover' who responded to any hint of a rhythm and a sense of fun, which inspired many flagging parties.

Joy's ballet teacher was a homely, rotund lady who one could never image performing a pirouette. But she was a lively happy person who engaged well with her pupils. Much to Molly's delight, the teacher encouraged them to visit performing arts productions as often as they could, or she would chaperone a class visit to a theatre, sometimes in neighbouring towns. It was on one such visit to see a new production of 'The Firebird' ballet, that Molly had taken Joy to meet the rest of the class at the bus station. Joy started to cry because she didn't want to leave Molly behind. Somewhat mystified, because Joy was a gregarious and independent young person, Molly felt she had no choice but to hop on the bus! On arrival at their destination Molly telephoned Ian with news of her whereabouts. "Surprise, surprise," he said laughing because he knew Molly's love of the ballet.

It was not unexpected that both Joy and Gavin were musically gifted within a family where music was enjoyed for its own sake ... even including Ian's, if somewhat self-deprecating, accomplishments as a drummer and piano accordionist in various groups! Joy played the piano, clarinet and guitar but it was as a Clarinettist that she was selected to play with the City's Senior Schools' Concert Band. – a vinyl record of one concert is a family treasure! Gavin developed considerable flare as a Cornet player in his School's Band and later in a local

Brass Band where he soon rose to the position of Principal Cornet player in the Junior Section.

Needless to say, Ian and Molly attended the children's appearances at school concerts, events in the local parks and Joy's performances on stage. A family first came the year Gavin's Brass Band successfully reached the semi-finals of the National Brass Band Competitions held at the Royal Albert Hall. Sadly, Gavin's band did not qualify for the finals but it was a most proud and memorable occasion. The experience alone of sitting in the vast ornate space of the Royal Albert Hall in the heart of London was out of this world and one that would never be forgotten.

When they went to stay with Nannan-Rose, Joy and Gavin took their instruments with them – Gavin giving a short excerpt from the Royal Albert Hall performance, and Joy a clarinet solo from her Concert Band's recent concert. A fine time was had round the old piano with Rose accompanying them – her left hand playing the right-hand music as usual! Nannan-Rose and Auntie Kate always welcomed Joy and Gavin to their country retreats wondering what new interests they would produce and sometimes Joy and Gavin delivered one or two surprises!

One of the great rewards for Molly and Ian was to witness Gavin's quiet personality shining through at school – and to be noticed! For instance, at parents' evening the teachers would inevitably comment on his integrity and sense of fair play. One teacher said, "Gavin is not beyond a bit of mischief but when I ask the class for the culprit to own up, there is usually a deathly silence; except if it were Gavin and he would shoot up saying, "Me, Sir!" "I can tell you," the teacher would say, scratching his head, "it was a bit off-putting to be confronted with such honesty, it quite took the wind out of my sails!" These virtues were eventually to shine throughout in his business enterprises and married life.

THE WORLD OF DISTRICT NURSING:

Molly was counselled by her Health Visitor Superintendent that the decision to transfer to district nursing was a retrograde career move – it seemed there was always the suggestion of a white-collar v blue-collar worker issue between health visiting and district nursing! So, Molly felt she took a leap of faith as she made her application for a vacancy in an area affiliated to the Queen's Nursing Institute (QNI) - initially, titled the Queen Victoria Institute of District Nursing when on the occasion of Her Majesty's Jubilee (1887) she lent her name and invested resources to raising the national profile and standard of district nursing for the provision of expert nursing care for the sick and dying in their own homes. The QNI set and maintained professional standards by creating a Roll of Queen's Nurses, together with a syllabus of training and conditions of entry to the Roll for qualified General Nurses. Once qualified and admitted to the Roll, regular attendance at refresher courses, specific preparation for teaching and management roles, and periodic work-place inspection by QNI officers was obligatory. Professional regulation of district nursing was a huge step forward and one aided by earlier visionaries such as Florence Nightingale's contribution to a qualified nursing profession and William Rathbone's pioneering efforts at Liverpool Infirmary to equip hospital trained nurses with the skills to work in the homes of the sick poor in Liverpool.

Royal patronage was not a sleeping partner but one that showed particular regard for the 'foot soldiers' – the district nurses. For instance, invitations to the Royal Garden Party each summer were issued to the QNI for distribution amongst the nurses; and Queen's Nurses achieving 21 years' service were personally presented with the Long Service Award by the Royal Patron, or a member of the Royal Family.

In a lighter vein, the district nurse captured the imagination of lyricists such as Marty Feldman's 1970's rendition of 'District Nurse Hargreaves' portraying the district nurse as a figure of desire!

And so it was, nearly a century after the establishment of the QNI that Molly stepped into this fine tradition. On the first day of her appointment Molly reported to the Centre Superintendent, Miss Todd, where she met her course mentor, an experienced district nurse titled Practical Work Teacher. Molly was acquainted with her 'District' towards the outskirts of the City, provided with a Register of her patients, and briefly introduced to the team of variously trained nurses she would lead in due course. Molly was fitted with the distinctive 'Queen's' uniform comprising a mid-blue dress, navy-blue coat, and an airhostess type chip-hat; once qualified she would be presented with the QNI bronze medallion on a cord of the Institute's blue and silver colours to wear. Finally, Molly was issued with her nursing bags and equipment and given a demonstration of the contents and use. And she set off on her great adventure with her Mentor!

It surprised Molly that people in the streets readily greeted the nurses with a smile and gave them preferential recognition saying, "You go first nurse, we know you are busy"; the policeman on duty at the busy road junctions in the town would control the traffic in their favour; and in the inclement weather people were quick to help with a nurse's unresponsive motor car.

As Molly moved through the district nurse training, she discovered a new dimension of nursing. She found that whilst the home might be seen as a microcosm of the ward environment providing professional nursing care, support for relatives and friends, and working in partnership with other agencies - the reality was very different!

Eventually, the day arrived for Molly's practical assessment by a QNI Inspector (a Queen's Nurse). With her car and nursing bags in mint condition, her uniform freshly laundered and pressed for the occasion, Molly waited at the Nurses' Centre for the call. However, the call when it came was not the call she expected! The doorbell rang several times with a sense of urgency, Molly responded only to be grabbed by the arm by a lady shouting, "Come quick, my husband is bleeding to death." Molly looked over her shoulder to check that a colleague was aware of the situation before being led to the house and the scene of the crisis. The husband was indeed experiencing a severe nosebleed – there was blood everywhere. Molly gave first aid and eventually arrested the bleeding. She gave his wife follow-up instructions and suggested a colleague be asked to call and check on progress. Returning to the Nurses' Centre, Molly repaired the damage to her appearance and answered the ringing of the doorbell for the second time to greet the QNI Inspector ... thankfully her arrival had been delayed by heavy traffic! Not the start to her practical assessment that Molly would have planned but it was an interesting duty and one that ended successfully for Molly. The written examination proceeded with less drama!

Now a qualified Queen's Nurse, complete with bronze medallion, Molly and her team entered heart and soul into their work on the district. It never ceased to surprise Molly how often she encountered scenes reminiscent of Rose's sickbay in her childhood home. For instance, in circumstances where a patient's illness involved long-term disabilities, limited mobility, or end-of-life care a bed was brought downstairs and the patient was nursed at the centre of family life. But all too often their low, soft, and probably double sized bed was unsuitable for the appropriate care of the patent, the safety of their carers, and the district nurse. However, left upstairs, the patient was isolated and the repeated climbing up and down the stairs increased the demands on the relatives. So, whilst relatives prepared the front room or a corner of the living room Molly would be reunited with the hospital bed and probably a selection of the paraphernalia reminiscent to that in use on the Orthopaedic Ward! Such as an overhead pulley, or a rope ladder attached to the foot of the bed to assist the patient's independence; a freestanding hoist made moving the patients easier and more comfortable - the 'donkey' had long been discarded due to the risk of circulation problems.

Stanley was one example of a patient suffering with a chronic form of restrictive arthritis who benefited from such arrangements. A sofa bed was also transferred into the large bay window recess for his wife to 'put her feet up' during the day, or to sleep on when she wanted to be near to Stanley at night. The arrangement made such a difference for them – Stanley's wife would laughingly remark, "We just love our little bed-sit and I have the rest of the house in which to amuse myself!" They worshipped at the local church and Stanley had been a member of the local Masonic Lodge so they were never without visitors for moral support. Stanley was a jigsaw fanatic, now with his wife's help - "he sorts the pieces and I fix them together," she explained.

However, in some circumstances young children helped care for the parent. Such was the case with Nancy's children who, when Dad worked early shifts, prepared Nancy's breakfast, gave her a bowl of water to wash her face and a toothbrush to clean her teeth. The children went off to school and Molly arrived to give Nancy the attention she needed. Sometimes Nancy would shed a tear because she felt she was "putting old heads on young shoulders. They must have their childhood, Nurse." In search of a solution to Nancy's concerns Molly, together with the health visitor, explored every opportunity to ensure the children's needs were met and the family flourished. The plight of such young carers was poignantly highlighted by a study titled, 'Who cares in Southwark?' Nancy lived at the heart of the family performing the role and responsibilities of motherhood from her bed, or wheelchair. The Home Help Service also supported her in the form of a lady who was more of a companion and who respected Nancy's position in the driving seat of her own home.

By contrast, life was not so easy for Tony in a small-palisaded cottage living with elderly parents. Tony, a young man in his twenties was severely incapacitated in a freak sports injury; he was bedfast and nursed in the family living room. Whilst it was a convenient arrangement for his parents with their health problems, Tony felt he lacked privacy, particularly to continue his relationship with girlfriend, Sally and when his 'mates' came round. It was quite a challenge to reconcile Tony's need for privacy and self-expression with that of his care and family life. Practical problems were more easily dealt with; the demands of extra laundry were met by the Laundry Service, the Meals on Wheels Service provided a mid-day meal for them all, and once again the home help shared in their cleaning and shopping requirements. Molly worked alongside the social worker and remedial therapists to address Tony's more complex needs. Eventually, the family recognised that it was in Tony's best interest for him to reside in the front room and once the move was made Tony's horizons widened. He felt part of the street community as passers-by waved to him; and his private life and remedial activities looked more promising.

Provision of end-of-life care in the home followed similar patterns and the emotional demands on the family were equally challenging. Whatever the situation, relatives inevitably became very tired and weary providing full time care at home where they could not walk away after 'visiting times' for the ward staff to take over. In such circumstances day and/or night volunteer sitters from a local Charity would be arranged to give the relative a break. The break enabled the carer to visit the hairdresser, meet a friend for coffee, or just take time out in the garden and of course during the night, to take advantage of a night's rest. As Molly gained experience, she recognised that the district nurse was not only part of a nursing team, but of a complex team involving other agencies. Molly often said she felt like the conductor of an orchestra!

Consequently, these routines would involve complex planning activities. For instance, some patients required several visits each day, say morning, afternoon, early evening; and possibly during the night for which purpose a full-time district night nursing service operated from the Ambulance Station from 8pm – 8am. Molly also recognised the value of working closely with the family doctor by arranging bedside consultations because they demonstrated the important partnership in care between the doctor, nurse, the patient and family. In a similar way, she liaised with the clergy for pastoral care, the social worker, or remedial therapists for counsel and advice – spiritual needs were not necessarily ones of religion but those of uncertainty, loss of hope, and despair. There was so much more for Molly to learn – it was a whole new world outside the hospital!

The Centre Superintendent, Miss Todd was only too conscious of these demands and responsibilities as she buzzed around the districts in her Wolsey Hornet car waiting to spot one of her nurses' cars parked outside a patient's home. It was remarkable how well the Superintendent knew all the patients her nurses attended and their particular problems ... and the patients knew the Superintendent, or of her! So, she would nip out of her car, tap on the patient's door, open it and say, "Hello, Miss Todd here. Just thought I would pop in whilst nurse is with you." The patients and their families were always pleased to see the Superintendent but woe-betide the nurse if she was taking any shortcuts! On other occasions Miss Todd would spend the whole of the round teaching, supervising and working with a Nurse.

Some patients were very private, or proud and it was respected that they would not always wish to share their concerns. Nevertheless, it seemed to Molly that an experienced district nurse usually found a way round the stumbling block. For example, one male district nurse always shared breakfast time tea and toast with an elderly, genteel, diabetic lady who lived alone. The patient thought she was looking after 'her' nurse whilst the nurse was ensuring his patient ate breakfast after receiving her insulin injection and that she was left with a 'good fire'. Clearly, this was more than 'tea and toast'; it was pastoral care and informed altruism. These hidden talents of a district nurse bemused Gwen as she observed Molly developing her own repertoire of sensitivities.

However, when some ladies of similarly refined traditions gave up their home, they may choose to live in a hotel rather than a residential home. Molly attended two such ladies who enjoyed 'hotel life' because of the changing faces of the residents. They enjoyed eavesdropping, or even joining in with the young travellers (Reps) who sat at the bar exchanging stories following a busy day promoting their merchandise or delivering their services. The hotel was also patronised by actors due to perform at the local theatre and sometimes they would entertain the hotel guests with short excerpts from their performance – the ladies thought this was a great treat!

Molly, like her colleagues, was often quite concerned by the personal and physical demands some relatives experienced in caring for their loved ones, and some patients did not always make life easy for their carers. The district nurse in charge of an area adjacent to Molly's and whom Molly relieved on her day off, noticed the emotional stress a husband began to show in caring for his bed-bound wife. The nurse used considerable ingenuity one Christmas to help him find his own space and interests by presenting him with a set of painting by numbers cards and paints. This seemingly simple idea opened a new world of interest for him and one, with the help of a 'sitter' for his wife, which eventually inspired him to visit the library and art galleries in the town. The day came when he whipped off the cover from the easel secreted in a back room to show the nurse his developing talents in oils!

That same Christmas, a card from Tommy and Lizzy reminded Molly of the challenges they had faced in order to create hope and new aspirations out of despondency. Tommy told of the improved state of health he was maintaining with the help of his doctors and his continuing enthusiasm for his hospital work. Lizzy was well and now working in partnership with her father in the family business. Dear Lizzy, Tommy's praise for her was boundless. Molly happily returned their good wishes and told of the twists and turns in her own life and that of her family.

Molly identified with Lizzy because throughout her career as a district nurse her regard for the carers, or supporters was paramount. In fact, Molly may comment on occasions that she would not immediately recognise who was the patient and who was the carer – they might both appear to be frail. The words of

Molly's Tutor, Sister Sparrow, often rang in her ears, "Use your five senses, Nurse – and don't forget the 6th! A message echoed by Miss Todd who ran the District Nursing Course, to which she would add … "Always observe and act – if you start to step over the proverbial 'hole in the carpet', then, just like the patient you to will get used to it and forget it is there until one day it will be your down-fall too" Molly was to realize that the district nurse needed the tact of a diplomat; wisdom of Solomon; integrity of a saint, and the compassion of Mother Teresa.

District Nursing and Molly fitted together like a hand in a glove! Molly's 'District' was her special place: a place that probably, quite unknowingly, resonated with a distant memory of the 'Fairy Dell' of her childhood! And Gwen? Could it be that almost by symbiosis Gwen had infiltrated too when Molly fondly tapped the car roof declaring, "Min and I are a team"?!
Ian and Gavin, however, were less enamoured by 'Min' on account of the amount of time they spent in repairing the punctures Molly regularly collected on her rounds! This proved to be a good training ground for Gavin that was not appreciated at the time!

The residents living on her District knew Molly's visiting pattern. As 'Min' signalled her arrival, it was not unusual for a curtain to twitch and the occupant to nip out and make a request, or share a concern, for instance, one neighbour intercepted Molly on an early morning call saying, "I know it's not your day to visit Julie, but her downstairs light was on all night and I wondered if she is OK Nurse?" Molly assured the kindly neighbour she would, "look in." A less direct approach might be a note left under Min's windscreen wiper – say, "Can you call at No. 14 before you leave, please Nurse? Dads stubbed his toe and it looks nasty." Or, "Can you pop into 'Goodwin's (the corner shop) please nurse? Our Fred woke up covered in a rash and he is not himself." Molly always responded - no plea passed unheard.

But contagious diseases required a sensitive, well-informed approach - the right decisions were critical within the test – trace – treat framework. The role of the district nurse was largely involved with 'treating' - 'hands-on' activities involving 'Barrier nursing' routines combined with health teaching and other preventive measures.

Barrier nursing, as set out in the textbook, *'District Nursing'*, by Merry and Irven, could be a considerable imposition on the family. It required the patient's crockery and linen to be stored and washed separately and used solely for the infectious patient. The district nurse's protective clothing and the equipment needed to nurse the patient safely were retained in the sick room, together with separate protective clothing for any relative who might need to attend the patient in the nurse's absence. Molly often recalled how smoothly and efficiently it all worked once the routines were set up and the goodwill of the relatives achieved. The nurses were also required to arrange other safeguards such as the management of 'Fomites', which included books, jigsaw puzzles, and soft toys used by the patient. Fomites remained in the patient's room throughout the period of infection and destroyed or sent to be autoclaved if removed. When the patient had recovered, the nurse notified the local health department who may arrange for fumigation of the sickroom.

However, sometimes both district nurses and health visitors would find their visits complicated by 'Household Pests', or patients infested with hair and body lice; scabies and ringworm. Thankfully, their training and textbooks gave explicit safeguarding measures for themselves, their patients, and the community in which they worked. Fortunately, Molly's district was not known for such hazards but she was always prepared should she need to relieve colleagues whose patients were in a different position.

In rather moving and sometimes subtle ways, the patients and their families 'cared' for the nurse. For instance, on a cold, wet day the nurse's coat would be warmed at the fire along with her gloves and scarf, notwithstanding the strict codes of practice to prevent cross infection and infestation from home to home (the coat and nursing bags were always placed on clean newspaper laid on a hard surface). The patients and their families loved to share hospitality and celebrations. A hot drink in the winter and cold drink in the hot weather was offered, "To keep you going, Nurse." Even forbidden fruits would be made available, "a drop of toddy in your coffee this morning nurse, it's cold out there?" And one winter's evening one elderly patient asked, "Would you share a nip of Ginger Wine with me Nurse? It's my birthday today," her hand hovering over the nicely presented tray of glasses and birthday cake. Just the same concern was shown to the nursing equipment left in the home where it was almost always, regarded by the family with the respect of the crown jewels and the brown envelope containing the nursing notes, which sat on the mantelpiece, was guarded with the diligence of the Official Secrets Act.

Trust was critical; patients trusted the nurse with their secrets, intimate moments, their welfare, and the freedom of their home. On the other hand, the nurse trusted the patient to be honest, to fulfil their part by alerting the nurse about any concerns. The relationship was very special and most district nurses can tell of the most touching moments. For instance, Molly will always remember the young executive, Adam and his wife, Beth who had recently moved to the town on promotion. Shortly afterwards Adam became ill and diagnosed with a terminal malignant condition. One morning after completing his nursing care it was clear Adam's condition was deteriorating and Beth said, "Please will you say the Rosary with us Nurse?" Molly was not of the Roman Catholic denomination but as she knelt at the bedside with the wife of her dying husband, she realized the privileges afforded to a district nurse were indeed unique. To be in a position to meet a patient's, or a relative's spiritual (not necessarily religious) needs in such times of uncertainty and loss was really quite humbling.

However, there were occasions when the district nurse became involved with religious practices in different ways. Molly often recalls the occasions she was assigned a new case of male child circumcision. Sometimes, such cases were referred by the hospital following surgery but on others a leader of the Jewish tradition would request assistance with the religious ritual at home – usually on a Sunday morning. Molly attended but found she was not required to participate merely to provide support as required. Once the ritual had been performed Molly checked the dressing and left the family to return the same evening and for several following days to check on the infant. Life as a district nurse was certainly full of variety.

Once a patient died, the district nurse usually continued to 'support' the bereaved for a while. Molly often recalls the impact on two brothers following the death of their bedridden mother for whom they had cared over many years, assisted by Molly during the last weeks of their mother's life. Now the brothers were in need of support themselves. Bereavement visits were usually arranged for mid-morning when 'coffee time' provided a quiet, relaxed atmosphere to talk about the loss, reflect on the impact of the changed circumstances, and to unobtrusively check on the health and well-being of the bereaved. One winter's morning just before Christmas, Molly arrived to check the brothers were organised and OK about Christmas – the first without their mother. Isaac, the elder of the two seemed to be the more outward looking but George was usually quiet and introspective ... "always got his head in a book," tutted Isaac. Neither of them was interested in the local church of which their parents had been members all their lives, so Molly touched on the facilities of Age Concern knowing the local organisation provided for a wide range of interests. She gave them the contact details and left the brothers to make up their own minds ... and they did just that. Molly learned later they were collected by a local volunteer and taken to the Christmas Party and in the spring, Molly met them on the local park pulling their little cases on wheels saying they had joined the local outdoor bowling club ... they had made it!

Later in the summer she met Nancy on the park. The family had moved into a nearby bungalow; Nancy had a motorised scooter and her children were on their bicycles riding beside her on their way to the play area. The 'District' was just an amazing community – just like the Policeman's Beat', Molly supposed; she and her little 'Mini' were well known and it was where Molly felt district nurses made a difference to people during times of sickness and uncertainty.

But there were surprises off the 'District' too. One night on Front of House duty at the local theatre, a young woman and her companion offered their tickets before entering the auditorium. They smiled at each other and froze in sudden remembrance ... it was the wife of the young executive with whom Molly had said the Rosary as he lay dying. "Beth." "Nurse." they exclaimed in unison! Beth turned to her companion saying, "Robert, this is the district nurse who cared for us when Adam was dying." Molly knew Robert; he worked in the 'Lighting Box'. "Whoa! Whoa!" he said. "You certainly hide your light under a bushel, I didn't realise you are the Florence Nightingale Beth often speaks about!" Memories flooded back and they agreed to meet in the Bar after the show. In the Bar, Molly listened whilst Beth reflected on her life since Adam's death, her meeting Robert and their pending move to a seaside town in Cornwall to set up a 'Novelty shop and Ice-cream Parlour'. 'Well, well, well!' Molly smiled as she drove home that night.

Not all bereavements and adversities in life ended in these ways; it seemed that some carers invested so much of themselves into their difficult times they found it hard to reinvest when the time came. Molly was always overwhelmed by the privilege of being able to play a small part in restoring poverty of spirit and personal aspiration ... a mission triggered by Miss Smith, her English teacher all those years ago!

By contrast, there were many humorous situations 'on the district', particularly those involving the patients' pets. Take for instance the morning Molly was scheduled to take another nurse's patients! Each morning the Superintendent, or a deputy checked the post and the telephone-answering machine for any messages, or perhaps take a call from a nurse who had fallen ill. The extra work was then distributed to the nurses on duty. This routine took place at 8am, 2pm and 4.30pm every day.

On the morning in question, Molly received her call at 8am from one of the Senior (male) district nurses relieving Miss Todd's day off. He gave Molly the additional patients to visit and when it came to the last one, he said "Just mind the bird". Hearing Molly's exclamation he reassured, "Don't worry, it is in a cage but can be noisy." Molly duly arrived at the house where the door was ajar and as she entered, she called, "Hello, district nurse." The patient responded and Molly walked through to the living room where she was greeted by a loud whistle and "I say, what a smasher." Molly saw the 'speaker', a bird – a beautiful, black as coal Mynah bird. Its large cage seemed to extend from floor to ceiling and protruded into the room about the width of a sideboard; several large branches crisscrossed the cage and there perched the bird. Greeting over, Molly carried out the treatment, prepared to leave and following her farewells came the call, "OK. Buggar off then."

The presence of a bird was totally unacceptable in a room where the nurse was treating a patient, the cage was either removed or the patient taken to another room. One lady Molly visited from time to time was well used to this routine and as usual her pet budgie, Gertie, was taken into the kitchen. After the treatment was completed, Molly returned the birdcage and said, "Goodbye." As Molly reached the front door, she heard, "Oh, by the way, Nurse ..." This, not unusual tactic, is known as the 'door knob syndrome' - a burning question the patient had been longing ask but felt she/he couldn't until this desperate attempt. So Molly turned her head to listen ... and returned to sit with the patient. "Could you have a look at Gertie before you go please? She flutters to the bottom of her cage because she cannot stay on her perch?" Adding, that she thought Gertie's toenails were too long and prevented her from gripping the perch. "Could you give her nails a quick trim with your clippers, Nurse?" Molly, fearing that the bird's nails were perhaps not the problem, suggested it would be best to have

Gertie checked by the Vet, "He's the expert." "OK Nurse you are perhaps right. My nephew is coming tonight I will get him to see things. Thank you ... You are a love." The next time Molly visited the birdcage was not in the room. The patient was very upset, "Gertie only just survived the journey to the Vet, Nurse. He told my nephew that Gertie was much older than we realised and was very frail. He sent me his condolences with the reassurance that Gertie had such a long and happy life because I had looked after her so well. I felt better knowing she hadn't died through my neglect." Molly made a cup of tea and as they sat and drank it together, they talked about Gertie. "What shall I do? Gertie was such company for me!" Bereavement came in all forms on the district and grief from the loss of a pet can be quite profound and a situation the district nurse ignores at considerable cost to her patient.

Molly quickly began to appreciate that when she lifted a ringing telephone, or opened the door to step inside a patient's home to always be ready for the unexpected. Perhaps one of the most unexpected and exciting (in retrospect) began with an eight o'clock telephone call from Miss Todd. Would Molly make her first call to a young lady who had unexpectedly given birth during the night? Mothers who gave birth without any antenatal care and therefore screening for hazards such as infection were not assigned to the midwife but to the district nurse in order to protect other mothers and their babies. The QNI training prepared district nurses to manage these extremely occasional events and Molly's midwifery experience held her in good stead.

Molly arrived to be greeted by the girl's anxious parents with an account of the situation. Their daughter had not been feeling well for a day or two when this morning they awakened to the sound of a baby crying. Rushing to their daughter's room they found the baby still attached to their daughter and lying on the bed crying. The doctor was called and had "attended to things"; now it was over to the district nurse. Molly peeped round the bedroom door to find a frightened looking young Mum cradling her baby son. The girl was very tearful and whilst Molly was taking her history, "…. I didn't tell Mum the full story because I was afraid I was seriously ill. I went to bed early last night and woke up with griping pains in my stomach and back followed by a flood of liquid, I thought I had an accident - the baby just came out."

Molly listened sympathetically and made preparation to wash mother and babe and make them comfortable – the doctor had done the rest. First Mum, who when settled in a clean nightie, her hair brushed and swinging in a ponytail sat on the edge of the bed and took great interest in what Molly was doing with her baby. After washing him and dusting him with powder he smelt like a meadow of wildflowers. Next, to weigh him and for this purpose a net bag and a pair of spring scales were included in the 'midwifery bag'. A photograph displayed on the QNI publicity material of a district nurse weighing a baby suspended from the scales in a net might have been Molly!

The baby weighed in at a healthy 7lbs; the little fella didn't have a name and to keep calling him, he, and 'it' was unacceptable. So as the secrecy surrounding the black cat at home flashed before Molly's eye, she suggested 'Moses' because he too had been hidden away! So Moses was named and thrived during the time Molly attended and his mother positively blossomed.

Certainly, one of the most challenging situations in which Molly was ever placed on the 'District' was the day she conducted a routine supervision with a district nurse student. All district nurses were first required to possess the SRN qualification, together with experience as a ward staff nurse, or a post-basic qualification. This particular student was experienced in heart and chest specialties. The task that morning, to clean a tracheotomy tube, was one with which the student would have been very familiar (*A tracheotomy is performed when a patient's upper respiratory breathing is compromised. An incision is made in the throat and a device is inserted into the windpipe to keep the airway open. The device includes an inner and outer tube; the inner tube is rigid to keep the opening patent and the inner one flexible to be removed and cleaned free from debris).*

As usual, before entering the home they discussed the case, and confirmed the student's understanding of, and competence to deal with the procedure. "Sure," said the student, "no problem, worked on the 'Chest Ward' too long to mess it up!" However, Molly sitting close by during the procedure became aware that the nurse was rather quiet and seemed a little flustered; the patient's breathing was also becoming laboured. The nurse had taken out both tubes and the soft tissue was beginning to swell from her attempts to re-insert the outer tube. A '999' call was made and the situation resolved by the arrival of ambulance personnel who administered oxygen and transferred the patient to hospital for the tubes to be reinserted. All's well that ends well thought Molly as she planned to suggest a study session around the procedure.

Life was full of surprises 'on the district' but Molly's encounter with a house of multiple-occupation was particularly memorable! Her visit was made in response to a hospital referral to a young man following an appendectomy operation. Having located the address at a large Victorian Villa, Molly rang the bell and waited ... and waited. On the third ring a dishevelled young man answered the door and Molly introduced herself. She was guided upstairs into a very large bedroom packed tightly with beds, all touching each other and mostly occupied by sleeping men. Turning to her escort he pointed to a bed in the far corner of the room. Molly raised her eyebrows, opened out her hands and said, "Come, please." "No, very sick you go," came the reply – was he really expecting Molly to climb across the beds she wondered? After some negotiation the young man scrambled across to sit in a chair placed in the space created by the open door. His post-operative recovery was progressing satisfactorily and he was fit and able so Molly suggested he attended the District Nurses' Clinic in town. The Clinic was the brainchild of Miss Todd for such occasions to ensure a safe and convenient environment to carryout sterile and other risky procedures.

Situations on the District were becoming more complex and with the increasing influx of people from other parts of the world the district nurse encountered many new challenges due to language barriers, different lifestyles and health issues. Health Visitors were using graphics to aid communication; some health visitors and district nurses were learning the new languages; the Health Education Department prepared notices and leaflets in multiple languages; and district nurses were also challenged to become inventive. Although a rather fearsome lady, Miss Todd was far-seeing and generally acknowledged to be ahead of her time; she broadened the teaching on the district nurse course and developed new ways of working long before they appeared on the National Curriculum, or as local policy. Furthermore, Miss Todd knew her staff well! She made every effort to utilise and develop their particular areas of interest and expertise. Molly's potential seemed to be recognised by offering her teaching assignments and involving her in inter-agency meetings. On one occasion Miss Todd surprised Molly by inviting her to an open meeting of her Soroptimist Branch. It was many years later that Molly realised the opportunity she had been given ... like the 'School Certificate Stream' of years gone by!

In these early days of Molly's District Nursing career, disposable equipment was in its infancy and in the home, the long-standing fail-safe methods of the QNI were still employed. For instance, a surgical dressing would require the patient/family to provide a saucepan containing two cups with handles and a saucer; the saucepan filled with water to cover the contents and placed on to boil ready for the nurse to add her instruments and boil for twenty minutes. In addition, a medium sized (biscuit) tin would be requested and the patient/family shown how to prepare a sterile dressing pack. First to cut a square of greaseproof paper, or clean white linen, say 10"x10"; then several strips of gauze cut from a roll to make a square dressing, with frayed edges turned inside, were laid onto the square, topped with a number of cotton wool balls made from a roll of cotton wool and finally, folded into a parcel. Then, to line the tin with greaseproof paper and fill it with the dressing parcels, the lid would be left loose and the tin baked in a moderate oven for 20 minutes. Finally, the tin was removed from the oven and the lid immediately secured in place ready for the nurse to use.

It all sounds a bit archaic now but it worked well. Only very occasionally would there be some slippage when the dressings were scorched and unusable and the saucepan presented with bits of potato floating in the water, or porridge stuck to the bottom! Molly always tried to recognize these issues needed to be approached in a kindly but meaningful way. As one senior nurse taught her in the early days, "You catch more bees with honey than with vinegar, Nurse."

Each Monday was designated 'Bag Day'. It was on this occasion that all the nurses were required to attend the centre to maintain their nursing bags. The bags were stripped, cleaned, relined with a fresh white cotton lining; instruments cleaned and hinges oiled; containers washed, relabelled and the contents replaced; and new emergency dressing packs placed in the nursing bag. The nurses rarely met together informally so this time was equally valuable as a means of peer support. Nurses might mull over (or bemoan) changes introduced, or talk about some difficulty they might be experiencing on their District, and, dare it be said, indulge in a bit of gossip!

On one such occasions Molly shared with her colleagues the difficulties she had recently experienced when attending a case of severe constipation, which the GP had been treating for some time with medication to no avail. Molly, identified the constipation was long established and quite severe. Spurious diarrhoea was present *(spurious diarrhoea can be likened to the eye producing tears to wash out a spec of grit, the intestines act in the same way when irritated by hard and impacted faeces)* ... This needed to be regarded with extreme caution. The patient was experiencing considerable pain when Molly tried alternative ways of relieving the problem. Eventually, the enema ordered by the GP was gently administered and the patient sat on the commode having extreme difficulty in passing the blockage; she was perspiring and feeling faint and did not look well at all. Just as Molly was about to seek further advice the lady made a concerted effort and then with a loud shout said, "Done it!" with the heart-felt, "Gosh, that was awful ... really nurse, it was far worse than having a baby." "Well," recounted Molly, "I suggested we name 'him' Joe Soap "This caused an explosion of laughter but none of the nurses had any advice so Molly was acclaimed 'Enema Queen!"

District Nurses cared for, and about each other in many different ways. For instance, in a heavy snowfall, a nurse after finishing her own list would ring the Nurses' Centre to ask if anyone needed help. It was an unwritten rule that a nurse did not go off duty if a colleague was known to be struggling.

Likewise, the same peer support sprang into action when the time came for the familiar bicycle to be replaced by the motorised 'cycle-master' and later when the Ford Popular car was introduced! The nurses helped each other, even husbands came to the rescue! District nursing was a family affair as the following experiences tell:

The wife of a District Nurse:
He was due to leave for his evening round. It was a dark, cold evening and a thick freezing fog had suddenly descended. He couldn't see to drive safely so I went with him as a second pair of eyes. Where the visibility was particularly bad, I got out of the car and guided his way by torchlight from the pavement. The children stayed at home – they were sensible and used to making such sacrifices for their Dad. Well! What else could we do? Dad had to visit his patients and I wanted him back home safely. (Beryl 1998)

The daughter of a District Nurse:
As a child, my heart always sank into my boots when I heard the telephone ring followed by Mum going into the cupboard under the stairs to collect her coat and her black bags. But I was so proud of her and fascinated by her work. I vowed that

when I grew up I would be a District Nurse ... and here I am. I have never been disillusioned – frequently challenged and overwhelmed by human endurance; and the lack of it! To be a District Nurse is a great privilege, it is my life and I wouldn't have it any other way. (Anne 1998)

CHANGES AND CHALLENGES:

The avalanche of change heralding the 'seventies' was unprecedented as technology and new thinking made its impact on Molly and her colleagues and the way they worked. Changes such as the introduction of pre-sterilised and disposable dressings and nursing equipment were welcomed; whilst others, namely the development of information technology (IT) systems took time to fulfil their potential; and some, like the 'Attachment' of district nurses to general practice were like the curate's egg, good in parts!

Few could deny the value of close working relationships between the district nurse and GP but whilst the experience of some 'Attachments' were like marriages made in heaven, others presented all the friction of 'shot-gun' weddings and struggled to get going. For instance, unlike the geographically defined boundaries of the 'District' many GPs did not circumscribe their catchment area, several different GPs might visit the same household, there might be a private patient arrangement in the practice, and access to the GP was not always easy. This resulted in several challenges for district nurses; they criss-crossed each other's visiting routes across the City, duplicated visits to households, and access to a GP by the nurse was often difficult due to arrangements within the practice.

Management arranged a meeting with the GPs. A graphic was presented showing something of this confusion and waste of resources by tracing each nurse's visits in a different coloured thread. Suffice to say the white board on which the graphic was presented was obliterated by a sea of haphazard coloured meanderings – a grossly frustrating and waste of resources which could not be denied! But where attachment worked, it worked well and benefitted the doctor, the nurse and the patient. This relationship was important in many ways but not least insofar as the GP was often thought of as the 'gate-keeper' to the NHS because patients generally gained access to other parts of the system by referral from the GP.

Molly was invited by one GP on her district to consider employment by the practice as a district nurse/health visitor, suggesting it would be helpful to know her current terms of employment, which the GP assured her he would at least match. Molly was very cautious! GPs were not generally known for their understanding of employment legislation, neither were they necessarily well-versed in the professional accountability of the Registered Nurse! However, Molly was saved making the decision because the GP replied, "Thank you, Molly but we can't afford you!" In the fullness of time GPs began to employ their own nurses designated 'Practice Nurses' and the district nurse situation became more manageable and achieve its potential.

But other factors came into play as increasing specialisation and expensive technology made their demands on human and financial resources. Whilst the diversity of change was a source of clinical interest, pride and challenge, resource issues created apprehension and dissention. Molly and her colleagues were well aware of on-going Government Inquiries into nursing management (Salmon Report, 1967 Hospital Nursing; Mayston Report, 1969 Community Nursing). The eventual implementation of 'Mayston's' recommendations introduced significant changes from the grass roots upwards as the ethos of corporate management replaced professional leadership

The new community nursing management structure was introduced across the City, with Molly's Centre retaining responsibility for district nurse training. Miss Todd retired and Molly was encouraged to apply for one of the new posts. This she did and approaching her first Christmas in post a seemingly innocuous breeze heralded momentous winds of change in community care. The first waft came when the Chief Nurse instructed, "No 'social' baths to be given over the Christmas period." Only in very exceptional circumstances was 'Social' in isolation to 'clinical' care remitted to the district nurse; and the nurses responded accordingly. Not to be convinced, the Chief Nurse issued the definitive instruction, "No baths during the Christmas period" and the rest is history, as might be said. The seemingly indivisible was divided; and over time the ambiguous category, 'social care', was syphoned off to the Social Services Department and the ministrations of non-nurse Care Assistants.

This executive, rather than clinical, decision seemed quite unexplainable to Molly and her colleagues, and to the more enlightened GPs; all district nursing teams included at least one 'Nursing Auxiliary', a non-nurse trained to provide personal care to patients in conjunction with a QNI qualified district nurse. The explanation could only evolve around finance and the apportionment of budgets ... and that was sad!

Given the apparent perilous situation of nursing and the implications for patient care, a parallel activity engaged the minds of nurse scholars in the form of a quest to establish the hallmarks of Nursing. Virginia Henderson (1960s) was amongst the first scholars to take up the challenge by defining the unique function of the Nurse in the modern idiom from which she created a model for the guidance of nursing practice and the education of nurses. Henderson's model became known as 'The Nursing Process' and her thinking was widely appreciated in the UK. Molly and her colleagues, readily adopted Henderson's inclusive approach, which set the patient as the defining point of Nursing Care, thus representing a distinct move away from the disease focussed medical model to one that captured the essence of district nursing.

Molly's employer was a renowned trailblazer who embraced change. A new post of Public Health Nurse Tutor was created in the School of Nursing and Molly was faced with the choice of staying in Management or moving into Education – Education won!

CHAPTER 9

WAS IT ALL IN VAIN?

BEDSIDE TO ACADEMIA:

The next step for Molly was to train as a Nurse Teacher; this she did and qualified with a distinction in Education. The Course was an inspiring experience and one that gave Molly confidence to take on her new post and enthused her to emulate Kahlil Gibran's vision of a teacher ...

"If he is indeed wise he does not bid you enter the house of his wisdom, but rather leads you to the threshold of your own mind."

It was during her studies in London that Sam told Molly he had been admitted to Hospital. When Molly visited him, it upset her to see Sam looking so poorly; gaunt, pale and very tired. Sam assured Molly "they think they have put their finger on the problem and I shall soon be on my way again." Then he smiled. "Something to do with the old ticker ... seems you've not been alone in tugging at my heart strings dearest Molly!" Molly gestured with a playful rebuke as Sam continued in a more reflective mood. "Sarah and I are firming up our plans to revisit the Mission field, partly out of nostalgia but mainly for a hospital sponsored support visit. I hope this lot doesn't get in the way but to stay in the Paediatric Department would be just as satisfying." As Sam talked about their plans, he became more positive and he looked somewhat happier when she left; but Molly carried a heavy heart.

At this time of change in Molly's career, family life was also making moves. Molly and Ian found the new house they had long sought – a detached house adjacent to the City's 'Green Belt'. From the windows Molly could see the cows grazing in the field and the horses cantering around – just like her childhood and perfect. She was always pleased they made the effort to afford a detached house with some space, not least so that Gavin could practice his cornet without disturbing the neighbours, but it gave them all private space to pursue their own interests.

Their new neighbours were friendly and they had many interests in common; they were there for each other in times of need and grateful to have Molly's nursing expertise to call upon! For instance, one lady, having dined out and attended a concert with family and friends was taken very ill on her return home. Molly was asked if she would help and told that the doctor had been called. The lady had struggled upstairs and lay on the bed in an extremely dire state, Molly did what she could to maintain life until the young doctor quickly came bounding up the stairs - Molly knew him well from her time 'on the district'. They worked together on the lady but eventually the doctor said, "I'm afraid, Molly … don't you think?" Molly called the family and the doctor confirmed that the lady had died.

Then in almost identical circumstances a while later, the son of the family next door to Molly called late one night saying his father was ill, they had sent for the doctor but would she come and see what she could do. Molly followed the son into the house and upstairs to where his fortyish year-old father lay in bed with his wife sitting silently crying by his side, gently calling his name and caressing his cheek. Molly felt she could usefully commence resuscitation until the doctor came but his wife was adamant that the doctor had said, "Don't move your husband, and I will be there immediately." The same young doctor arrived, smiled at Molly and with such youthful and spontaneous compassion asked what had happened. Almost identically the couple had dined with friends before attending a concert and returned to the house for a nightcap. When the friends had left the house, the couple retired to bed. The wife then struggled to tell that as they settled into bed her husband, "started to snort and then seemed to stop breathing. I thought he was fooling around." He was indeed dying.

Molly's change of career direction as a nurse teacher, with a return to a 9am – 5pm day and 5-day week routine, was a great advantage to the family and much to Ian's delight. Joy and Gavin were approaching their longer-term career choices with Joy's ambitions directed to university and Gavin's towards craft and technology. Ian was promoted and holidays abroad might become an option!

That summer the family celebrated Ian's success by taking a holiday in Wales where one of the high spots of the holiday was the day they climbed Mount Snowdon. Ian, being a keen amateur photographer caused everyone to be wary when, "Dad's camera was at the ready." And so, it was on Mount Snowdon when Gavin and Joy nipped behind the next corner to recover, Gavin shot to his feet as soon he sensed the camera was about, whilst Joy, who didn't seem to give a jot, remained on the ground! But Ian was able to capture some amazing memories: the breath-taking scenery, the atmosphere of the mist in the valley below, clouds so low you felt you could almost touch them, and at one point an aeroplane flying through the valley below them. The event was made even more memorable because the returning trains were all fully booked and the only way down was to walk - this was certainly not the original plan!

Shortly after Molly commenced her new post disaster struck; an undetected lower spine abnormality created serious problems, which necessitated complicated surgery. An extensive period of recuperation included a trip to Majorca - it was a magical holiday – their first abroad. Leaving Luton airport, the weather was wet and miserable but on arrival in Majorca they were greeted by sunshine and warm spring weather. They wandered through the blossoming almond groves and orchards on the hillsides and visited the local village harbour with its busy fishing fleet provided hours of interest in the early morning sunshine. Molly eventually returned fit and well to her teaching position.

Molly and Sam sometimes spoke on the telephone comparing notes and encouraging each other following their episodes of ill health. Sam, who seemed to be making a fairly promising recovery, was discharged to his parents' home for a period of convalescence whilst Sarah continued her work commitments.

THE BEGINNING OF THE END OF AN ERA:

Alongside such rejoicing and happiness on the one hand, Molly struggled with a deep sense of foreboding. Sadly, Wills' health did not recover from his collapse under the hedges from which Kate rescued him and he became increasingly frail. Kate and her three sons supported Rose in caring for Wills during the week and Molly took over from Friday night to Monday morning. It was a sad time to see Wills fighting against his growing weakness and immobility – he longed to get out of bed. In fact, one night whilst in the care of his youngest grandson, Wills persuaded the lad to get him out of bed. In the morning when Rose got up she went into the room to find Wills happily asleep on the rug in front of the fire and his grandson asleep in Wills' bed! But Wills was 'as happy as Larry' and as they propped him up resting with his back against the sofa and toasting his toes by the fire Wills could see no reason why this arrangement could not continue.

One weekend Molly found Wills considerably deteriorated, with Rose and Kate sitting wringing their hands at his bedside. "I think this is the end," whispered Rose and so they sat in their twilight vigil of sorrow. Suddenly Wills moved his head to look at Rose, then pursing his lips and tapping them with his finger, he called, "Mum." with a kissing sound. It was heart breaking as Rose went over to Wills, Molly just couldn't watch and intrude on this precious moment - moments that Wills had probably longed for all his married life. Molly just hoped and prayed Rose would summon the long-stored years of love and compassion to kiss her dying husband. When Rose eventually turned away from the bed she sobbed, "Molly, go and talk to him."

Molly knelt by her father's bed talking to him about the wonderful life they had shared; of his faith and his hope of glory. Wills looked at her, smiled and gradually drifted away. Molly treasured that moment because she felt she had at last been given permission to care and show the love she felt for her beloved father.

Molly went to the village telephone kiosk to tell Ian her sad news. They cried over the 'phone with each other until their tears were spent. Molly walked through the village in the darkness thinking about her father's life in the community and the respect in which he was held; she stood at the Lych Gate guarding the drive up to the church and remembered the day she walked through as a bride on her father's arm to her wedding. When Molly arrived home the undertakers were laying Wills to rest in his coffin which replaced the black iron bedstead in the alcove.

Wills lay in his open coffin for several days during which time, the neighbours curtains remained closed, visitors came to pay their last respects, and Molly stayed in the house with Rose. One night, seemingly out of the blue, a strong wind blew across the open fields; the windows and doors rattled, structures creaked, and the wind howled across the chimney top. It was frightening and Rose was very unnerved. Molly went downstairs to look at her father and he had changed, it seemed as if his restless soul had flown and he was at peace with his maker. The next morning the undertakers came to seal the coffin and it was time to say their last goodbyes.

Wills' funeral service was held at his beloved Pentecostal Church in town with his brethren glorifying Wills' life and reverencing his passing. The congregation 'raised the roof' by the volume of their songs of praise and worship and the sheer joy of Evangelicalism. Wills was taken home to his village and buried in the churchyard to wait for Rose.

Rose was amazingly strong. She downsized and moved into a bungalow in the centre of the village near to the church. Kate, who had been unhappy in her marriage for many years felt able to petition for divorce now that her father was not alive, two boys were in the services and one at University. Kate set up house in a nearby village and Rose was a frequent visitor to give a hand with the 'tacking' and menial jobs of tailoring. Kate had also perfected upholstering skills and frequently visited the large houses to fit new chair or settee coverings, and even hanging curtains at tall elegant Georgian windows. Rose was in her element visiting her old stomping grounds.

LIFE'S TWISTS AND TURNS:

Molly's spinal surgery was a great success and she returned to continue in her teaching position. District nursing, was in the process of far-reaching changes. Different patterns of working and wider responsibilities were introduced to respond to the changes taking place in society; the expectations (and limitations) of health care reflect the increasing prominence given to the experience of illness alongside the medical diagnosis; and the management of human resources both at the bedside and within the organisation. A national qualification in District Nursing replaced the QNI arrangement; training was made mandatory; and the curriculum broadened its scope and depth, particularly in relation to the study of the behavioural, social and political sciences. Also, because no one profession works in isolation within the broad landscape of health and social care, a more interactive learning environment between students became a priority. Such opportunities were at hand for courses situated in higher education but in single disciple establishments such as the School of Nursing, Molly negotiated a contract with the local University to bridge the gap.

Consequently, the updating needs of teaching staff both in the school and the students' fieldwork placements were pressing.

Molly encouraged enrolment on an Open University (OU) short course to study abuse within the family because of its emerging significance and for the underpinning the subjects would provide for other aspects of practice, such as a more systematic approach to the assessment of need and the delivery of care e.g., Models of Nursing. Some, 6 nurse and practice teachers, plus 4 practitioners from other disciplines enrolled on the OU course, with the OU tutorials held at their teaching base. It was quite fun to be 'students' together with the 'boot on the other foot' as it were. The initiative proved to be highly successful and a few participants, including Molly, went on to graduate with a Bachelor of Science Degree. Under the Directorship of Mr Pete, the School of Nursing became a vibrant environment, spearheaded by Molly and fostered by the young academics who readily broadened their teaching assignments to include students and staff in their research interests! Mr Pete, whilst encouraging Molly's creative mind always warned her ... "bring to me a well-argued case and I will give it serious consideration but no half-baked ideas, they will be a waste of your time and MINE!" The Director need not have had concerns because Molly's experience with Miss Todd had been a master class!

Alongside her own studies and teaching remit, Molly was sought to represent district nursing at national level where new legislation was about to change the regulation of the nursing profession. Also, an enthusiastic supporter of her professional organization, Molly held office at her local branch ... and later served as President.

Episodes of ill health continue to beleaguer Molly. Having recently recovered from a serious bout of pleurisy, she visited a teaching centre in East Anglia. Returning home, Molly noticed a significant degree of discomfort in her left leg and driving the car was quite a challenge. A visit to the doctor's surgery that evening was met with absolute horror as he examined her painful, blue swollen leg. "You should have gone straight to the hospital, Molly," he advised. *"Sticky blood following Pleurisy," he murmured almost as an aside.* "But all is not lost, I will call an ambulance and you can go direct from the surgery." Ian returned home to collect a few bits and pieces for Molly and went to the ward.

Friday night and the Consultant had finished for the weekend. The Registrar and his colleagues gathered round the bed; a blocked artery, possibly a vein was diagnosed with a decision to operate. The doctors left the ward and Molly was prepared for theatre. After a while, the young Australian sounding Registrar returned looking ponderous, he confirmed the diagnosis but continued by telling them of an alternative form of treatment. "I have just been re-checking a paper I remembered reading recently in our professional journal about the efficacy of Streptokinase administered intravenously to disperse such blockages: but it is very toxic. Would you try it?" Molly and Ian looked at each other, neither speaking. Molly immediately shared her concerns with the Registrar by telling him that she had used the drug to clean suppurating leg ulcers!! The Registrar knew about its use as a de-sloughing agent since the thirties but assured Molly that it had been approved for use by intravenous administration quite recently, mid-nineteen nineties in fact. "I'll leave you to mull it over," he said, "it is very toxic but safe if given under close supervision." Ian and Molly, after discussing the pros and cons, agreed to accept the experimental treatment as a welcomed alternative to further surgery.

The drip was set up and Molly given strict instructions on the number of drops per minute at which the drip had to run. "Could you please be another pair of eyes, Molly?" However, Molly deteriorated into a mild state of delirium whilst the drip continued throughout the night but on Saturday the leg began to show small signs of improvement. The Consultant visited on Monday and progress had been maintained but instead of praising the Registrar, he seemed to challenge him on the accuracy of his diagnosis!

Once again, Molly duly recovered and was soon back on form again. When 'clot busting drugs' came into more general use, Molly often wondered if she had been one of the guinea pigs and hoped the young Australian Registrar received just recognition for his initiative!

Shortly after this episode, Molly's neighbour whose husband had collapsed and died placed her house on the market in preparation to downsize. An early middle-aged German businessman, Hans, was quick to show interest in the impressive large, white house. Hans had such a story to tell from his days as Prisoner of War (POW) in a camp situated in the neighbouring village. He told of his origins in Germany and his time in the 'Hitler Youth' prior to joining the armed forces and being captured. In the 'forces' he told how they were all warned about the brutality of the 'Brits' and, should they be taken POW, the devious methods of interrogation they would employ to disadvantage the 'Fatherland'.

Hans described how he woke up to find himself in what he began to think of as, "the glorious English countryside." The guards were pleasant and polite, and the accommodation, although stark, was warm and comfortable. 'Ah! Ah!' he thought, 'this must be the warm-up to interrogation.' But it never came. Instead, they worked in groups on the local farms and in the fullness of time they were allowed into the City centre on Saturday afternoons. He told how he began to develop a fondness and respect for the 'Brits' and especially one young lady who worked in the coffee bar frequented by the POWs. Meanwhile, he continued to gaze out from the camp and across the village to where he could see the lovely white house ... 'One day,' he promised himself, 'I shall live there.' And so he did.

But first, he married his English rose. They set up their first home in a terraced street in town to incorporate a small manufacturing industry in an adjacent property; they produced seven children; "and the rest is history," as Hans often said. But it was Hans' wife who told of the hardship they experienced in making a success of the small factory. "We all worked at it; Hans in the factory, me and the kids at home!" She told how she worked during her confinements with the eldest child standing on guard watching for the midwife! On seeing her, the child ran upstairs and helped her mother to pack up the work and push it under the bed! Home working had a long tradition in the town as William Felkin described over a century earlier:

'I found a female at work between 9 and 10pm, with her husband and two journeymen at work above her head up the stepladder over the kitchen she was occupying ...' (Bowles and Kirraine, 1990).

When Hans and his family moved to the white house with their robust seven children it was quite a shock to the neighbourhood! Hans' eldest daughter, Tina, was about the same age as Joy. She worked as an apprentice beautician with a highly esteemed company in the city centre. Tina took every opportunity to practice her developing skills on the only too willing Joy but on one occasion with unintended effects. Joy was a member of the PHAB (Physically Handicapped and Able Bodied) Club and on that particular occasion Jimmy Saville was to be the celebrity guest. Eager to look her best and inviting Gavin to join her, Joy came downstairs dressed in 'hot pants', the fashion of the day, her coiffeur and make-up gave evidence of Tina's artistry. Gavin took one look saying, "If you think I am travelling on the bus and walking through town with you looking like that, then you need to think again." They met at the venue but Gavin maintained a safe distance and departed early!

Joy's appetite for fashion was insatiable. Ian became exasperated, reminding Joy, "the family budget isn't a bottomless pit, you know!" One day he announced they were each to be given a monthly clothing allowance and a rather generous arrangement was negotiated. Joy's eyes sparkled. However, her excitement was short-lived in spite of Molly's creative fingers and the help of her Singer sewing machine, Gavin's moneybox began to fill with IOU's. Molly invented an imaginary friend for Joy she named Fred. 'Fred' was a very generous benefactor whose gifts were found amongst her birthday and Christmas presents and at various stages in between! Dear 'Fred', by now a family joke, continued his generosity into Joy's adult years. He even funded her Christmas shopping sprees to London, plus a matinee performance, which had now become an annual event for Molly and the children - one year the arrival of the Maxi Coat surpassed all others! Molly was becoming more like her mother, Rose, every day!

Family life strummed along nicely. The open-house Christmas arrangement at Molly and Ian's home had become a family tradition since the early days in their terraced house. As usual, Rose came in advance to supervise the preparations and cooking; bringing her homemade Christmas pudding and cake and enjoying family time. As time passed Joy appeared with her latest beaux in attendance and Gavin with his friends.

Sam and Sarah kept in touch with Molly during his convalescence. Sadly, Sam's recovery was slow due to his worsening heart condition – Sam's aside that Molly was not the only one to tug at his heartstrings gave a little light relief. Molly and Ian found Sam very frail but still smiling. He was "well cared for by the district nurses" he assured Molly roguishly … "I bet you made a wonderful district nurse," he mused. Sam talked about his "wonderful life" and the encouragement he had received from his family; "the happy times with you, Molly; meeting Tommy and setting him on his way." Sam reminisced about his life in the Mission field; but most of all he spoke adoringly about the love he and Sarah had for each other and their baby, which "might have been. Yes, life has been good," he sighed contentedly and drifted off to sleep. Molly and Ian had supper with the family and just before they set off back home, Sam woke up. "That's better," he said "just to think I can have a snooze whenever I want and not in anticipation of being disturbed by the telephone!" It was a quiet, sad journey home for Molly whose every instinct wanted to stay and care for her beloved friend. Sam died within a few weeks; Tommy was inconsolable and Molly … well? It only seemed like yesterday that they had all celebrated Sam and Sarah's wedding – now almost 20 years ago!

They all attended Sam's funeral with the pride of having been part of Sam's life and privileged that he had chosen them to be numbered amongst his friends. Sam was laid to rest in the village churchyard next to his grandparents, with the symbolic posey of deep yellow roses gracing his coffin top. Sam's mother walked away with Sarah saying in the silent agony of prayer, "Why our Sam?" Molly found solace in sharing time with Sam's family during the wake as they tried to make sense of the mystery and the "unfairness" of life and death. They were very proud of their Sam and rejoiced that his short but honourable life had been spent in the service of others. Interest turned to Tommy and Lizzy as they described the comfort and convenience of their new home. Tommy falteringly expressed how humbled he felt by all that Sam had made possible for him and Lizzy, the quality of health he enjoyed and the success it enabled him to achieve at work. He told of his recent promotion and his ambition to "get nearer the top!" Lizzy showed such enthusiasm for Tommy's future and the City and Guilds Management Course he was studying to secure his future. "One day, I might be a graduate, like you Molly!" Tommy speculated with a smile on his face. But the mood changed and for whatever the reason, Tommy shared his doubts about having a family.

In the wake of Sam's untimely death, Ian and Molly's twenty-fifth wedding anniversary was drawing ever nearer. On the day, Ian surprised Molly by producing a bright red sports car, which they named Rosey. Their first trip in Rosey was an adventure organized by Ian on a tour of Scotland. They travelled up the West coast, then via Edinburgh, climbing to enjoy the vantage point of King Arthur's Seat and back home via the East coast calling for an overnight stay on Holy Island. Later they both qualified with the Institute of Advanced Motorists, "so that we can drive Rosey properly," said Ian. Ian became a life-long member and enthusiast of the Institute.

Ian had a feel for Scotland; the 'Highlands and Islands' from his wartime posting. Another year on a similar tour in 'Rosey', Ian discovered The Hawes Inn, Queensberry at the foot of the

Forth Railway Bridge. They stayed in the 'Robert Louis Stephenson Room' (RLS) complete with a huge four-poster bed and the desk at which RLS was said to have written 'Treasure Island'. The room looked out on to the magnificent bridge spanning the Firth of Forth. For Ian, who after his demobilization spent time on the footplate of a Garret steam engine, the rhythmical rumble of the trains and the smell of steam intrigued him. And the walkways across the bridge enabled Ian to get closer to these sensations.

Some while later, Ian's sister, Joan and her husband Len shared a holiday with Molly and Ian at the Hawes Inn. The holiday was not altogether a happy experience. The old Inn and its history spooked Joan and Len and they found the sound of the trains irritating in the extreme. But worse was to follow. Molly had observed Joan getting out of their Renault Scenic and noting the difficulty she had judging the distance to the ground and her initial instability when standing ... 'Parkinson's', thought Molly, 'dear me, I do hope not.' Sadly, these were proved to be the early signs of this cruel condition, which progressed slowly over time. Joan was a lovely human being; kind and gentle just like her father. Joan qualified as a midwife and spent the remainder of her career delivering babies, supporting Mums and safeguarding their health – she must have been a wonderful midwife to have by your side both as a Mum and as a colleague. Joan had experienced two extremely painful broken love affairs but third time lucky when she met and married Len, Ian's friend, who had adored her from afar for a very long time. Joan and Len were blessed with two girls and the joy of grandchildren who gave amazing support throughout Joan's long illness. Ian and his sister were very close and his beloved Joan's situation was overwhelmingly distressing. Ian spent many hours 'talking' to Joan in the loneliness of Parkinson's, which gradually invaded her limited world.

MAGICAL HOLIDAYS:

Ian once again turned his mind to organising family adventures. A holiday in Tunisia with 'wifey' and Gavin gave Ian all the scope he needed and when the opportunity to stay at a discontinued French Foreign Legion Fort in the desert was included as an option, his enthusiasm knew no bounds. Molly was concerned that it might be too costly and Gavin was not over keen at the idea at all. Ian made his usual remark, "We may never come this way again, so take the opportunity while you can!" It proved to be just the right decision. The accommodation whilst very basic stirred the imagination and everyone on the excursion joined in the fun – Camille, the tour host was amazing. After supper in the stark canteen-style dining room, Camille organized a party in an adjacent hall, again not exactly equipped with creature comforts! They danced the night away to a bespoke dance band – Camille beating out the rhythm of a drum on a tin tray, Ian making a tune by blowing through a comb covered with tissue paper and two of the German tourists tapped out a rhythm on two spoons – Magic!

The following year Molly and Ian travelled to Australia, to visit Ruth and her family in Melbourne. They lived on the edge of the Dandenong Mountain Range, a beautiful part of the State of Victoria. Puffing Billy, a small steam engine took them up through the tree-topped mountains where they discovered magnificently coloured birds and the sounds of unfamiliar bird song, such as that of the 'bell bird', which sounded like its descriptive name. They took a short safari and stayed in a lodge bounded by the sea on one side and the open country on the other. One bright starlight night they walked to a neighbouring community – no streetlights in what seemed like the 'outback'. The night animals could be heard foraging at the roadside and the Koala Bears were bustling about in the trees to settle down for the night – quite a night to remember. Of course, they visited the Zoos and animal parks where they had close up views of kangaroos, some with a Joey in their pouch.

The Fitzwilliam Aboriginal Museum opened their minds about the heritage, culture and traditions of the Aboriginal people; an experience that was rounded off by the Labour Day festival of Moomba – in aborigine meaning, 'let's get together and have fun'. The carnival floats and bands paraded through the streets of Melbourne and across the River Yara where the boats mirrored the carnival's splendour. A mid-day break at a pub for a 'Counter lunch' of sirloin steak on a sizzle dish was the height of fulfilment for Ian. Two sizzle dishes were purchased to take home but the steaks never tasted the same away from the magic of 'Oz'!

During their five-week stay, Molly spent time with the Victoria District Nursing Service established under the same Royal patronage as the QNI in the UK. Molly accompanied a district nurse on her rounds, which included pre-discharge visits to patients in the large ultramodern hospital. The hospital was an amazing place; spacious, copiously signposted, and a paging system, which included the district nurse! Arriving at one patient's bedside, Molly was introduced as a district nurse from the UK - the patient seemed quite bemused and curious! Molly was encouraged to tell them about health care in the UK. First, however, Molly applauded the facilities of their hospital, explaining that many of the hospitals in Britain were historical monuments upgraded for present day practice, with a spate of municipal hospital building from 1930s, until the recent ambitious facilities. Molly briefly explained the health and social care facilities in the UK; the apparent freedom of the NHS intrigued her listeners! Once the nurse began her interview with the patient Molly was on familiar ground ... until the district nurse, before concluding the arrangements for the home visits asked, "How will you pay?" Such a conclusion would not have been heard in the UK since pre-NHS when the Lady Visitors from the local voluntary district nursing associations would have pursued the same line of enquiry! For Molly, it was just wonderful to experience the kindred spirit of district nursing taking place on the other side of the world!

Always ready to get into a classroom, Molly also spent time at the higher education establishment providing education for the public health nurses and social care specialties. The approach seemed rather more systematic and relaxed giving students the freedom to learn as a priority to being taught. This approach, Molly found quite thought provoking at the start of her relatively new career in teaching and certainly more in keeping with the wisdom espoused by Kahlil Gibran!

Dear Ruth had always been an enthusiastic craft person but in Australia her ambitions seemed to know no bounds! She proudly showed examples of her work in the local church, her own home and her exhibition pieces. Molly already knew of Ruth's talents from the hand-woven gifts she received from her friend but Australia had fuelled her ambitions – Ruth had invested in a spinning wheel, a large weaving loom and expanded her interests to making stained glass leaded-windows and ornaments!

They went here, there and everywhere with Ruth. The lasting memories were visits to Ruth's 'weaver' friends and the groups of which she was a member. One of the last visits was paid to her sheep farmer friend. It was here where Molly and Ian caught their first glimpse of the 'Chastity Apron' a leather garment worn by the rams to prevent unwanted pregnancies! They were shown how fleeces from the sheared sheep were processed and the different stages through which they passed before being spun into wool. It was a productive home industry and one, which also formed the foundation for vibrant social activities. Molly's next Christmas present from Ruth was a personally designed blanket created from the fleece to the loom; its soft muted colours were a testimony to Ruth's personally made vegetable dyes – another new interest!

Ian, in particular, was quite taken with the Australian people: their "get up and get it done" attitude; their openness; and the hands-on, physically active interests in which he participated. Molly was half afraid Ian would want to follow their friends and emigrate! Whilst it would be good to live within closer contact to Ruth, and to practise within a different clinical ethos, Molly's family had a far bigger pull. Thankfully, they boarded the Jumbo Jet looking forward to be going home. Throughout the long journey Molly entertained herself reading a recent best seller set in Australia, 'The Thorn Birds' by Colleen McCollough; a gift from the sheep farming ladies.

But another adventure was 'just round the corner' when Ian discovered the Greek Island of Rhodes in the early 1980's. They arrived at their beach side hotel in Falaraki in the early hours of the morning and immediately fell into bed. The next morning Molly heard Ian 'swish' open the curtains and gasp, "I say Wifey, just look at this." Thinking she was going to look out onto the golden beach and rippling blue sea, Molly shot out of bed to see they overlooked a village-like scene and a large field with a man tending his goats. Several small wooden sheds were situated on the field from which the goats had emerged to be caught and tethered on a long rope to a fixed point in the field. When Ian and Molly returned in the evening to sit on the balcony with their Ouzo cocktails the man was busily returning the goats to their sleeping quarters before nightfall.

During the evening Molly and Ian roamed around the quiet village streets, probably have a drink at a taverna on the beach and back to bed by a reasonable hour. In later years when Faliraki hit the headlines as a hot spot of drink and debauchery Molly and Ian could not believe they had been to the same place, as indeed questioned their friends! Faliraki changed over the years; the fields and the goatherd disappeared to be gobbled up by a concrete jungle of hotels and the simple bars and solitary beach tavernas were swamped with modern facilities.

For many years Molly and Ian spent their holidays on the Island during the first two weeks of September and always stayed in Faliraki. Ian hired a motorbike and they travelled around the Island. They spent time exploring the towns including the capital city of Rhodes with its huge 'Colossus' statute to the Sun God, Helios, guarding the entrance to the harbour. The motorbike, equipped with balloon tyres to give a firm grip on the rough country roads, continued on its adventure throughout the week. Passing through the mountainous regions they occasionally dipped back down to the deserted coastal region for a 'skinny-dip' before wending their homeward journey. Riding through the mountains was a memorable experience. The tall green spruce trees exuded a pungent almost heady aroma, a taste found in the honey collected from the bright blue beehives peppering the hillside. The quiet roads could spring surprises in the form of the sudden flash of a snake as it slithered across their path; the unexpected appearance of a goatherd with his flock; or a small village where luscious honey-coloured figs ripened on the branches of the rambler-like trees growing at the edge of the roadside gardens – a few figs always happened to fall into their hands!

Boat trips to the ancient town of Lindos at the far end of the Island and to the neighbouring Island of Simi became an important part of the holiday. The large pleasure boats waited a distance offshore whilst a small motorboat transported the tourists from the beach out to sea where they climbed aboard by the heavy metal ladders on the side of the ship. The first time it was a bit of a surprise for them both but for Molly, who hated not to be able to "touch the bottom with my toe," it was scary!

Each year when they arrived for their holiday, some local people greeted them like old friends. The Greek husband and wife owners of the motorbike hire shop became especially friendly, often inviting them to an alfresco supper, or a glass of Ouzo under the stars. The young Greek lady who managed the harbour-side café would run across the quay calling Ian's name with her arms out-spread to welcome him. Molly found a craft shop in Rhodes town where she became a well-known customer and each year, she bought a tapestry to take home. The tapestries she made into cushions continue to adorn their home with pride.

Ian's passion for motorcycling and adventure seemed to be absorbed by Gavin. Gavin bought his first motorbike when he was aged 17. And with their hearts in their mouths Molly and Ian watched Gavin embark on numerous adventures. On one occasion that Molly and Ian will never forget, Gavin decided to visit Joy at her University in the South West with a supply of Molly's famous mince pies. Molly made mince pies all year round regardless of Rose's warning, "Food out of season, trouble without reason!"

Without access to satellite navigation, Gavin methodically listed the key points of his journey down the Fosse Way and attached the paper to the petrol tank of his motorbike. The route was carefully planned to take account of re-fuelling (the petrol tank was not very big) and a trouble-free run. Gavin set out at midnight, probably to enhance the adventure, although he said it was to avoid the traffic! Molly and Ian went to bed, not sleeping but waiting for the 'phone call which they hoped they would not receive. Sure enough, the call came in the early hours - Ian had misjudged a bend entering a small village on 'the Fosse' and was in difficulty. Taking details of the village Ian mapped out the journey and set off in the car with Molly.

Arriving in the village Ian spotted Gavin's motorbike outside a cottage. Knocking at the door a kindly man invited them into his home where Gavin was enjoying a breakfast of bacon and egg with all the trimmings. They inspected the motorbike and Ian was able to fix it to enable him to ride back home. Gavin, who was shaken (although wouldn't admit it) and disappointed, travelled home in the car with Molly. The phone call to Joy explaining that her delivery of mince pies had been temporarily suspended faded into insignificance compared with her concern for Gavin.

CAREERS AND RELOCATION:

As time passed Ian gained another promotion to a position he had longed for in External Planning; he also began to think in the longer term by anticipating possible retirement opportunities. Molly and Ian enjoyed many visits to Joy during her time at University in the South West and they had liked what they had experienced; they had also taken an interest to the golfing environment of Sandwich in Kent.

Joy was about to complete her studies with plans to gain access to a Missionary programme on graduation. Sadly, her ambitions were thwarted for a time whilst she consolidated her postgraduate experience as a teacher of music and mathematics.

To gain this experience, Joy was successful in her application for a teaching post at a Church of England boarding school where she also performed the role of housemistress. During this time, Joy formed a close association with the Anglican Community of Nuns linked to the school and after one year she prepared to enter the Convent. Whilst Molly and Ian were proud of Joy's calling, Molly was bereft at the thought of losing contact and what the future might hold. But once again she reflected on the wisdom of 'The Prophet', Kahlil Gibran...

"Your children are not your children.
They are the sons and daughters of Life's longing for itself ...
You give them your love but not their thoughts, for they have their own thoughts.
You may house their bodies but not their souls for their souls live in the house of tomorrow, which you cannot visit, not even in your dreams.
You may strive to be like them, but seek not to make them like you ...
You are the bows from which your children as living arrows are shot forth."

Molly and Ian, like other parents, were called to dwell on these pearls of wisdom many times as the children carved out their own lives.

Meanwhile, Gavin was excelling at such subjects as technical drawing, music and art; he was taking an interest in jewellery and attending Silver Smith classes at the local 'Tech' where his demonstration pieces included a neckpiece and a silver ring set with a large amethyst for Molly. In Gavin's final year at school, he worked on a project about 'Pearl Diving' and this, together with a visit to Birmingham's Jewellery Quarter with Ian, seemed to cement a career working with precious stones and jewellery. A Gemmology degree was muted, but like Molly and the School Certificate Stream, Gavin was having none of it!

Gavin eventually combined his interest in jewellery with a Diploma in Management and entered the retail jewellery business where he met his future wife, Dana, a shop assistant. In the fullness of time they set the date for their wedding. But it was to be a day of joy and sadness: Gavin had realized his heart's desire but there were heartfelt gaps in the family ... Wills had died and Joy entered the Convent. This left Rose, Molly and sister Kate, who in true Dolman-girl tradition, attended the wedding and celebrated Gavin's happiness - but it was hard. The future looked good for Gavin and Dana. Gavin bought a terraced house and settled in with his bride; he took the entrepreneurial step to invest in his own retail jewellery business, which with a touch of genius and hard work showed promise as a successful enterprise. Meanwhile, Molly responded to Dana's interest in nursing by introducing her to a Ward Sister friend who arranged for Dana to spend time on her ward. Dana's interest was captured and she took a tentative step as a Nursing Auxiliary, and eventually enrolled for nurse training.

With the family engaged in their own pursuits Molly again took the opportunity to respond to a new assignment. A Mid-West USA, University had established a British Campus for Nursing Studies in the neighbouring County. The campus was situated in a large Country Manor surrounded by extensive gardens threading through which an impressive drive led up to the house. The nursing students spent a semester at the British Campus to study health care in the UK and extend their clinical know-how to which Molly and her colleagues made a contribution. It was their first encounter with the 'Loomis and Wood Model of Nursing' in action. The Model was complex and not as easily digested as Henderson's, 'Nursing Process' but Molly recognised its potential and happily took the advantage to learn more. It was whilst undertaking this commission that Molly made contacts through which she would extend her appreciation of nursing education.

Sadly, Molly's insatiable ambitions caused her marriage to falter quite severely. Following an assignment where she commuted to London daily for two separate periods of six months, a permanent teaching post became available. Molly put the opportunity to Ian saying she could easily stay in London from Monday to Friday and spend the weekends at home. With hindsight, Ian did not seem to agree or disagree but gave Molly her head. However, the night before Molly's interview, Ian broke down ... "I never thought it would end like this, Wifey," he sobbed inconsolably. Molly attended the interview but was not appointed. "Time to take stock" Gwen tried to signal to Molly, 'listen to your better judgement and value what you've got.'

It had indeed been a 'wake-up call' for Molly and time was needed to repair the world she had so nearly shattered. Walking was a recreation they shared, so Molly began to think of some 'time out' on holiday whilst things were at such very low ebb. To relieve Ian of the planning, Molly suggested they joined a 'Walking Group', or take a 'Holiday Fellowship' walking holiday either at home, or abroad. But, "No", said Ian "It would not be the same as when there is just the two of us, Wifey." And that about summed up their relationship; it was all Ian ever wanted - to be with 'Wifey'! So they packed their bags and went to Falaraki!

REINVENTION:

The 1980's continued to be a bag of mixed blessings. Molly graduated with the Open University, a ceremony Rose proudly attended with Ian and the family. But during this time Molly again fell victim to ill health – removal of the thyroid gland due to early malignant changes, followed by the removal of a malignant melanoma from her leg. Barely out of recovery, Molly was to re-invent herself as a scholar and figuratively speaking, to don academic dress over her nurse's uniform – Molly was first and foremost a nurse! The Nursing Council promoted the transfer of Health Visitor and District Nurse Courses to University or Polytechnic establishments. The edict was resented in many parts of the country; Molly's teaching contracts with the local University sufficed in the short term, but eventually the local Health Visitor Course relocated to the Polytechnic with plans to include the District Nursing Course.

This was a disappointment to Molly because to develop the existing connections with the University would have been her choice.

Returning home from a London meeting one evening, Molly seemed unusually light footed on arrival at the station after a long and demanding day. Ian commented on her apparent exhilaration – "Not half, Hub." said Molly "I have been invited to apply to a West Country University to head its Public Health (Community) Nursing Courses and develop a degree programme." Ian registered his surprise, together with a frisson of interest knowing that retirement in the West Country had been a venture they had considered. However, this time Ian's position was the primary consideration.

Molly attended the interview with Ian. She was offered the post but on a two-year contract about which the University was apologetic but openly declared that in this transitional period from in-house nurse training to higher education they were unsure of the long-term financial commitment by the sponsoring authorities. In one way, this was music to Molly's ears because it bought time for Ian to relocate. Everyone who knew Ian doubted whether even his versatility would enable him to settle as a West Country local. But he did and with amazing success and personal enjoyment. The deal was done and the contract continued to be reviewed every two years because Molly would never consider a fulltime commitment – just in case.

Molly and Ian bought a quaint bungalow in a small village adjacent to Dartmoor; descending into the village when it was shrouded in mist resembled Brigadoon! The bungalow, which needed converting from its 1930's style to a modern home, made Ian's DIY fingers twitch with excitement. He was in his element sourcing materials and fittings across the South Hams and further afield - often on the motorbike he had brought down from the North. During the turmoil of refurbishment Gavin and his wife were regular weekend visitors, on one such occasion, they announced their forthcoming new arrival. Molly was ecstatic at the thought of becoming a Grandma but "Oh, I shall be so far away," she fretted.

Rose and Kate also came to stay. Village life was not new to them and they enjoyed the quaintness of the locality, and the simplicity of the church services. One family Christmas after a stay at Gavin's home, Rose was unwell. Molly took her mother home with her to Devon where she stayed until she recovered. Rose returned to her own home but it was not a success; she was forgetful, lonely, and unwell. Kate found it difficult to take full responsibility for Rose on account of the nature of her work and the necessity to spend time away from home. Rose agreed to stay with Molly and Ian with the possibility of settling with them in the West Country.

Again, it was not a success, Rose worried about Kate being divorced and on her own now that her three boys had left home. She was also concerned that as the oldest person in the village Rose was presented with one shilling every Christmas and she was afraid she might lose this if she moved to Devon! Rose returned home. Sadly, it didn't work out and Kate encouraged Rose to move into residential accommodation. Molly was angry with Kate and for many years their relationship did not recover from the disagreement. The one saving factor was that the Home was owned and managed by two district nurses, a mother and daughter, with whom Molly had become friendly whilst serving on one of the national committees. The owners were involved in 'hands-on care, with the attention to detail that only a district nurse could give,' thought Molly; and she felt encouraged.

Meanwhile, Ian began to find his way around. He enjoyed trips to the coast on his motorbike – always taking the back lanes to avoid the 'Grockles' (tourists) who clogged up the main roads. Ian found this a wonderful life; "I feel as if I am on permanent holiday walking along the pier with the holiday makers." When Molly had a day off, armed with her bathing clothes, she would nip onto the pillion seat to enjoy a trip to the coast and a swim in the sea. It really was a magical place to live. One night Ian said to Molly, "I would love another dog, a pet like my old pal, Jimmy would be wonderful." Molly raised no objection and the next morning Ian wrote out a notice asking for 'Border Collie cross puppy' for the postmistress to display in her shop.

Before lunchtime Ian received a call from a local farmer to say he had just had a litter of puppies and Ian would be welcome to take his pick with one proviso that it must be a male. The farmer believed his ladies were more loyal, reliable and "got stuck into work," whereas he found the males to be irresponsible and unreliable and "off the moment they were on the trail of an interesting scent!" And so Ben or 'Mr Ben' as Ian titled him, arrived as a ball of black and white fluff with little pink paws. Ian adopted a rather protective attitude, not least because he would not ever let Mr Ben have the 'snip' because it would rob him of his 'manhood'! Mr Ben was Ian's soul mate for nearly 15 years, everyone in the village knew him and if ever Ian was to leave him at home, the first question he would be asked was, "Where's Mr Ben?"

The University presented extremely fulfilling assignments but like Miss Todd, her inspirational District Nurse Superintendent, Molly regarded spending a duty with the students as equally important. Not only did it provide time together to foster the teacher - student relationship outside the classroom, it kept Molly focussed on basics, and also brought her into direct contact with the unique culture and traditions of the South West. For instance, whilst visiting with a student in a tin mining area of Cornwall one patient gave them each a banana saying, "For your 'Crouch', nurses." The student enlightened Molly that when the tin miners stopped for a break, they 'crouched' in a warm corner to eat their food - the bananas were for their lunch! And in Devon Molly began to warm to the spontaneous burr of "my loveerr."

Meanwhile, Molly's responsibilities at national level were unrelenting. The 1980's – 1990's were a time of unprecedented change with a restructuring of the Statutory Committee framework; a reconfiguration of nursing as an academic discipline; and a move from a qualification for life to evidence of continuing competence as a pre-condition of Registration as a Nurse. In addition, attending the meetings in London was far more demanding than travelling the shorter distance to and from the North. Nevertheless, the big bonus was the opportunity it gave Molly to visit her mother, or Joy for an overnight stay. Joy had now left the convent to take up a teaching post in a deprived area of London. And true to form, Joy also worked within the local church community to provide pastoral care to the under privileged children and their families, she sang in the church choir and acted as relief organist – services Molly was proud to attend from time to time.

The close contact previously enjoyed by Molly and her friend Petal was greatly missed by them both. The telephone was better than nothing but it was not the same, they even swopped plants from their gardens and regularly presented each other with gifts to ensure they had a bit of each other nearby! However, as time passed by Molly began to feel reassured as Petal described the home-comforts she was enjoying including a lovely new kitchen and small cosy sitting room constructed from a space at the far end of the hallway. But Petal's pride and joy was the reconfiguration of the entrance porch to the Hall now graced by gothic pillars, inside the restoration highlighted the wonderful stained-glass windows and made an impressive entrance to the ballroom ... "The effect is truly magnificent, Mol!" But there was more as Petal told of the marquee being erected on the pristine lawns in readiness for a friend's early summer wedding ceremony, to be followed by a fundraising Garden Party for the local Soroptimist Branch of which Petal was an active member! The new baby had now grown through the toddler stage to a schoolboy despite all her misgivings about the inhospitable environment in which they lived. Life was looking good for Petal and she sounded happy.

Much to Molly's surprise, and it should be said, 'against her better judgment', Ian revealed his ambition to have a boat to sail on the many and varied local waterways. Molly came home one night to find he had heard of a sailing course based on a retired Liverpool Ferry boat moored in the estuary. "How about it Wifey, shall we enrol?" Molly, unlike Ian who was well prepared following his experience with the rowing club, did not enjoy deep-water activities. "I shall need you to crew when we get a boat," said Ian persuasively. And so it was that during Lent they set forth on their sailing course. Each day began with the theory of certain sailing activities followed by practical sessions on the river. So far, so good - Ian and Molly got on quite well. The instructors then began to segregate the 'slow learners' from the more progressive sailors and Molly was assigned to the first group with a different partner and that was where it all started to go wrong. Molly was apprehensive, uncertain and hating every minute of it, whilst she could hear Ian romping up and down the river on his dinghy with his equally competent buddy. Molly knew Ian would be just longing to cross 'the Bar' and head out to sea!

By contrast, Molly and her equally hesitant sailing partner were given extra tuition but even that ended in disaster when the instructor, attempting to tie up at one of the buoys, fell into the water! Enough is enough thought Molly. However, as they were approaching the end of the course, she was persuaded to qualify for her certificate by completing the last two exercises, one of which was 'capsize drill'. The day arrived and suitably equipped Molly and Ian took their turn on the boat to complete the exercise. First the boat was tipped on its side and Molly plunged into the water to swim around the stern, continue along the underside, climb on the keel and haul the boat upright! Having navigated her way around to the keel she seemed to lose all power in her arms and legs and the chap who manned the safety dinghy placed an oar between her legs and helped her on her way. No sooner had she righted the capsized boat than she was propelled into the water again whilst Ian undertook his task!

Holding on to the side of the boat, Molly paddled the water until Ian had completed his exercise and the boat was righted again. Safety was paramount and officials observing the scenario from the boathouse sent a recovery boat to collect

Molly. Feeling nauseous, faint, and with pains in her neck she was advised to lie down in her bunk. An Orthopaedic Consultant member of the course was sent to assess Molly. He arrived rather apologetically saying he was only a 'saw-bones' but he was happy to help if he could. Listening to Molly's symptoms he said, "I think you and I both know what is the problem, don't we?" Molly nodded because she too feared she was having a heart attack, which the local GPs tests eventually confirmed. Molly was admitted to hospital.

Four weeks later she was discharged home and greeted by the news that she had a granddaughter and to her delight Gavin and Dana brought the new baby, Jayne to see her. Molly's convalescence was going well and, as she approached what she hoped was the end of her enforced rest the Head of Department paid her a visit. The developments Molly had put in place were promising but needed tighter co-ordination, would Molly consider a promotion as Head of Nursing Studies to take forward a combined graduate programme for nursing and related professions? Molly accepted the challenge but knowing that her health would not sustain the additional demands, together with her national commitments, she resigned from most of the external appointments she held.

Ian really experienced a time of 'reinvention'. Not only were they both on a different trajectory, Molly in academia and Ian in retirement but the culture and conventions of the rural South West were very different to that of a Northern City. The village population presented a similar picture from the national one, insofar as there were more elderly women in the community than men! Ian's services were in great demand, "The car will not start," and "OK, I will be round." ... "The tele's flashing," "OK, I will be round." ... "The light bulb in the kitchen has blown." "OK, I will be round." But one morning Ian received a call that was beyond his comprehension ... "Can you come Ian, a calf has run up the silage heap and is sinking?" On arrival Ian found the farmer and his wife trying to lasso the calf with the clothesline but the calf was sinking rapidly. 'Take the line, get in the dingy and lie flat, Meg" the farmer said to his wife "You,

Ian, slide the dingy up the muck heap." It was far from easy but Meg managed to loop the line around the calf's head and together they pulled it away from a certain death. The farmer hosed down the calf, loaded it into the back of his truck and drove off to market. Ian went home 'smelling of roses' and into the bath.

But as time passed Ian and the farmer formed a great friendship. They enjoyed times of revelry and the farmer's wife regularly joined in! A favourite escape after milking on a summer's day was to pack a picnic, including a supply of local Cider and take the boat on the river for the day. Ian always came home exhilarated – the experience undoubtedly recalled memories of his youth.

Ian readily made friends in the village but his true mate was Charlie, a recently retired farm worker. Charlie was Devon born and bred and he taught Ian many different ways of doing things and seeing the world! Ian also made friends with Derek and his wife who moved into the village shortly after Ian arrived. The three men would meet up on a fine day to 'take the air' around the Parish – they were fondly referred to as the 'Last of the Summer Wine' trio: they even had a bonny widow vying for their attention! Derek's wife wrote a poem about Ian's outgoing way of life, – here's a taster:

Our Ian

He always has time to give a helping hand to someone in need;
A chauffeur, a plumber, or a load to be taken to the rubbish tip down the lane.
Should the village hall need attention, Ian is bound to be there;
Just ask our Ian he will always assist.
The Post Office also has been in his care –
Yes my dear, your pension is here – let me just find the key,
Ah it is in this drawer, I see.
Then the village pantomime, and his hour of glory came as the Pantomime Dame.
Our Ian, What would we do without him?

After the May Day celebrations with the young folk dancing round the Maypole on the village green, the next event was the Annual Sports Day and Garden Show in August. Early one morning prior to the appointed day Ian was given the job of clearing the cow pats from the two fields where the tents and show rings would be prepared - 'So much for country living', thought Ian whilst loving every minute of it! Early morning on the 'Show Day', Ian was assigned to the hall to check-in and place the exhibits against their allotted number on the tables. Later he assisted the judges by recording the results and finally placing the First, Second, or Third prize cards against the appropriate exhibit. During the show Ian helped with the 'Nine-pin Bowling' and in the late afternoon when the races began he officiated as one of the umpires.

Ian became such a popular member of the village community he was invited to stand in the Parish Council elections to be elected with a nice majority! However, if there is one thing that the Devonians do not like it is to be organized and coming from a different culture, Ian could be rather insensitive to their way of doing things ... he learned the hard way sometimes.

One year, the by-gone tradition of a village Christmas Pantomime was revived. Auditions for 'Jack and the beanstalk' were held in the village hall and Ian came home with the part of 'Widow Twankey', Jack's mother: Molly made his costume; and Ian learned his lines whilst walking Mr Ben. After weeks of rehearsing, the first night arrived. The 'Panto' was a huge success and Ian's name shot into the bright lights.

Next, it was Molly's turn. Having joined the Women's Institute a request was made for volunteers to organize the annual harvest festival supper in the village hall. Molly and two other newish members stepped forth. For the Menu they decided on a 'Summer Casserole', much to the disdain of some village people. "What's that?" they were repeatedly asked. "Oh, well I'll bring along a few slices of roast beef and boiled ham just in case ..." came the dubious response. "Will you be making a salad?" "Well, we thought perhaps jacket potatoes this year," came the reply. But some were not pacified and suggested they provided a variety of salads – "just in case, mind."

The three, new to the job, volunteers looked into the cost of various brands of cream to accompany the apple pies and cider to drink. Needless to say, the supermarket brands came quite cheap compared with the same products from the local farmers' market. As rumours began to circulate about the famous 'threesome' intentions they were reminded, "We always have farmer 'X's clotted cream with the apple pie and Scrumpy from farmer 'Y's orchards – we don't like that foreign stuff." The threesome conceded and all seemed well on the night – well fairly well!

But change was inevitable, even in the South West! The long-serving incumbent retired and a new Vicar arrived – a Cornishman who was received with caution solely because he came from "t'other side of the Tamar"! The new Vicar and Ian got along famously, even though Ian was not a 'church person'. The Vicar, believing there were many ways to heaven and thinking Ian was a good man asked him to step into the breach when unable to fill the position of Secretary to the Parochial Church Council (PCC). "Always willing to help if I can. What do I have to do?" enquired Ian "A brief outline of the appointment was given. "But," said the Vicar "You must first become a member of the Church." "How do I do that?" asked Ian somewhat mystified. "Are you Baptised and Confirmed in the Church of England?" enquired the Vicar. "Yes," replied Ian. "OK, I'll get it sorted." came the assurance. And so Ian took on another key responsibility in the village and relished every minute of it.

Anyone planning a wedding, a funeral, or seeking information about Confirmation classes dropped in to see Ian to set the ball rolling as it were. For a funeral Ian met with the family, the undertaker and the gravedigger – there was definitely a hierarchy in the churchyard; you could not go in any old plot you fancied! The Vicar who lived in the next village had three extensive rural parishes was only too happy for Ian to do all the administration. Ian came to refer to the vicar as the 'Revd. Delegator'!

However, the day came when Ian made a most unusual and unexpected contribution to the wedding of his stage 'son' from 'Jack and the Beanstalk.' Ian decided to perform the old northern custom of dressing up as a chimney sweep to bring the newly-weds 'good luck'! But very few were familiar with this 'up country' custom, although one or two people recognized Ian wearing grimy overalls, his sooty face topped with a black leather cap and chimney sweep brush over his shoulder. As one might imagine Fay, was astonished to be greeted by a chimney sweep as she left the church on the arm of her groom but when she recognized Ian, her 'stage Mother', smiles bathed her face followed by big cheers all round. The photographs said it all.

In addition to his village commitments, Ian readily volunteered to escort Molly throughout the South West, and beyond when she visited her students on their placements. Whilst Molly met with the students, Ian investigated the local area, had lunch and they met up late afternoon to return home. These excursions stood Ian in good stead for the times he was called upon to entertain visiting University dignitaries.

The Nursing Department offered a three months placement to American University students, this time from the 'Deep South'. The visiting Professor usually spent about one month with the class. This was to be the second hands-on exposure Molly experienced of teaching within the framework of a Nursing Model – this time American nursing scholar, Betty Neuman's Systems Model. The Model was yet another approach to defining the growing complexity of nursing in a changing world. The profession now seemed to be awash with 'Models of Nursing' for which there was a general tailing-off of enthusiasm in the UK on account of the perceived constraints, confusion, and 'jargon' – perhaps Neuman's contribution could be seen to be rather typical. Nevertheless, Molly was disappointed by what seemed to be an arbitrary rejection of these more systematic approaches to the identification of health limitations and patient need as the means by which both clinical practice and professional education can be informed.

Whilst in the UK, the visiting Professor looked forward to experiencing something of the geography and culture of the South West of England, and its health and social care provisions. Ian happily dealt with the former by escorting the Professor to eating-places of historical, or popular interest for lunch, such as Jamaica Inn on Bodmin Moor the location for the famous film of that name. He also found places of interest, or macabre curiosity in the Cathedral Cities, seaside resorts, and across the Moors. For instance, the famous Benedictine Monastery at Buckfast Abbey on Dartmoor offered visitors a veritable feast walking through the sensory gardens, sampling the well-stocked shop of fine examples of religious artefacts, and of course the temptation of the Abbey's home-brewed 'Tonic Wine'!

Ian's visitors were also fascinated by the vast open space of Exmoor, particularly 'Doone Country' the area Blackmore chose for his seventeenth century novel, Lorna Doone. The intriguing story was a fictitious reflection of earlier times but it was in the church where the sad story of Lorna's fate was most poignant. A memorial plaque to the author is situated in Oare Church, a replica of which Ian's visitors would have noted during their visit to Exeter Cathedral.

The coastal areas inevitably captured the fascination of the visitors; from the rugged cliffs of Land's End, to the quaint fishing harbours such as Falmouth; and the touristy attractions of the seaside resorts such as Paignton and Torquay with their wide promenades, piers, novelty shops and theatres.

Ian invariably came home with tales of his visitors' wonderment, disbelief and sometimes, sheer terror especially when driving along the narrow lanes encased by high walls and hedges. On occasions a party, including the students, would spend the evening walking along Plymouth Hoe, each reciting the bits they remembered of Sir Frances Drake's bravery in defeating the invading Spanish Armada. One particular area on the quayside marked the sailing of the Mayflower - the large imposing plaque recording the historic event attracted time for reflection. To lighten the feelings this brave and significant event had provoked, supper on the Barbican was the next stop! The historic area with its magical lighting effects was often likened to that of stepping into a fairy tale but nothing caused more amusement than to find 'Faggots' on the supper menu – in the States they had a totally different meaning!

The group departed at the end of their studies with much appreciation and the assurance of a very warm welcome should Ian and Molly ever wish to visit the Carolinas.

In the light of her promotion, Molly was keen to advance her academic status by researching a Master of Philosophy degree (MPhil); her thesis, 'learning together promotes working together', was inspired by Allport's (1971) assertion that positivity is the glue that cements a society together. The Dean of Faculty gave approval and her research was supervised by the Department of Psychology. Ian re-jigged a room at home as Molly's study and the ancient Brother typewriter was exchanged for an Amstrad computer – what a transformation!

Unexpectedly, Molly was invited to participate with a team of academics at an Inter-professional Learning Conference at Helsinki University in June. The papers presented by the team gave an evaluation of their experience of shared learning between community nursing specialities, general practitioners and the remedial professions. The Conference was a stimulating experience for Molly on the brink of her MPhil research but of equal interest was to discover the beauty of Finland now waking up after the long dark winter and realising at first-hand what it meant to the people of Helsinki.

Molly's love affair with the pen never waned; her ability to 'think outside of the box' was widely acknowledged. She was an innovator, thanks to Miss Todd; and no stranger to the conference platform! Preparing conference papers and articles for publication in the professional journals was a regular feature of Molly's career. But her great ambition was to write a book! A quite unforeseen opportunity came along when her Head of Department, suggested he introduced her to his publisher. Molly's proposal was received with interest. However, for once in her life she realised she had too much on her plate!

But Molly never lost sight of her ambition and the next time it was literally handed to her! A publisher approached Molly following the publication of a Report by a nursing review she had chaired. Unintentionally, the book became co-authored to accommodate the ambitions of two colleagues – it was quite an experience! But the book was published; it was well received by their peers; and later translated into Polish!

But, was it all in vain? What would her parents have thought about Molly's achievements? Would they have met Rose's ambitions? Would Wills have considered Molly had earned her Gold Medal for keeps?

CHAPTER 10

LOVE: THE PRIZE AND PRICE

THE ARRIVAL OF GRANDCHILDREN:

As Molly's career and Ian's involvement in the village flourished in many and varied ways; life was embellished by the joys of grandchildren and extensions to the family but overshadowed by losses that would be unredeemable.

The over-riding attraction in Molly's life was granddaughter, Jayne, later to be joined by a brother, James. What a pair they were! They came to stay with 'Nannie and Granddad Ben'- so named after Ian's dog, Mr Ben. Once again history repeated itself as Nannie-Ben took Jayne and James beneath the sheets into Benjamin Bunny's burrow! Gwen's unseen presence snuggled in between them felt the same warmth of previous generations; it seemed only yesterday when she, Kate and Molly were with Rose and listening to her tales. These were such happy but heart-breaking times for Molly who just longed to live near to her grandchildren, saying 'Goodbye' at the end of a visit was painful for everyone – Jayne was inconsolable.

Jayne and James filled Molly's life during the vacations and any other times she could get away to their home, 'up country', as they say in the South West! It seemed like an all-embracing matrix in which experiences, like gems, would be embedded forever. The children sailed their little boats at the seaside, competed with each other at crazy golf on the promenade and played Bingo and Drop-Penny at the end of the pier. Visiting a local shopping complex was also an attraction with its child-friendly boating lake, a dodgem car track where Jayne was greatly dismayed one day when the money did not run out and the car seemed destined on a perpetual journey round the circuit. James couldn't wait to drive himself round a motor car circuit and at every visit he stood tall trying to meet the minimum height bar – one year he did and off he went.

Organising fun times, which included elements of teaching and the development of new skills was Ian's speciality! One such activity involved 'survival exercises' on Dartmoor. The children were equipped with a compass and a map, a stick, protective clothing, a rucksack with a survival kit including chocolate, barley sugars and fortified drinks – a 'sin-bin' never allowed at home! As the exercise unfolded on Dartmoor it all became very realistic, particularly on the day that the treacherous mist descended. At some point in 'the game' Molly and the children would hide under a rocky outreach, or in the hollow of a dislodged tree root pretending to be lost and taking shelter whilst Ian went through the motions of finding them. During their wait out came the 'sin-bin' and by the time Ian 'found' them their lips were caked with chocolate and the drinks containers drained dry. With sparkling eyes and bounding energy they leapt out in response to Ian's call to be 'rescued'.

Part of such expeditions, included the recognition of animal tracks, "to help if you lose your way," Ian advised. He explained that some tracks gave a lead to safe ground, whilst others signalled caution. For instance, they were always to lookout for the large shaggy footprints of the legendary 'Beast of Dartmoor,' which they knew not to follow towards his secretive and dangerous lair!

On rainy days when the children were housebound Molly organized cooking sessions using the 'out of date' ingredients she had saved for the children to invent their own recipes. One favourite cake was named 'slobbidob' and a slice always awaited Granddad-Ben when he came in for tea. Ian pretended to eat it but it was totally inedible – even the birds wouldn't peck at the crumbs when they were thrown onto the lawns!

Jayne was studious and frequently brought school projects to complete during her stay. One holiday she had a 're-cycling' exercise to complete. Jayne carefully noted on her teacher's checklist Molly's routines to dispose of food waste, tins, plastics and paper waste. When Jayne returned to school and her project was marked, she proudly telephoned Molly to say that her teacher had awarded Molly top marks. Well, nothing was ever wasted at Nannie-Ben's home – "wilful waste brings wilful want," warned the age-old adage frequently quoted by Rose.

But one of the most intriguing enterprises was yet to come - the making of a costume for Jayne's part in the next school play, Hiawatha! Jayne and Molly went shopping, they bought a length of brown fabric for a tunic, some fur fabric and a length of multi-coloured webbing, but where to buy feathers became a challenge. However, they started work on the tunic, edged it with fur, measured the webbing for the right length of a headdress to trail down Jayne's back. But they were still without any feathers. Jayne was suddenly inspired, "What about the beach Nannie, there are lots of sea gull feathers there?" So off they went and when they returned home with their bounty the feathers were cleaned and then patiently sewn onto the webbing. A pair of brown tights and a smidgen of fur on her shoes – magnificent!

At a very early age, Jayne learned to knit, sew and embroider; on one occasion she made a nightgown for herself and wore it with justifiable pride! Molly tried to entice James to make a nightshirt of the type his great-granddad Wills might have worn. He thought Molly had taken leave of her senses and would have none of it! However, James conceded to drawing some small sports pictures on graph paper for Molly or Jayne to embroider on his pyjamas! With an eye for colour and mathematical design Jayne produced some exquisite tapestry work which she gave away as birthday or Christmas presents, or to take back home to Dana's mother, "with love from Nannie-Ben."

Jayne, a lover of nature worked tirelessly in the garden with Molly. She filled the birdbaths from her little watering can, "so they can have a drink and wet their feathers in the hot weather, Nannie." She set seeds for next year's flowers; dug out the weeds and popped the worms back into the soil, "in case they get lost away from home, Nannie!" It was at times like his when Nannie and Jayne were playing together that sensations came flooding back of Molly and Gwen playing in the Fairy Dell!

But Jayne was also keen-eyed and ready to take charge!! One afternoon Molly, Jayne and James went to the cinema to see the film 'Pocahontas'. Molly asked at the box office for tickets to see 'Hocus-pocus', a little face quickly popped up over the counter saying, "She means Pocahontas." Likewise, Jayne enjoyed taking charge as 'teacher'. With her dolls and soft toys sitting on the sofa, or her bed she would assign Molly the role of 'teaching assistant'. Drawing herself up to her full height, Jayne greeted Molly at her classroom door saying, "Good morning Molly. Would you help with reading practice this morning please?" Jayne's eyes would twinkle at the daring use of Molly's Christian name instead of Nannie.

By contrast, James was action packed and crazy about football, cricket and karate – in fact any sport! But they all shared in the fun when Molly and Jayne joined in with his games, even to the extent of dressing up in their pyjamas for early morning karate exercises on the lawn in the mists of their 'Brigadoon village'! James marshalled them to form his well-organized karate class, or cricket team and put them through their paces. He was exceptionally strict about following the rules of the game; no shoddy practice and certainly no concessions allowed. During one game of tennis on the playing field, Molly thought she qualified for two bounces of the ball because she was Nannie and therefore of a great age. "Absolutely not," said James.

On the lighter side of life, James' one-time all-consuming interest was the 'Back to the Future' films in which Michael J Fox (MJF) played the leading part. MJF became James' hero. True to his nature, James took it all very seriously as he placed himself out of sight behind an armchair and whilst humming a tune, he gradually unrolled a scroll of paper to appear above the back of the chair as if introducing the film credits. James then leapt out to become MJF – in fact, James really began to look like MJF as he emulated his every characteristic. It all provided great entertainment for his audiences if somewhat disconcerting for his parents perhaps!

The grandchildren loved the challenge of competition in any form. One opportunity presented once a year when the whole village prepared for the Annual Sports Day and Garden Show. This was not to be missed. Jayne and James came prepared to make an entry in the 'Children's Handicraft Competitions' and together they created such exhibits as wind-chimes out of Ian's collection of odds and ends in his 'Just in case' box, or Jayne used her developing horticultural flair to make a miniature garden or an unusual flower arrangement. Jayne's entries were always perfectly presented and she regularly came away with a first or second prize. James quickly became bored with such trivia and went off to pursue his latest craze. But one year Molly and Jayne persuaded him to make a collage of a scene on a Rugby pitch – success! They used a green carpet tile for the pitch and under James' instruction they patiently produced the players and officials in the right coloured felt and appropriate poses. However, James was only interested in instructing Molly and Jayne on what to do, who went where on the pitch, and the motion of the player in relation to the ball in action! The collage made a very attractive entry and won first prize, which needless to say Jayne and Molly claimed as theirs but James was having none of it because he said he was "the brains behind the idea".

The Annual event ended with a series of races carefully organised to secure fair competition. There were 4 classes: all classes, women, men; children. James was in his element and

Jayne, always the good sport joined in with gusto!! Some races where quite adventurous competitions; one in particular went up a steep hill, around the farmer's tractor parked on the top, down the hill, through the farm yard, and back to base ... whew!! But James just loved it and he was always amongst the first 'home' in his Class.

James had long since grown tired of 'kids' stuff' like Benjamin Bunny stories at night so with a bit of quick-thinking Molly capitalised on his noncommittal curiosity in the legendary 'Beast of Dartmoor'! They invented their own stories and together concocted outrageous exploits, which sometimes caused Jayne to be a bit afraid of the monster. However, most had a double meaning, for instance, 'The Beast' enjoyed Branston Pickle and Peanut Butter sandwiches but sadly he didn't clean his teeth and one day a peanut got stuck in a decayed tooth which sent him howling to the dentist. Magical times, as one imaginative exploit led to another.

The late Norman, Anglican village church, became part of their adventures of fun and discovery. Although baptized in the Roman Catholic Church, which they had not attended since their Baptism, the little village church was a kind of novelty for them. Taking account of Jayne's love of a project and James preference for activity games Molly produced a Quiz Trail to explore some of the interesting features of the old Norman Church. 'The 'Trail' included the unique Italian Sgraffito plasterwork embossed with symbols and figures from earlier civilisations which lined the church walls; the red and grey sandstone Norman font; the ornate Rood Screen dividing off the Sanctuary; and the striking stained glass windows depicting stories from the Holy Bible. The 'Trail' usually ended with a tune on the old organ! Joy sometimes played for a service when she visited, with Jayne, or James sitting with her on the long bench-like seat to turn over the pages of music; or Jayne might accompany the organ on her Recorder. The organ was a monumental piece of history – hand pumped until 1951 when electricity was installed, which always brought back memories for Molly who as a young girl pumped the church organ and sometimes played the pedal organ for the hymns at the Chapel services – always with Gwen in tow, of course!

The gentle Cornish Vicar was an imaginary preacher who inevitably involved his congregation in one-way or another. For example, the Holy Bible story of Jesus washing his Disciples' feet always engaged the Vicar in washing the feet of (volunteering) members of the congregation – Jayne and James were always willing volunteers! When the grandchildren visited the South West for their Easter holidays, they came prepared to make an Easter Bonnet for the Easter Day church parade. James nearly always chose a baseball cap with no adornment other than the peak tipped at a rakish angle! Jayne, on the other hand, made the most original creations using tiny yellow chickens, miniature Easter eggs or small flower heads to decorate one of Molly's hats – the yellow hat with the ornate veil was a particular favourite.

The church was a source of new interests and experiences in many other ways. Molly had joined the 'Cleaning Rota'. Jayne and James readily volunteered to give Molly a hand when her turn came, although rather subdued because they thought being alone in the stillness of the church an eerie experience. It didn't help when they knew the church housed a colony of bats that sprayed acid urine as they flew around in the dusk. Removing the spray stains on the wooden pews and beautifully coloured floor tiles was a difficult task for the cleaners. The children thought it was "disgusting' and frequently looked up to the rafters to dodge any spray that might come their way! But it gave the children a useful understanding of the life, habitats and habits of the bats, which they might never otherwise have encountered.

The cleaning routine was somewhat lightened when they came to Angie's pew. Angie was not terribly tolerant of children in church, she would turn and scowl if she heard them whisper, or give a chastising 'tut-tut' if they should accidentally drop their books. So when Jayne and James arrived at Angie's seat they gave it a special polish so that the shiny surface would cheer her up and make her friendlier towards them. Sadly, none of us noticed any change in Angie's behaviour! However, during one cleaning session Molly overheard James whisper to Jayne, "Put plenty of polish on Angie's seat and give it a good rub then she might slip off when she turns round to scowl at us!" Seeing Molly's frown, he sensed that whilst it might be fun, he realised it was most unkind and thought better of the idea!

Summer holidays unfolded with the usual round of adventures, mishaps and inevitably tearful partings with the promise of Christmas at the children's home, or maybe the half term break if all went well! Gavin now hosted Christmas in the lovely old family home, which much to the grandchildren's and Molly's delight lasted from Christmas Eve to New Year's Day. It seemed never ending but of course when the end came the inevitable tears were shed. Early into the New Year on one particular occasion, Molly's telephone rang and when she answered she was delighted to hear Jayne's voice. "Hello, darling" said Molly as she listened to Jayne talking and Dana's off-stage whispering. "Hello, Nannie. The bungalow opposite my house is for sale, Mummy says if you buy it I can come over for tea." 'Oh dear, how are you going to deal with that?' Gwen thought because she just knew Molly was thinking, 'if only'.

THE END OF AN ERA:

However, later in the year Molly was brought down to earth with a message from the residential home to say Rose had deteriorated and was calling for her. Molly drove 'up country' and really appreciated her IAM driving skills and discipline, which concentrated her mind on the road.

On arrival at the Nursing Home Molly found her mother fairly lucid but clearly approaching the end of her life. Just as she had done with Wills, Molly held her mother close and talked about their wonderful life and the hopes of glory ahead. Rose smiled and stroked Molly's cheek saying, "Oh Nitto!" as she drifted back to her dreaming's. Now closer to the point of death Rose's all-knowing eyes peered closely at Molly; she smiled, closed her eyes and her face became transformed by the tranquillity of death as Rose drifted away.

Gwen felt Molly's overwhelming grief and was greatly moved by her murmurings, of comfort and love as she searched for the answer to a question that Rose would take with her to the grave ... "Oh Mum, what did happen all those years ago to blight the love you and Dad once shared?" Just how long Molly sat there holding her mother she never knew but Gwen did and it was a long time before the nurses were called and the eventual rumble of the hearse was heard on the gravel drive followed by the undertaker's trolley. A final "goodbye" as the wheels rumbled back over the stones and carried Rose away to close Molly's childhood forever.

The funeral was held in the village church and Rose was laid to rest by the side of Wills – it was a heartfelt prayer in which Gwen joined with Molly as she earnestly said, "May you rest together in peace and love". Now there was only one of the five Dolman girls left – Jane, Rose's youngest sister.

Life goes on, and the day came when Jayne and James were to join their cousins on a visit to Disney Land. "Please come, Nannie," said Jayne. But Molly couldn't join them – she hadn't been invited, if she had Gwen just knew she would have moved heaven and earth to go with them! So, Molly did the next best thing by going to Heathrow Airport to wave them off. Just in case there was any tears Molly had designed a storybook about 'The Beast of Dartmoor', which she gave them as she said 'Goodbye' and the moment of sadness was diffused.

NURSING IN USA:

October 1990 and the 'boot was on the other foot'. Molly was awarded a Travel Fellowship to study Community Nursing education in the USA. The study would have a particular focus on inter-professional learning between health and social care practitioners. Her willing hosts were the well informed and generous of spirit colleagues from the American Universities she met during their UK placements.

Molly wrote to Sarah to tell her about her award and to share some of her apprehension about Ian's possible reluctance to accompany her. In return, Molly received surprising news from Sarah to say that she and her professor, who was recently widowed, had accepted academic appointments in New Zealand. "Well, Molly there will never be another Sam. Gerald and I get on well together, we share a common professional interest and Gerald's eldest daughter migrated to New Zealand many years ago. Marriage? Well, who knows?" Then Sarah went on to say, "Sam thought the world of you, Molly, and I seemed to think you thought of him that way too. Sometime, you might feel like telling me why you never got together. I know one thing for sure; if Sam were around now, he would be on that 'plane with you to the USA like a shot!"

The prospect of having to leave Ian at home began to cast a shadow over Molly's enthusiasm, until by sheer coincidence Molly heard from her friend, Cindy who had been in a similar situation. Cindy held the position of Director of Nursing Education at a prestigious specialist hospital where a multidisciplinary team of medics, nurses and therapists regularly participated on Conference platforms at home and abroad. On this occasion the team had just returned from America and talking to Molly, Cindy happened to comment on how much her husband, Syd, had enjoyed the trip. With some amusement Cindy described Syd's involvement and his expeditions on the Greyhound Coaches to "somewhere, anywhere and maybe staying overnight. Syd always gave me a ring at the Conference Hotel to say where he was and when he would return!" Magic, thought Molly, Ian loves an adventure but was he really that adventuresome?

Molly proved to be right – in part! Ian was enthusiastic and the more so because he knew the professors from hosting their visits in the UK. Arrangements were made but the nearer to the date of confirming the airline booking approached Ian seemed to 'go off the boil' as it were, whilst insisting everything was "OK." Time went by and during breakfast one morning Molly reminded Ian that they needed to pay for the airline tickets by the end of the week. Ian replied, "I'm not going." Molly was dumbfounded but Ian went on to explain, "I shall be on my own all day and I shall miss you, Wifey ... and then there is Mr Ben!" Molly prepared to look for a compromise asked, "Well, what shall we do, Hub?" But there was no compromise to be found. Molly felt she had no option at such a late stage but to go ahead. Hurt and puzzled by Ian's behaviour she set off for the first phase of her study in the Mid-West.

Arriving in Minnesota, Molly stayed overnight before flying to the local airport. Morning arrived and she found her room overlooked a wide expanse of water on which a number of distinctive looking ducks were paddling. The waiters told her the 'ducks' were Loons, the designated 'State Bird' who, it was believed, had special significance of tranquillity; just the message Molly needed! The Loons certainly presented a majestic sight of caring as they gently paddled through the water carrying their young on their back safely folded between their wings.

In the crystal brightness of the sunny morning Molly set out on the final stage of her journey to be met by two nurse teachers. They were welcoming and friendly, chattering away during the car journey and pointing out places of interest. The University was situated in a stunning environment with a river running through the campus to offer a marvellous opportunity for water sports, or for just dreaming away on its banks in the autumn sunshine. One side of the campus was bordered by a forest noted for its rich variety of trees and wetlands, an ideal area in which to find rare botanical species and wildlife, whilst the other side bordered suburbia with the sounds of a busy city echoing in the distance. Molly stayed in 'Halls' and most evenings she strolled through this glorious setting, which was even more exhilarating in early October when the autumn colours could be seen in all their glory.

The City housed a rich and vibrant culture partly inherited from earlier times when industrialists from Germany, Norway and Finland were attracted to live there; and more recently a diverse mix of peoples including a large community of Vietnamese. A close-knit Amish agricultural society also had long established its roots in the area and their distinctive black horse-drawn carriages mingled graciously with the busy city traffic. Molly expected that the challenge of providing integrated nursing education within such cultural diversity and geographical expanse would be an interesting and meaningful experience – and it was!

The University, dating back to 1916, was proud of its standing both in the local community and the academic status it had achieved in wider circles. The School of Nursing, now approaching its 25th anniversary, was part of this kudos. The School's baccalaureate and post-graduate nursing degrees reflected the American Nursing Association's definition of nursing as "the diagnosis and treatment of human responses to actual or potential health problems". But, the coherent and comprehensive construction of Loomis and Wood's Model of Nursing was applied to give structure and meaning to the practical application of nursing at all levels and in a variety of settings, including education and research. In a bizarre sense, Molly likened the multidimensional model to the Rubik's Cube with its multiplicity of colours and options of alignment but one that required more than a random manoeuvre to calibrate!

Molly's participation in inter-faculty debates and seminars, in addition to practical teaching sessions produced some lively encounters between the different disciplines. For instance, because students were recruited from a widely spread geographical distances, they met together less frequently at the parent University but in local groups to participate in tutorials, seminars and one-off lectures. An arrangement that had some similarity to Molly's 'satellite' programmes in the South West peninsular, However, at the Mid-West University teleconferencing played an interesting and important role in distance learning. Molly led such an event shortly after her arrival; it was an illuminating experience of a resource that could be more widely used as a forum for integrated learning activities in the UK.

Working with the Community Nurses in the USA, Molly experienced the now familiar 'zing' of inter-national nursing kinship; even their role titles were similar to those of their counterparts in the UK! Molly accompanied the nurses on their home visits where she felt immediately in her comfort zone participating in various activities and talking to the patients and their carers. She also joined in diverse social and rehabilitation activities with voluntary agencies and charities such as the Lutheran Community. Wherever Molly worked, the universal guiding principles of patient care and family welfare seemed to be grounded in the preservation of dignity, a respect for individuality, the fostering of hope and aspiration for a future yet to unfold whether it be a brief, or long journey. The American people Molly met had a gracious disposition and a delightfully expressive and open style of speech with seemingly few inhibitions and a kind of directness that hit the spot! The nurses were generous hosts and happily provided an insight to their work and aspirations whilst equally interested to know about Molly ... "Is there a Mr in your life; do you have kids?" And about health care in the UK, they frequently asked, "Would you do it like this?" Or, "How would you make such arrangements?" Or "Is the NHS like an all-inclusive insurance policy – what happens if you don't pay your premiums?"

The patients generously extended their hospitality to "our honoured guest from the UK." They were curious about Florence Nightingale and frequently asked whether Molly had actually seen her lamp, or visited the famous St Thomas' hospital. No, she hadn't; but Molly delighted in relating an account of a visit by the President of the American Nursing Association to her School of Nursing and the President's reaction when given its treasured bronze of Florence Nightingale to inspect. Molly did so wish she could have shown the press photograph of the occasion! The endless questions provided an opportunity to fill in the gaps in Florence

Nightingale's family background and the lesser-known aspects of her work, such as her support for district nursing and health visiting ... interests that had brought Molly to the States she explained!

The concept of 'Royalty' was intriguing and inevitably, curiosity was aroused about the QNI and its 'Royal' connection. Molly found herself talking about the origins of Royal patronage from the times of Queen Victoria; describing the Institute's historical headquarters in Belgravia; and the ceremonials held to mark achievements in district nursing. The 'Long Service Award' to mark 21 years as a 'Queen's Nurse' was one such ceremony ... "Do you nurse the Queen and members of the Royal Family, then?" Of course, Molly didn't but she explained that Buckingham Palace was part of a London district nurse's designated 'District' to visit and serve the needs of the staff.

Had Molly ever met the Queen or any member of the Royal Family? In response, Molly frequently made reference to the event 5 years ago when the Queen Mother presented her with the golden medallion to mark her 21 years' service; the afternoon tea taken with Her Majesty followed by the photograph of the whole assembly tiered up the magnificent ornate spiral staircase. Her hosts sensed this was a very proud moment in Molly's career inquired whether Molly wore her Long Service medallion. - it only appeared on ceremonial occasions; she would explain. Inevitably Molly was jokingly challenged, "Well, you should have brought it with you; this is a worthy ceremonial visit – we shall expect to see it next time!" Molly began to wish she had taken a collection of the QNI almost military like insignia for her hosts to inspect.

Molly's hosts were always curious to known whether she had visited Buckingham Palace? And so Molly was able to tell of the bright summer day she, together with other Queen's Nurses, attended the Royal Garden Party as guests selected by the QNI. Molly described to her avid listeners her feeling of wonderment as she walked through the entrance, up the impressive stairway and out on to the raised terrace to look out over the gardens and lake. The colourful sea of guests assembled on the lawns in becoming outfits; not forgetting the men in their immaculate uniforms or well-tailored suits. White gloves were essential should you be presented to a member of the Royal Family on their walk-about - Molly was glad that her gloves were fit for purpose when her turn came. Finally, Molly described how the afternoon proceeded with strawberry tea in the large marquees and finally home to reality! "It was a day to remember," said Molly whose entertainment was met with the animated response ... "and a day we shall remember too!"

Interest in the UK by the people Molly met was quite overwhelming – she had few opportunities to talk about the USA way of life so all five senses, and her sixth sense, were highly tuned! Sometimes, her host's interests could take the most surprising turns. One husband, a retired engineer, was most interested to know that Molly lived in the vicinity of Plymouth, the stomping ground of his idol Isambard Kingdom Brunel! Was Molly familiar with his famous bridge over the River Tamar? "Yes, it's a route I often use in the course of my work," she told him. "What does it feel like to look at from close by?" he asked. "Awesome," said Molly as she reinforced his already extensive knowledge and admiration of the structure; she also expanded on the mini 'playground' for fishermen and leisure activities on the embankment at the foot of the bridge. However, when told of the recently installed pay-barriers on the bridge, Brunel's devotee did not regard the barriers be-fitting for such a noble piece of engineering architecture!

Sometimes memories of visiting the South West during a tour of the UK would be recalled. Occasionally a man would reminisce about his time at Dartmouth Naval College – or maybe recall the pride of a fellow student who one day returned to Plymouth with his ship! There were often moments of merriment when reflecting on the reputation of home brewed Mead, Buckfast Abbey's Tonic Wine, and 'Scrumpy', a rough cider in which fragments of its progress through the Cider Press remained! It was always a cause of amusement when Molly explained how the result of over imbibing would be described by the locals as, 'ere be maized, 'ere be! One family suddenly remembered the long-forgotten bottle of Plymouth Gin they had once brought home as a souvenir!

A rather surprising turn, and this time nearer home, came during a visit to one of the social centres when Molly met a man who was eager to hear about the University of Leicester's Space Centre Project in the Midlands. "Oh! Don't start on that!" declared his wife rolling her eyes in mock frustration. "His work related to the space industry and he has been obsessed with the outer universe all his life!" she declared. The man smiled and raised his eyebrows as if encouraging Molly to tell what she knew. Molly agreed that it would be an invaluable resource – due to be opened as a celebration of the millennium in ten years' time. "My grandson has an apprenticeship in the space industry – only just started, but what prospects!" he proudly concluded.

At the mention of grandchildren, his wife came alive to regale Molly with the details of her grandson's achievements at school and in sports; also, those of her granddaughter, an airhostess. "Aviation crazy they are; they would live above the clouds if they could - and it's all his fault!" It was lovely to hear the couple's banter – nothing changes, thought Molly.

But it was not all work and no play, as they say! The opportunities for Molly to savour a first-hand expression and understanding of the Wisconsin culture were many and varied. From the informal occasions to which she was invited such as student gatherings in Halls, to family suppers in the homes of her hosts where she might help with bedtime reading and other end of the day activities. Bedtime stories seemed to be enjoyed by children the world over and as she thought of her grandchildren, Molly sometimes shared a story of Benjamin Bunny! She was taught how to make popcorn by one family and given the recipe to take home!

Visits to local craft markets immediately attracted Molly's interest with her involvement in handicraft work at home and her acquaintance with Ruth's masterpieces. The different textures, colours and motives demonstrated the distinctive characteristics of the cultural setting from which they originated. Cushion covers, hats and gloves were easy on the eye and Molly found the odd purchase hard to resist!

Excursions to the surrounding countryside clothed in its vibrant autumn colours were inspiring and as Molly rested on the banks of the St Croix River in Stillwater watching a paddle-steamer sail by her joy knew no bounds – Gwen sensed that Molly was just imagining Al Johnson singing 'Old man River ...' Her hosts were proud to remind Molly that the 'pop-up bread toaster' was invented in Stillwater in 1926!

The end of Molly's time at the University was all too quickly approaching. It had been a wonderful experience in every way friendships, camaraderie, and new insights for the job ahead!
At a jolly farewell gathering with her colleagues Molly gave them all flower bulbs to bloom in the spring; her colleagues presented Molly with 'Wisconsin's Poet's Calendar' (1991). Opening her gift at random in the month of October, Molly experienced the imagery of the poet as if it were her own:

October Pantoum

October is wearing bittersweet
one last fling in golden dress.
One last look and then goodbye
to summer and the greening days
(Yvonne E. Yahnke p83)

Finally, she met with the Head of Department for a formal debrief and then to prepare for the grand finale. Molly's last evening coincided with a formal function in celebration of the 25th Anniversary of Nursing as an academic discipline – an impressionable evening laced with academic achievement, professional pride and a spirit of camaraderie.

The following day Molly left the glories of the campus and the comfort of her homely residence to head for the airport to begin the next stage of her journey to the Deep South' Having boarded the inland airlines flight to Columbia Molly was reassured to know she was still in America when the steward came round asking "Any traaash, Ma'am?"

Academic colleagues met Molly at the airport and greeted her with the famous 'Southern' hospitality; but they were dismayed to find she was travelling alone. Molly gave a brief explanation of Ian's absence, which she could see was very disappointing to her hosts, not least because Ian and the professor had bonded very quickly during her time in the UK. After 'refreshment' Molly was driven to the campus where she had been allocated a house designated for use by visiting professors. It was late, dark and Molly, now dead-tired, went straight to bed where she slumbered until the morning.

A lovely sunny morning greeted her and downstairs a 'welcome' card was attached to a large basket of fruit from the Faculty. Looking through the windows Molly realised she was in a woodland area of the campus. Venturing outside the birds were chattering and singing in the trees – she even spotted bluebirds nearby. It all seemed like a film-set.

Later in the morning the Professor, who Molly had known from the UK, came to greet her. After hoping Molly had slept well she proceeded to express her disquiet about Molly being alone. It is an expectation of the University that a visiting professor occupies the house with a travelling companion for security reasons. Molly was explained the risks with which she could be faced and the fact that a murder had been committed on campus last term added to the concerns. Molly, far from feeling comfortable with the situation, assured the Professor she would be watchful and security conscious … and Molly's assignment began.

An arrangement had been made for Molly to spend time with the Dean of Faculty. At the meeting the Dean spoke about the fine traditions and high standards to which the University had aspired since its establishment in 1872 and acknowledged the contribution the Nursing Department had made by its academic rigour and diversity. He emphasised the basic motivation of the University was to produce well-rounded graduates, cultured people who make a lasting contribution to society. The Dean expressed the hope that Molly would observe this to be so during her sabbatical. Indeed, she did; and in ways that would make a lasting impression.

For instance, Molly's visit took place in the aftermath of Hurricane Hugo where she witnessed at first-hand the devastation on the coastline of South Carolina and the considerable disturbance and distress for the local community. Molly was told how the University nursing students decamped to the stricken area to care for the sick, injured, isolated and homeless. It was an amazing story, the philosophy of which is one that should be seen to underpin the ideals of best practice across the nursing profession.

The Southern States experience certainly encountered the footprints of both present and past as a source from which present-day nursing ideals and practices originated. Molly's academic programme was integrated with visits to heritage sites, participation in local traditions and an appreciation of its cultural roots alongside its undisputable contemporary achievements. For instance, a visit to the 'Slave Market' in Charleston was a graphic reminder of past traditions across the world where freedom was not the value it aspires to be today. A reminder of that past was represented by the congenial smiling black ladies sitting cross-legged on the ground at the entrance to the market weaving their intricate and colourful baskets and offering them for sale.

In contrast to the streets of spectacular colourful houses, Charleston also presented large square, almost Georgian, plantation houses with spacious ventilating balconies to capture the sea breezes. The balconies were equipped with the traditional long swing canopied seat on which the plantation owners and members of their family might spend their leisure; the swing movement provided by the sea breezes, augmented by human hands gently adding to the motion. Inside, the impressive dwellings were defined by their spaciousness and emboldened by high architrave ceilings, the opulence of highly polished dark-wooden floors, and furniture adorned by rich soft fabrics. The Plantation Houses told an impressive story of the grandeur of past-times.

Rambling through the highways and byways of Charleston, Molly seemed to walk through this mist of time; a contrasting time which celebrated both the best of human virtues and violated then. Almost on cue they arrived at the famous City square named 'The four corners of the Law'. Here a dominant building on each corner gave a graphic message of the four pillars of Law: City Hall representing Municipal Law; the Post Office and Court House depicting Federal law; County Court House emphasising the authority of State law; and the Church illustrating the centrality of faith and God's Law. Out of town, a tin hut was the place of worship chosen by the black community for their more exuberant forms of evangelical praise and worship.

Next for an experience of 'medical law', one might say! One of Molly's clinical experiences included a visit to a grand private hospital where opulence alongside clinical excellence functioned hand in hand. Throughout her stay, health promoting behaviours were most noticeable and Molly found the commitment with which healthy choices were absorbed into everyday life quite illuminating. Raw fruit and vegetables were available at every meal; iced water freely accessible; and in the Carolinas sugar was omitted by request whilst in the Mid-West it was added by request … an interesting experience of the inter-relationship between health care values and culture that Molly could identify with the UK.

Later in her placement she was given the opportunity to attend another such hospital for a 'Breakfast meeting' where teach-ins and other formal gatherings were not uncommon at this time of day. On this occasion Molly was invited to lead a 'Breakfast teach-in' on UK nursing. She had prepared a questionnaire to explore her American colleagues' concept of interprofessional collaboration. Once again, the relationship with other professionals and agencies seemed to be regarded as an important but parallel activity – self-sufficient but not insular. For the second time Molly's perspective was challenged; was this contradiction the root of the difficulties experienced back home, she wondered? Nevertheless, it was an unusual and exhilarating experience to be alert and functioning at breakfast time and one that set the tone for the day.

Perhaps one of Molly's most impressionable on-site learning was a combined health and hygiene screening session at a middle school session involving teaching staff, student nurses and medical students. The participants worked seamlessly together and, as if by osmosis they seemed to absorb specific and interchangeable roles and responsibilities. The reality setting appeared to be fun both for the school pupils, their teachers, and the university students. The learning experience undoubtedly had the potential to be more effective than didactic teaching, or artificially constructed learning assignments. Another idea for shared learning to be explored back home!

Betty Neuman's mid 1970s Model of Nursing had been adopted by the School of Nursing to construct a curriculum of education and direct clinical practice. Once again this systematic reconfiguration of Nursing was equally complex to unravel at first glance! However, Molly's understanding was enhanced by her mentoring Professor during a friendly 'tutorial' as they strolled along the beach in South Carolina and a tiny crab provided a representation of human complexity under stress. Here's how Molly described the tutorial as she opens her section in the third edition of Betty Neuman's textbook (1995) …

"... we found a crab on the beach experiencing great difficulty in surviving because it could not respond to the environmental stressors and establish stability. We analysed the situation with reference to Neuman's Systems Model:
What factors are normally present to enable the crab to maintain viable balance between the external and internal environment?
Why is the crab unable to adjust to the present circumstances?
How can the stressors affecting the crab be prevented, corrected, attenuated?

At the 'Health and Hygiene' feed-back session in school the nursing students were obviously familiar and adept at using Neuman's themes as a framework to investigate health problems (stressors) and construct appropriate nursing responses; even the medical students quickly got on track; and the teachers clearly appreciated its logic! Modelling seemed to offer a template by which the core elements of inter-professional education could be distinguished from the discipline specific. This hands-on approach to shared-learning felt so right; it was fun, it was sparky, respectfully challenging and left Molly feeling greatly enthused.

Back in the University Molly recognised the friendly face of Monica, one of the undergraduates who formed part of the South West UK international class. The first session centred on the Nursing role in the maintenance of child health and well-being. The students were clearly more familiar than Molly in manipulating and applying Neuman's theoretical concepts! Nevertheless, the environmental factors conducive to positive health promoted by Nursing were hotly debated, whilst the nursing response to their prevention, or treatment of adverse influence (stressors) was less contentious, a consensus was not easily achieved. It seemed that the assessment of 'intuitive' aspects of Nursing proved less easy than the scientific, or objective aspects.

Once again, it was not all work and no play! The State of South Carolina was as varied in its terrain as in its culture. So from the ocean and its beaches and the sophistication of the City, Molly and her supervising professor headed for the Blue Ridge Mountains. It was here that Molly enjoyed a 'real' hot-dog from a fast-food stand. The hot-dog looked a work of art; the light golden-brown sausage was garnished with different coloured sauces which trickled down the side of the bread roll; it's looks did not belie its taste – all washed down with 'Coke'.

Caesars Head, a huge over-hanging granite rock resembling the headdress of a Roman General, was a local beauty spot in the Mountains to which Molly and her host headed with a sense of adventure. Quite a wager could be earned by anyone brave enough to stand on the plume of the general's helmet – and Molly was assured that the view below into the valley was awesome! "I'll take your word for it," said Molly!

Next for some folklore originating out of a geological phenomenon created by the freezing and expansion of water which split a huge rock vertically to form a deep ravine. According to folklore, the steep ravine between the two rock surfaces, was created by the Devil himself when he accidentally spilt some potent illicit home brew, hence named 'The Devil's Kitchen'. Indeed, to peer down this deep, seemingly bottomless, narrow gorge was an incredible sight accessed by a flight of steps – but not for the faint-hearted!

From folklore and geological phenomena, they visited one of the modern-day wonders of scientific developments: the Oconee Nuclear Power Station, the first of its kind built in 1973 on Lake Keowee, near Seneca. The scale of the building and the realization of its potential contribution across a spectrum of industrial, scientific and domestic functions was awe-inspiring to the extent of disbelief. Sated with wonderful experiences they headed back home exploring the often imponderables.

Molly was now beginning to feel 'at home' in her house on the campus where the sun shone in through the sitting room windows to greet her each evening. Sleep came easily on the lovely soft mattress of the large double bed, and she even began to welcome the musical interlude of a passing train that roused her from her slumbers on occasions – the first time she heard the sound she thought she was in heaven listening to the harps of angels! The exceptionally large trains seemed to signal their presence quite near to the campus – it was not unpleasant and quite different from the harsh whistle of the UK trains.

The rewards of looking through her window each morning where she could see the campus amphi-theatre, a creative arrangement in a woodland area of the campus, and the bluebirds flying around were a sight to remember. Classical productions were regularly staged in the amphi-theatre but Molly did not have the opportunity to see one during her stay. However, she was able to attend a moving production of 'Steel Magnolias,' a play set in the 'deep south', which made the sad story seem so real. Knowing Molly's love of the theatre one of the lecturers invited her to see a production of 'Jekyll and Hyde' at her local theatre. The theatre was quaintly classical – old London style; the play was very well cast and expertly directed but it was strange to hear the brave translation of the cockney accent by the American actors!

During the evenings Molly wandered around the immediate environment of the campus and the local shopping malls. It was approaching the end of October and the celebration of 'Halloween'. Nevertheless, it surprised her to see the elaborate decorations festooning the local homes – ghosts, corpses and coffins, and of course pumpkins with faces lit up by candles. October 25th was Ian and Molly's wedding anniversary and it was a very emotional telephone call they exchanged on that day. But, Dolman-like she put back her shoulders to face the remaining days of her placement.

Molly felt at home with her colleagues and their infectious zest for learning. From models of nursing and their application and manipulation, to the collaborative inventiveness of health and social care agencies. A nursing visit to a Residential Home for the Elderly was such an example. The residential establishment combined the twin programme of childcare for working parents with the care and well-being of the elderly residents. The children arrived with their parents before school each morning and the parents left the children in the care of the staff to go to their work. During their stay, the children took breakfast with the residents – sometimes climbing on a resident's knee to eat their cereals. It seemed like they were enjoying a 'Nannie-Ben' experience! The school bus came and the children left for school with some residents waving them off at the windows.

Later in her placement Molly was fortunate to observe the reverse process as the school bus brought the children to the residential home for tea with the residents, prior to being collected by their parents to return home. Whilst waiting for their parents the children read stories to the residents, some continued with their jigsaw puzzles, whilst others involved the residents in their homework! It was such a thriving, exhilarating experience for Molly and Gwen sensed she just wanted to tell them her story about 'The Beast of Dartmoor' or 'Benjamin Bunny'!

A follow-up classroom session demonstrated the ease with which the students were able to orchestrate the process of nursing as a welfare function within the Neuman framework. For Molly too, it was a learning curve as she began to appreciate similarities in the disciplined approach taken by various nursing scholars to define nursing practice, theory and critical enquiry. Certainly, 'Modelling Theory' was universal and widely accepted across all disciplines - nursing should not exclude itself was the message she wanted to take back home!
Time with a group of mixed discipline students later in the week provided Molly with the opportunity to explore the relationship between home and professional life. Much of the domestic routine was the same; childcare varied very little but the family economy provided an eye-opening discussion.

The married students, particularly those with children, agreed that it was difficult to sustain the family budget and meet the financial outlay of their course. Most told that they held at least one form of employment in addition to their fulltime academic studies. One student explained, "In the States, we are encouraged to budget for our education from a very early age so we save from our pocket money and eventually get a day-job!" Another lively participant told how she held down three jobs: one evening at a diner, another evening at a gas station and Saturday work at a superstore. Her colleagues peppered her with questions about how she coped with it all ... not forgetting the studying and project work; husband time as distinct from children time; and time for yourself to come up for air? One chirpy young student roguishly asked, "What are the stressors? How do you maintain a balance between the internal and external stressors?" and even a greater challenge, "how do you prevent stressors getting out of hand?" Silence was broken by laughter! Then the student with the three jobs jauntily replied, "Oh! We get by; my husband is good with the kids; we are able to fit around each other's commitments; and still have our 'special' times!" Seeming to reflect, the student looked at Molly who nodded saying, "Yes, it all sounds very familiar."

Then a student from the Amish community explained how unusual it was to be allowed to distinguish one's self by studying at University. She was humbled by having been given the opportunity and was clearly enjoying her course and the contact with other students. "But it took some working out and lots of understanding," she admitted with a smile. "However," she continued shyly, "I am so looking forward to taking the benefits of my profession back to the Community."

"Now your turn. Molly," hooted the students! So Molly presented the two examples she described from her district nursing experience namely Beryl, the supportive wife of a district nurse; and Anne, the district nurse's daughter with her dread of the telephone ringing, to illustrate the stressors families can encounter and the ways in which they can be reconciled. Molly wished she had brought more material from home, although the University allowed her access to various workrooms to produce visual aids. Nevertheless, if only she had a 'tablet' or a laptop'!

Turning the tables Molly suddenly challenged the students, "Is there anything you want to know about the UK, or share from your experience of visiting the UK?" And just like the interests exposed by her colleagues and the people she met in the Mid-West, Molly was asked about the Royal family, Florence Nightingale and this time there was a keen interest in the Mayflower and the people who sailed from the UK to settle in America. Fortunately, Molly had a brochure featuring the famous plaque on a street corner in the Barbican area of Plymouth listing the names of all those who had sailed on the perilous journey into the unknown. This time it was good to have Monica in the group to share at first hand her experience of the UK and living in Plymouth! Needless to say, Monica remembered the 'faggots' she had eaten at the Barbican restaurant and tales of the Scrumpy Cider. Once again, the group was amused by Molly's acquired Devon accent as she repeated the Devonians description of a alcohol jolly person – 'ere be maized, 'ere be!

Returning to the house, Molly packed an overnight case for a stay in South Carolina to attend the State Nursing Association Conference. Much to her surprise she was allocated a seat on the platform and asked to respond to the Chairman's welcome to the "Visiting Scholar from the UK". As Gwen looked on she smiled as Molly carried it off with aplomb. Her mentoring professor, who was getting to know Molly very well by now said, "Well done! You always steal the show because you are a performer – a real show off!!" Molly didn't quite know how to take those remarks: compliment or criticism? Hey Ho, she thought, does it matter? As her father would have said, "Always do your best, Nitto!" And she had.

Molly's stay concluded with a farewell celebration hosted by her fellow academics. It was a happy evening; Molly expressed her appreciation and summarised the highlights and insights of her time at the University. The Faculty responded by presenting her with a silver plaque embellished with the University crest.
Molly packed up her borrowed home in the woodland for the last time and made a call to Ian who lovingly announced that he

would be waiting for her at Heathrow. The next morning, she realized how sad she was to leave – it had been her kind of place; a long-term opportunity she would have explored under different circumstances!

On the long flight to the UK Molly had lots of time for reflection as she revelled in the re-booting of her passion for nursing: reflected on her USA colleagues' response when health and well-being was jeopardised; and their seemingly practical and opportunistic approach to inter-professional learning. However, Molly remained committed to the need for caution in slavishly adhering to the structured modelling approach. As a nurse of some considerable experience, she recognised the value of intuition – her highly developed sixth sense, aided by Gwen her alter-ego?!

But now it was time to enjoy the feeling of going back home to Ian and the family she loved.

CHAPTER 11

RASPBERRY SPONGE PUDDING

BACK HOME:

The long air flight over and Molly arrived at Heathrow to find Ian standing there like a vision of loveliness. He opened his arms, her luggage trolley sailed away across the concourse and as she drifted into his warm embrace all misgivings were forgotten. Molly was at home with Hub, her soul mate. The next weekend Molly and Ian travelled 'up country' to visit the family and to give Jayne and James their presents from the USA. James was delighted with his transporter loaded with a space rocket and Jayne just couldn't do anything for a while but to gaze on her new doll with a full wardrobe of clothes.

As Molly recounted her adventure, she hoped for the opportunity to repay something of the hospitality she had received from her American hosts! A short while later the opportunity arose when the USS Guadacanal LPH-7 arrived in Plymouth harbour. Local naval connections invited villagers to host crewmembers for a 'taste of British home life in rural England'. Two sailors stayed with Ian and Molly in their quaint little home and as usual Ian sprang into action as 'tour guide'. There were a few confusing moments when hosts and guests considered each other with amusement – just like the ones Molly had experienced!

Returning to the University Molly was rewarded by the success of her MPhil thesis, with the encouragement to convert to a Doctorate. However, Molly hesitated, she was beginning to recognise the need to relax the demands of her career and come up for air to enjoy more 'family time'. By the end of term Molly had decided not to renew her University contact but to accept occasional assignments and further her interest in the voluntary sector. Whilst she missed University life, the change was a good decision. It was one that expanded her professional horizons and led her to new insights within the courts, as "Victim Support' (children), and as a telephone listening volunteer.

Needless to say, the more relaxed and flexible lifestyle was a bonus for Ian and one that also enabled Molly' to enjoy more family time and adventures with the grandchildren. Gavin's business had flourished, probably beyond his wildest dreams, whilst he too became involved with voluntary work through membership of the Rotary Club. Dana was enjoying her work as a qualified nurse in the private sector. It was a full and busy family life but they still found time to visit the South West.

Unfortunately, for Joy this was a challenging time as she bravely tried to surmount the traumatic consequences of leaving the Convent; the guilt and disappointment of not fulfilling her Calling weighed heavily. However, she embraced her work within the local community with vigour and commitment. Her contribution as youth worker, teacher of Mathematics at the local senior school, together with the input she made to the local church, not only as a talented organist but as a member of the choir enriched the lives of many but, sadly, did little to assuage her 'guilt', or console her sense of bereavement. It is said that, 'time is a great healer' and so it proved to be. Joy formed many varied and interesting friendships; Molly visited regularly and Ian gave his usual DIY support. Joy seemed to enjoy the opportunity to give a helping-hand in one of Gavin's shops during the Christmas period and to reconnect with the family and old friends.

Eventually, Joy met Jimmy. They had a happy and loving relationship and were married during a holiday in Scotland. In the fullness of time they moved to start a new life together in the South East. Sadly, Jimmy became inextricably involved with a situation from which there was no easy way to withdraw and they parted. The bottom seemed to have fallen out of Joy's world. "Please never let me go down that road again, Mum," she pleaded as she stoically carried on inspired by the challenges of her career, community responsibilities, and with the support of her friends and family. In the fullness of time romance was in the air again when Joy was tricked into a Blind Date where she met Stevie, also struggling under the distress of a broken marriage.

The force of the next blow rocketed through the family like an earthquake and left deep scars of indescribable pain. Gavin and Dana's marriage fell apart, they separated and Dana left Gavin, and her young children to form a new relationship. Life changed forever. For Gavin and the children, life inevitably set forth on a different path but one that did not altogether exclude Dana, who fortunately continued to live in the area. Molly was so thankful that Wills and Rose were not alive to witness the position in which their grandson and great grandchildren found themselves. The memory of Wills' distress, in the wake of one of Kate's boy's difficulties was indelibly marked in Molly's mind ... the tears streamed down her father's face as he quoted his version of Jesus' words, 'For as much as you do unto these little ones, you do unto me.'

READJUSTMENT:

Ian was eerily quiet and morose in the face of the tragedy his family were facing; he began to look pale and drawn and he lost his zing. At the time he was involved with a local project to build a new Village Hall - the 'tea boy' he was named because of the copious amount of tea he supplied! After much thought and talk he and Molly began to think about returning to live closer to his son, "to be at hand if needed." The move was made and in the longer term it was a good, albeit traumatic decision for everyone – particularly for Ian whose grief was palpable.

It was a sad day for Ian when he left behind his home in the South West. But when Dana's father reached out to him, Ian soon became aware of the anger and raw heartbreak the break-up was causing her parents. It seemed that in consoling Dana's father, either as they spoke on the telephone, or on the odd occasion when they met in Dana's father's 'local', Ian began to assuage his own grief and anger.

The sadness lingered on but the time came when Ian experienced a reprieve from his turmoil. The self-build project in the village was completed and Ian was invited to perform the official opening of the new Village Hall! A plaque on the wall bears testimony to this ambitious achievement but it also reflects the esteem in which Ian was held in the village, his dedicated contribution to village life, and the unstinting help he gave to anyone in need.

Little by little Ian's new surroundings seemed to bring some consolation. He grew to love the new bungalow; when he first visited the overgrown garden he said to Molly, "Do you know Wifey, I think I could feel at home here." And so he did! The bungalow was situated in a beautiful preservation area on the City boundary. It was large and spacious, newly updated and refurbished with a sky-blue carpet throughout. The bungalow was enclosed within a wrap-around garden, which although very overgrown was a desirable feature. Molly stripped out the brambles and undergrowth from the rear plot from which Ian created a vegetable plot and just like his father, produced his famous harvest of runner beans and onions.

Taking a friend round a part of their garden covered with ivy, she was startled to see movement beneath the overgrown area. "I'm not sure what it is but I definitely saw something move." Ian pulled back the ivy to find a fishpond with three beautiful Koi carp swimming around! Molly was left to sort out the garden and the fish pond whilst Ian continued to find interest in attending to real, or imaginary DIY concerns in their new home but something was missing.

Life went on: Molly and Ian helped with 'school runs', swimming lessons and other 'baby-sitting' or taxi services. When the children slept overnight, then once again they visited Benjamin Bunny and The Beast of Dartmoor under the bedclothes and make-believe continued to engage the children's imaginations. Jayne set up 'shop' in the back bedroom as 'Jayne's Everything Store', whilst James created numerous exploits with his hero, MJF (Michael. J. Fox) and organised cricket matches on the back lawn. And of course, various school activities began to call upon their spare time.

'Jayne's Everything Store' was a great source of fun! Molly would dress up to be the student paying her rent for the flat she occupied above the shop – sometimes she was in arrears and would be gently admonished by Jayne! Old Mr Taylor (Molly in Ian's work clothes) coming in for his 'baccy' and Jayne kindly enquiring about his wife; Mrs Townsend (Molly in jeans and sweat-shirt) whose children were all "down with the fever', she wanted some 'Beechams' which attracted Jayne's comfort and advice; the local Councillor (Molly, teetering on high heels in a posh frock and fancy hat) would drop by on a good will visit. The look on Jayne's face as she tried to anticipate who would be the next 'customer' through the shop door was bemusement personified!

Ian continued to mix play with learning. For instance, he found a leaking tap and asked for volunteers to repair it. As usual, Jayne's curiosity got the better of her and she was soon involved with sorting out a washer from Ian's 'just in case' box and the spanners from his tool kit. But first and foremost, to turn off the water at source, "or you will flood the place out," warned Ian! James came in "to supervise," he said dribbling a football at his feet! Jayne soon had an audience of admirers as she manipulated the tools with her little hands. Finally looking round with a huge smile of satisfaction as Ian pronounced, "Job done. Well done, Miss Jayne!" 'Miss' was Ian's special term of endearment; James was known as 'Buster'.

James continued to organise the sports and keep fit sessions for anyone willing to join in. He supervised karate classes and cricket games on the back lawn. They played tennis on the local tennis court where Molly would make her usual case to be allowed two bounces of her ball instead of one on account of her 'great age', or 'sore elbow'! James would never concede, "You either play properly or not at all," he said.

Gavin invited Molly to accompany himself and the children on their first holiday without Dana. They went to a holiday park in Barbados. It was an action-packed week; they learned to play golf; went sailing on a boat that capsized; and jet-skiing with Gavin in the driving seat. They travelled from the park to the sea front in a rickety old bus with reggae music blasting away in their ears. Reggae music was everywhere; at the socials in the evening; on the bus into town where the passengers swayed to its rhythm. It was all great fun.

Then out of the blue, Tim, a friend from the village in the South West spoke to Ian and asked how he felt about sharing a holiday he and his wife were considering to the States. "We usually plan our own route, stay in 'Best Westerns' and see how it goes." And that is what they did ... and it was just what Ian needed! It was an amazing adventure – a round trip from arriving in San Francisco and back again. They spotted 'Spruce Goose' a Howard Hughes creation in San Francisco harbour, later removed to a museum in Oregon. The journey continued through Yosemite National Park admiring such unbelievable sights as the Redwood forestry, the Bride's Veil Waterfall, and evidence of the brown bear's foraging. Death Valley lived up to its acclaim from the golden desert floor to the huge rock faces with their ever-changing perspective in the sunlight. It was at a restaurant park at the end of Death Valley that Ian had his first close up encounter with one of the large American road transporters. The driver was surprised by Ian's intense interest and was only too pleased to explain the mechanics of the huge beast and to invited him to sit in the driver's cab. Ian undoubtedly enjoyed the experience more than Death Valley where he rather dryly observed, "one rock is like any other!"

The friends motored along Route 66, paying tribute to the relocated London Bridge at Lake Havasu ... and what a moving sight to see this well-known piece of London's history set in the heart of America! Arriving back in San Francisco, time was spent exploring the famous steep jig-jag Lombardie Road, making several journeys across 'Golden Gate Bridge', and visiting Alcatraz. Alcatraz was an amazing experience and offered the sensation of a functioning 'correctional' institution! The prison almost came to life as they walked around the complex on the pre-planned tour, listening on headphones to the history of the prison. From time to time the tape included realistic snapshots of stories as if told by a prisoner, or member of staff, together with background sounds of prison life such as clanging gates, and noises from the dining room. The guided tour included the cell from which 'the Birdman of Alcatraz' escaped and the balcony from where the famous prison riots began! It all seemed so real and a fitting climax to quite an adventure.

Following this amazing adventure, Molly once again turned to academia. She registered for a PhD with a research proposal focussed on District Nursing from early to late twentieth century. Molly also applied to transfer her volunteer interests from the South West to her new location. Gwen, although she knew she was virtually receding from Molly's orbit, sensed enormous relief to see Molly re-engaging with, and even extending, the caring and enabling work she loved.

Once 'back-home' the district nursing support group re-emerged as part of Molly's life and friendships were renewed. A Retired Community Nurses Association had been formed to promote continuing contact between colleagues and provide a welfare function in times of need. In the fullness of time some nurses produced artefacts, documented evidence, and oral histories to inform Molly's PhD research; in return Molly amused them with familiar and hitherto unknown stories.

With the passage of time, some nurses were now widows and Ian, once again came to the rescue as 'handyman'. Other nurses reached the end of their life to be mourned by a whole community ... the headlines in the local paper for one nurse read 'Belgrave Mourns its Angel'; the Parish Church was full to over-flowing at her funeral. The new Association tried to ensure that no district nurse at her life's end was knowingly left unacknowledged by her peers. Looking in on this vibrant peer group relationship it seemed that the funerals of a colleague not only provided an opportunity to honour the nurse and give respect to her life's work; it was also a time of reunions for her surviving peers. The funeral of one district nurse nick-named 'Lady' on account of her regal demeanour, genteel ways and well-educated presence was one such occasion that Molly will long remember.

The funeral was held in an impressive church in a part of the town where the 'well-to-dos' used to live. Walking into the front vestibule on the morning of Lady's funeral was breath-taking as the sun shone through its delicately stained-glass windows and glittered on the highly polished wooden furniture and impressive winding staircase – the central feature of the vestibule. The service was held on the first floor to which access was gained via the staircase, or a small 2–3-person lift. After a simple but very meaningful service the funeral officials stood in conversation with the mourners at the foot of the staircase admiring its wonderful features. Molly commented to a funeral official that it must have been very difficult to carry the coffin up the staircase. "We didn't use the staircase, me' duck," he said "we took 'er up in the lift." The official must have noticed the perplexed expression on Molly's face as she looked across at the small lift because he then explained, "We stood her up in the corner." The look on Molly's face eased into a smile that ricocheted around the small group of nurses like a flash of lightning to reveal but a single thought, "Lady would NOT be amused!"

So, what of Ian? 'Mr Ben', Ian's old Border Collie died soon after the move from the South West. Ian, at a loss without his pet, promptly visited the RSPCA. A young Border Collie cross who had recently given birth to ten puppies lay exhausted in her pen with the puppies nuzzling around her; the dog's name was China. Ian gazing into her soft brown eyes, spoke her name softly and China gave a slight twitch of the white end of her tail, almost like a purr. "That's my dog," said Ian and when the puppies were weaned China came home with Ian. "There's just one thing," said Ian rather hesitatingly, "I don't think I can call 'China' on the park!" The lovely Cornish Vicar from their parish in the South West and his wife were staying with Ian and Molly. "How about Chy? Cornish for house-dog," they suggested. And 'Mrs Chy' she was. Mrs Chy and Ian were inseparable – he had found another soul mate just like Mr Ben.

Ian's parents had downsized into a ground floor flat nearby to daughter Joan before her illness. Lily became increasingly frail and whilst Joan took charge, Harry had the occasional break with Ian and Molly at their home in the adjacent county. It was on one such occasion that Lily died. Poor Harry was heartbroken, "I've lost my mate and my sweetheart," he cried.

Harry continued to live in the flat but always joined Joan and her husband each day for lunch. It was Harry's usual custom to sit in the comfy fire side chair and read the local paper until they moved to the table for lunch. One morning, Harry arrived as usual and took his seat by the fire with the newspaper when Joan noticed her father had dropped some pages of the paper on the floor and seemed unable to sort out the problem. The doctor was called and diagnosed 'stroke'. Joan nursed Harry in her front room where he died. Harry's death hit Ian very hard; they had always been good mates. Father and son had served together in the same Home Guard unit prior to Ian joining the Royal Signals during the war; they celebrated victory together in their 'local' on Ian's demobilization from the army; and Harry cycled to various events to spend time with Ian and encourage his talents as a drummer in music group. This adventuresome pair enjoyed numerous other jollies too, including visits to relatives in neighbouring counties; trips to Harry's historical past in Sussex; and days out at the seaside on

Ian's motorbike! They also found common enjoyment in the TV series 'Dad's Army'! The death of his father left a big gap in Ian's life.

Life returned to some kind of normality for Ian and Molly as they formed new interests in the local Branch of the Institute of Advanced Motorists where for Ian membership became a lasting source of enjoyment and challenge to his driving prowess. Together they reinvestigated opportunities with the local amateur theatre society: Molly took up new interests as a Front of House volunteer and First Aid Person; Ian preferred to watch the performance but always willing to lend a hand.

Ian was led towards a surprising new interest as a volunteer providing breakfast for the homeless at one of the local churches! He cooked porridge, made toast and sometimes Molly made bacon, or sausage butties for him to take along; at Christmas, she accompanied Ian to help cook a full English breakfast for his guests. It all had a sense of deja vu as Molly recalled her times taking supper from the Mission to the homeless at the Salvation Army Hostel.

Back in their hometown once more, Ian renewed old friendships and re-joined the 'Retired Members' Club'. Molly and Ian's popular parties were re-established, including their themed evenings, which involved dressing up – the 'old boys' and their wives joined in the spirit of the event; Jayne and James were in their element wearing a wig, a moustache, or make up. Molly wrote the scripts for Murder Mystery Evenings and, along with everyone else, the grandchildren played their parts with conviction! One of Ian's former work colleagues said, "Its so good to have you back – you keep us all together." And indeed, 'the old boys' network was a vibrant community of like-minded engineers!

Jayne and James were growing up, almost overnight. They made close friends, had 'sleep-overs' and went into town as a group on Saturday afternoons. Gavin found he was able to pick up his pre-marriage pastimes such as scuba diving, sailing and hill walking; all of which he introduced to the children and supervised their developing prowess. In the fullness of time Gavin bought a motorbike but that was definitely 'out of bounds'!

As time passed Jayne and James succeeded at school and each gained a place at University – Jayne to read Law and James to read Economics. Molly felt that they now had their own story to tell.

PARKINSONS DISEASE – A LONELY ROAD:

However well life seemed to be unfolding on the surface, Ian was frequently dispirited and seemed to be grieving for the South West, a situation often made worse by return visits. Sadly, Mrs Chy died aged 14 and Ian began to look unwell. Molly feared he was suffering with depression but the mood would lift, although his spirits never quite seemed to return to his usual exuberance for life. As the years went by Molly noticed a light involuntary foot tapping movement whilst Ian was eating, or sitting watching TV. Molly recoiled in horror as she thought, 'No, surely not, could it be Parkinson's Disease?' But Ian didn't seem to attach any significance to his foot tapping and it didn't interfere with his various activities so Molly let it pass. One day Gavin said, "Don't you think you ought to get a doctor to see Dad about his foot tapping?" Molly reacted by saying, "Dad hasn't complained, so leave it until he does – there may be nothing we can do about it." But insightful Gwen was sure Ian had long since been aware but was saying nothing.

And so, they carried on in this conspiracy of silence, in which Ian busily attended to his DIY hobbies around the bungalow; helped at the theatre; and served his now famous breakfasts for the homeless. The day eventually arrived when Ian said he ought to see the doctor but Molly hesitated and seemed willing to bury her head in the sand. Really in fear, Gwen suspected. However, Gavin was persuasive and they consulted the GP. The memory of the doctor taking one look at Ian, lifting his shoulder dismissively and saying, "Parkinsons?" will be one that is lodged in Molly's mind forever. The doctor had no understanding of the death knell he was so frivolously proclaiming with a shrug of his shoulders ... and in the wake of Ian's sister's experience too.

When they arrived home, Ian said, "It's no use, I miss my dog." A quick call to the RSPCA and Ian's request was entered on their 'Wish List'. Within the week Ian received a call to say, "She has arrived, her name is Poppy and she is a Border Collie!" Poppy was wonderful from day one, obedient, clever, amusing and affectionate – a perfect pal for Ian. Everyone was so very pleased for Ian and for Poppy who had found a good home. 'Mrs Poppy' seemed to turn Ian's life around. Once again, he walked on the local parks, chatted with the gardeners and made friends. One day Ian returned home in jubilant mood having shared time with three 'breakfast clients' sitting on a park bench together. Perhaps things would not be too bad after all Molly prayed. The Consultant had advised Ian against taking any medication until the time was right. The challenge for the family was to sustain Ian's interests and creativity.

A sparing match of wit and teasing always brightened up Ian's day. His relationship with Rose's youngest sister, Jane, was no exception. Similarly minded, they enjoyed their times together to engage in their usual revelry. Although the Dolman Girls were rather wary of Ian, his roguish ways seem to fascinate Jane! But it was not to last and the day came when Jane's health suddenly deteriorated and she died in her nineties. Jane was the last of the second-generation Dolman dynasty and her funeral seemed to echo with the unseen presence of the 'Dolman Girls' all of whom, with the exception of Helen, had been gifted with longevity.

Kate and Molly met at Jane's funeral after several years of estrangement following their mother's death. Molly was horrified to see Kate in fairly advanced stages of Parkinson's disease. 'Surely not, this is so cruel' thought Molly, 'first Joan, then Ian and now Kate'. Reconciliation was an emotional experience but they recaptured a close sisterly fondness after some years in the wilderness. Kate frequently stayed with Molly and Ian; she enjoyed visits to their local amateur theatre – even giving an occasional hand at Front of House; and worshipped with Molly at her local church where she was greatly moved by its magnificent choir, and the highly polished Anglican traditions. For many years, in addition to her position as church organist, Kate performed the duties of Churchwarden, Sacrosanct and Pastoral Care Assistant in her village church. As Kate became more absorbed into Molly's family life and routines it was a most rewarding experience for them both … and Ian too! Although fairly incapacitated, Kate accompanied Ian and Molly on holidays to Gran Canaria where she and Ian showed the same feisty spirit as they walked with the aid of their walking frames, talking, joking and admiring the local coastal terrain. For Molly, it seemed just magical to have a sister again!

Petal, who knew Kate, 'Dukie' as she called her, was saddened to learn of her Parkinson's affliction but Petal had her own grief to bear. Timothy, Petal's husband, died of lung cancer just before Molly and Ian left the South West. Although Petal told how she nursed Timothy with the help of her boys for many months knowing that the end was inevitable, her grief was no less sharp and difficult to bear. Molly realised that one of the many joys of being 'back home' was the ease with which she and Petal could keep in touch during the time they called their 'Golden Years'. Petal's boys were married; two with children and those nearest home were continuing to make remarkable improvements to the Hall and promote its facilities – the most recent to host a wedding ceremony complete with magnificent marquee of the front lawn! Molly delighted in visiting Petal and to find her so comfortable in her magnificent surroundings. The parkland surrounding the Manor was glorious and each year Petal held fundraising Garden Party events.

And so the 'Golden Years' unfolded. Christmas was approaching and Petal's family wanted to present her with an overnight stay in London, to include the West End Show,

'Jungle Book'. Secretly, her daughter-in-law asked Molly if she would join Petal, explaining that the family thought it would be more fun for Petal to go with Molly than any of them. Molly unhesitatingly accepted and off they went – coincidentally to stay at The Strand Palace, Molly's honeymoon hotel! The young cockney taxi-man who escorted them from the station to their hotel was a chatty fellow and during the journey he almost seemed to become a life-long friend. He thought they were marvellous getting out and about in such a manner to celebrate an eightieth birthday. "Oh," said Petal, "We shall be back to the Royal Opera House to celebrate our ninetieth birthdays!" He laughed saying, "I wish my Nan could hear you. I hope I'm around for your ninetieth so that I can do you the honour again." Gwen absorbed the implications, feeling that Petal was perhaps being a touch over ambitious – but who knows?

Meanwhile, Molly continuing with her PhD research found Ian a tower of strength as he deployed his DIY know-how to create a comfortable and functional study; the technology was updated; and he continued to join Molly on various expeditions to archives and libraries - always doing his own thing whilst Molly was otherwise engaged. The journey back home was entertaining as they compared notes and stopped off for a meal! As her work progressed Molly would often sit at the computer long into the night, which Ian found disconcerting and bringing a cup of tea he would urge, "Come on Wifey, enough is enough!" But when she was confronted with one chapter she just couldn't get right, Ian, sensing her struggle would give the rather macabre warning, "If you don't get on with it, you won't live long enough to finish the job!" The day came when Molly's dissertation was finished, presented, and succeeded with the award of PhD. Petal joined Ian and the family at the ceremony of Molly's award and for the celebration lunch afterwards. Ian looked in an exceptionally good state and Molly was beginning to think his condition had stabilised; and so it did for a remarkably good span of time.

The following year Petal optimistically arranged another overnight expedition – a visit to the Chelsea Flower Show, which they enjoyed with a critical and appreciative eye - both being enthusiastic gardeners! It was good to have such uninterrupted time together. Gavin, who kept a watching eye on Ian, sensed that his father quite enjoyed the peace and quiet in Mrs Poppy's company! But Molly's excursions were also a bonus to their recently widowed friend, Grace, a kind and gentle person, whose company Ian had always enjoyed. The spaciousness of the bungalow with its colourful gardens seemed a real joy for her and Molly was content that Ian was safe in her care.

And so Molly looked forward to Petal's next adventure to Ascot Ladies Day. They did not win any money but Petal's hat of fine pale green feathers was the star attraction in their Grandstand - a prestigious position near to the Royal Box! Just before the arrival of the Royal party, Petal left to make herself comfortable for the afternoon. Molly's alarm was raised when the Royal Party in their carriages drove by and Petal was still absent! However, she need not have been concerned because Petal arrived back escorted by two handsome young men in top hat and tails having been invited to join them in a 'ring side view.' Petal had done just that. "Mol," she said on her return, "it was wonderful, I could have touched Her Majesty – she looked beautiful. "The account of Petal's 'ring-side view', and the graciousness of her young male companions became the highlight of their day at Ascot!

The last escapade by these two incorrigible friends was to the Festival of Remembrance at the Royal Albert Hall; what a spectacle but who would have imagined it would be their 'Swan song'. Sadly, Petal was not to realise her ambition to celebrate her ninetieth birthday at The Royal Opera House – Molly has yet to find out her chances!

However, soon it became like trying to juggle the possible with the impossible, even with Gavin's devoted support. Kate was deteriorating and Ian becoming irreconcilable with the limitations his condition was imposing. Ian's zest for life became transformed into a liability of self-determination, which inevitably led to a series of disasters but he rarely seemed aware of the effects of his behaviour and therefore unremorseful, or apologetic. Ian's stiff upper lip generation made it difficult for Molly to share his own personal burden of Parkinson's and the grief of his declining position as lover, provider, and caretaker of the family – if Ian really understood what was happening it must have been devastating for him. However, sometimes when the going got really tough and he became despondent, Ian would look around the bungalow, scan the family photographs and maybe gaze on 'wifey', or just to himself would say, "I have been so very lucky, lucky, lucky. What a wonderful life I have had." It was a long, lonely and distressing road insofar as Molly felt she could only stand by and pick up the pieces – there was no cure, limited remedial treatment (at least for Ian), and no hope. Thankfully they had dear Mrs Poppy-dog who seemed to boost their sense of togetherness and expressions of affection.

Gwen was sure Molly feared the future as much as she did, particularly after Kate's sudden deterioration. Kate had been reasonably well, she was taking experimental medication, which at first seemed to be a miracle cure. Kate's bubble burst as the winter approached and she found it hard to deal with the returning Parkinson's problems. April followed and preparations were in hand to attend Joy's second marriage but for Kate this was not to be. On the eve of Joy's wedding, Kate suddenly lost her sight and was admitted to hospital with suspected Stroke. In the depth of despair Molly attended Joy's wedding with Petal. Remembering Joy's plea and recognising Stevie's alcohol issues and personal problems, Molly was fearful of the step Joy was taking in her vulnerable state. If only Molly could have glimpsed the future with Stevie's problems resolved; the joy of Stevie's close and loving relationship with his school-aged twin daughters, Jessica and Florence, who still lived nearby; and a successful business enterprise unfolding. Sadly, we are not privy to such foresight ... as Sam would have said; "Only time will tell." And it did!

Two months later Jayne was married to Alwyn at St George's Church in Hanover Square. The wedding breakfast and overnight stay for the guests was hosted in the luxury of Mayfair. Kate had recovered, her sight had returned and with inspirational Dolman grit she was able to enjoy the happiness and splendour of the occasion. During their reminiscences Kate and Molly would talk about their lives together but Kate always concluded by saying, "Jayne's wedding was the last happy day in my life." Life was hard for Kate but, although she lived quite a distance away from Molly, she came to visit from time to time although it broke her heart to see Ian deteriorating so quickly. As Kate left to return home the unshed tears would flow and she would whisper to Molly, "He is such a good man ... Look after him Molly, you will only have one chance to do this."

Molly, with the support of Gavin, continued to carry the burden of Ian's long terminal condition, as well as Kate's losing struggle to out-wit 'Mr Parkinson' – always with her mother's plea ringing in her ear, "Look after Kate when I'm gone, Molly." But Molly lived with hope in her heart and never ceased to pray for better times ahead.

Early one morning as late summer turned to autumn, Molly found Ian drowsy and reluctant to take a drink. The traditional piece of pineapple Ian enjoyed to freshen his mouth was not an option. So, Molly gently freshened his mouth with a swab moistened with pineapple juice. Talking to sleepy Ian, she playfully said, "Now Hub, don't you bite my finger." Ian opened his eyes and with a twinkle gave Molly's finger a nip. Molly rolled her eyes saying playfully, "Ooouch" and Ian's face lit up with the most beautiful glowing smile of the like she had never ever seen him express before – like a lifetime of love in one smile. The smile gradually faded, the light went out and Ian was gone!

Sadly, there was no time to say 'goodbye' when Ian died; the final parting came so suddenly and unexpectedly when Ian's playfulness gave Molly new hope. Gwen knew the shock would shake Molly to her very foundations. Molly just could not believe her soul mate had left her after more than 60 years together - far longer than she had lived without him; and even in those years perhaps she had sensed her destiny! For three nights before the funeral, Ian lay at peace in his open coffin in the lounge of his home looking out on the garden he loved. Ian's death touched people from so many different walks of life and at his funeral the chapel of rest overflowed. It was a beautiful sunny day; the sound of 'Some Enchanted Evening' and the sunflower coffin top seemed to carry forth the message and inspiration of Ian's life.

Joy and Gavin paid tribute to their father, Gavin found it so very hard and James stood by his side ready for when he faltered. Kate and Petal both made their silent tributes from where they sat. Jayne presented a poem of memories and fondness to Granddad Ben –

Our Grandfather kept a garden; a garden of the heart
He planted all the good things that gave our lives a start
He turned us to the sunshine, encouraged us to dream
Fostering and nurturing the seeds of self-esteem.
And when the rains came, he protected us enough
But not too much because he knew, we would stand up strong and tough
His constant good example taught us right from wrong
Markers of our pathway that will last a lifetime long
We are our Granddad's garden; we are his legacy
Thank you, Granddad; we love you.

After the funeral, Ian's life was celebrated, as he would have wanted with a party on the lawn at his home in the sunshine. The next day, the family took the coffin top sunflower wreath to place on Ian's parents' grave. It felt to Gwen, as Molly stood there with Gavin, Joy and Stevie, they were returning Ian to his parents and saying "Thank you for lending him to us for a while." But what of Ian's ashes? Well, they are waiting to be mingled with his beloved Wifey's ashes when the time comes so that they can be joined to rest in peace forever.

Three months later, Molly suffered an acute heart attack, resulting in heart failure – a condition known as 'broken heart syndrome'. This was Molly's second near escape and the young doctor said to her as she prepared to leave the ward, "Take care, Molly, the third time you may not be so lucky!" But fate dealt another cruel blow when Kate suffered a second stroke and for the remainder of the year she spent struggling with deteriorating health and incapacity. Kate gradually became weaker and died in December, one year after Ian's death; she was laid to rest in the village churchyard by the side of Rose and Wills.

Molly once again seemed to gather her now incomplete self together; she gradually resumed her voluntary work and took on extra responsibilities at the theatre. Jayne and Alwyn bought a house, which they refurbished and made into a lovely home. Gavin and Molly enjoyed visiting from time to time - Gwen knew Molly just loved being consulted on their plans for the back garden! James announced his engagement to Linda so the wedding season would be starting all over again. To see such hopes for the future lifted everyone's spirits.

Life was becoming a busy roundabout for Molly. The church and her voluntary work took up quite a slice of her diary; her spare time was peppered with family involvement and the companionship of retired and practicing nursing colleagues. Links with the USA were maintained through her mentors, for instance one Professor planning a nurse education event in a Spanish speaking country asked Molly if she spoke Spanish and would she join the team of educators? Sadly, Molly did not speak Spanish! However, to Molly's delight, Monica, the nursing student from the UK semester, now a senior Oncology Nurse maintained regular contact – even calling to visit Molly during a family holiday to the UK and France.

THE JOYS AND TEARS OF FRIENDSHIP:

Needless to say, Molly and Petal kept in touch one way or another! They chatted and laughed together on the telephone and always lived in anticipation of their next adventure. But Petal was beginning to show signs of failing health and as time went by it became apparent that her heart condition was deteriorating. Two stair lifts bedecked the Hall's magnificent staircase; one lift was not long enough! Nevertheless, they tentatively talked about a River Cruise in Holland but sadly it was not to be when Petal died suddenly one night. The following morning Molly went to visit her friend. Petal lay in her bed almost sleep-like enfolded by a wonderful dream, overlooked by photographs of herself in nurses' regalia and Timothy in his RAF uniform. Her shining silver curly hair lay in the folds of her pillow, a child-like innocence on her face, and her lips pursed in a kind of whimsical smile, which Molly thought might burst into a smile, or a song at any moment. Molly, noticing with sad amusement that Petal had not applied her eyebrow pencil, she recalled the time Petal explained ... "Since the day my eyebrows were singed off, Mol when a flare shot out of the bonfire ...it is the first thing I do every morning. Eyebrows define your face, you know duckie-darling." Gwen the silent witness quietly absorbed the pathos of these precious moments, couldn't help but wonder how Molly would feel when their ninetieth birthday came around with the celebration they had planned at The Royal Opera House?

The village church was packed with mourners and as Petal left for her final resting place to the sound of 'Moonlight and Roses', just as she had on her wedding day, Molly could hear her friend's challenge, "Come on Mol, you have got to do it for both of us now!" Molly walked away from Petal's funeral bereft, knowing there would always be a big hole in her life, that special place which her friend had occupied for well over half a century.

But now it was 'back to the drawing board' and as usual Molly sought solace in academia. But first to join with Joy and her husband on the river cruise as Petal and Molly had planned. The cruise to Holland and the waterways of Amsterdam was a remarkable healing process. It brought together so many wonderful moments in Molly's life as if to equip her for the future. She swayed to 'Beside the Zuider Zee' as they traversed the water claimed from the North Sea; the fields of exotic-coloured tulips in full bloom triggered memories of Rose in full song; and the sight of the great Windmills provoked a splutter of laughter as she thought of Rose's performance when mimicking the mouse as she sang 'The 'Windmills of Old Amsterdam'. To walk around the

Windmills and observe their industry in the management of a vast network of waterways, and to discover the homes families made within their walls was truly fascinating. The day Molly confronted the reality of Anne Frank's small house stirred her memories of the times she pauses on the park whilst walking Poppy-dog to reflect at a memorial plague and the inspiration of its extracts from Anne Frank's diary. The holiday was a lesson in courage.

On arrival back home, almost as if in reinforcement of her need to move forward, Molly received a letter from Sarah inviting her to visit New Zealand. Sarah and her Professor, Gerald, shared a spacious house overlooking the bay. They continued their academic interests "on the fringe as it were", and taken up sailing. Gerald's family, although living quite a distance away, were very hospitable – "they know all about you, Molly!" Sarah went on to say, "Gerald and I do not feel we want to marry but we are very affectionate partners – it's a great relationship. Incidentally, you haven't yet told me yours and Sam's story – I'm waiting!" Molly also knew there was always Ruth's invitation too, "Come and stay with me, Molly; when you like; and for as long as you like!" One day perhaps! Meanwhile, Skype and Email conversations were just marvellous.

HOPE AND RASPBERRY SPONGE PUDDING:

In true Dolman fashion Molly recovered but it seemed that the zing had gone out of life; it had acquired the drabness of a colourless sponge pudding. Thinking she may never again find life's lustre, Molly and Gavin went on holiday to Gran Canaria, an old stomping ground of happier times. They arrived on a glorious spring day and as Molly felt the plane touch down on the tarmac she said, "I never thought it would happen." "Well, it has," said Gavin "and here we are, Mo*ther*." Gavin made his usual playful affectionate emphasis on the '*ther*' in mother!

As she walked down the steps leading from the aircraft with the familiar aroma of the Canaries in the air, Molly placed her foot on the tarmac saying, "Now to retrace old memories." "Well, no, not quite, Mo*ther*," said Gavin, "We shall lay new memories of our own." And that was the day that the dreary sponge pudding was turned upside down out of the basin and the bright red shiny jam trickled over the surface and began to seep through the sides.

As the holiday unfolded, they basked in the sunshine and sea breezes, played Pitch and Putt; and experienced the joy of just 'Being'. Molly glimpsed the future before her: the joy of family and anticipation of becoming a great grandma, the rewards of friendships at home and from across the world. She also anticipated renewing contact with the profession she loved by contributing as a hospital volunteer; her Faith greatly strengthened and renewed joy in her church; a return to the thrills and spills of Front of House; and a new home life to carve out at home for herself and Poppy-dog! Academia was also beckoning … but, first to complete this book as a tribute to Ian who, she asserts … "put the me into Molly."

For Gwen Sturdy, seeing Molly's journey unfold thus far has been a unique experience. But Gwen suspects Molly will be critical of the story by thinking she has helped to disguise Molly's failings … as if she would! Well, sobeit; the failings, if that is what they are, will be seen by the discerning eye! Tracing the numerous, and sometimes devious contours of Molly's journey, it seemed that was no real beginning and no real end. One generation did not stand alone; the spirit and characteristics of Molly's forebears, can be seen to spiral through her and in all likelihood, generations to follow. Pausing for thought on this journey, Gwen is reminded of Shelagh Stevenson's 1966 play, 'The Memory of Water,' once staged at Molly's amateur theatre. The play exposes the concept of water as a holding media for our 'memories' - the joys, laughter, loves and losses; anger and tears; and relationships that are part of everyday life and living. A blue-print, which might be seen as a kind of biography, that is laid down and added to by one generation through the next – a dynasty with no beginning and no end that influences the way its individual members are sculptured and what they then make of their lives.

CHAPTER 12

GWEN STURDY

WHO AM I? WHERE AM I??

Molly created me, she gave me my name and she saw me as her friend; a pretend friend who knew her like no other, one who shared her joys, regrets, sorrows, and innermost secrets. Throughout her life I remained in that special place where memories are stored ... and brought to life.

What did I look like to her? I often wondered if I ever looked any different to the little girl she created all those years ago? Did I grow older, or was I always a child friend? Did I look like a person? Was I man, woman, both, or neither – perhaps just a sensation?

Where did I live? Was it always as Molly's shadow, or perhaps not even as separate as that? Did I live as an integral part of her mind - her alter ego, her other but somewhat different self-maybe? At one time Molly assigned to me a pretend home of my own, a house she passed on the bus going to town. When the bus reached this house Molly imagined me to get on and moved along the seat for me to sit beside her. The house still stands and whenever Molly passes by in the company of others, she always points out the house and tells our story.

How did I exist in Molly's reality of life and living? Sometimes, I think she saw my presence in the eyes of people like Miss Bowen, the schoolteacher who foretold of a great future for Molly; in Sister Sparrow, her inspirational Nurse

Tutor; and Miss Todd who opened the door to the joys and challenges of district nursing; perhaps in Sister Starlight who always held the dignity of life so tenderly in her hands; or in the shrewd eye and kindly heart of the Yorkshire night sister; definitely in the complete trust and love-hugs she shared with Petal; and I entered into her spirituality as she prayed and said the Rosary at the bedside of her dying patient?

I would be proud to think Molly found me in her father's wisdom and compassion. I know I was under the bed sheets with her mother and Benjamin Bunny; I was there in the love she poured out to her babies, Joy and Gavin in the warm embrace of breastfeeding; in Ian's bottomless love and passion for 'wifey'; and in the unconditional love and boundless joy of her grandchildren. I am the glow she finds in Mrs Poppy!

However, sometimes when I doubt, I ask myself what will happen when Molly's spirit becomes part of the 'memory of water'. Will I remain part of Molly, or will I float along as a spin-off from the feisty 'Dolman Girls' and Wills' extraordinary family; or maybe a kind of Mary Poppins, or a Nannie McPhee ready to respond when someone in future generations needs an imaginary friend!

In truth, I know we can never be separated because I am Molly!

Printed in Great Britain
by Amazon